THINKING

Bridging the gap between theory and practice, this strikingly original analysis of the complex dynamics of high-risk fields demonstrates that teamwork is more important than technical prowess in averting disasters. *Thinking through Crisis* narrates critical incidents from initiation to resolution in five elegantly constructed case studies: the USS *Greeneville* collision, the Hillsborough football crush, the American Airline flight 587 in-flight breakup, the Bristol Hospital pediatric fatalities, and the US Airways flight 1549 Hudson River landing. Drawing on a variety of theoretical and real-world perspectives, this vivid, well-documented book provides innovative ways to understand risk management, develop new models of crisis decision making, enhance socially responsible leadership, and encourage deep questioning of the behavior of individuals and groups in complex systems. Its insights will resonate with professionals in a wide range of fields and with a general audience interested in understanding crises in complex systems.

Dr. Amy L. Fraher is Associate Professor and Chief Pilot of the Aviation Operations Program and director of the International Team Training Center at San Diego Miramar College. She is a retired U.S. Navy Commander, Naval Aviator, and former United Airlines pilot with 6,000 mishap-free flight hours in four jet airliners, five military aircraft, and several types of civilian airplanes. A crisis management expert with almost thirty years of leadership experience in high-risk fields, she is a member of the *Washington Post* Leadership Panel. As principal consultant of Paradox and Company and qualified Lean Six Sigma Yellow Belt, she consults internationally with a broad range of organizations. Her focus is on improving team performance in high-risk organizations by helping people understand how group dynamics can debilitate operations. She is the author of *Group Dynamics for High-Risk Teams* (2005) and *A History of Group Study and Psychodynamic Organizations* (2004). Her essays have appeared in journals such as *History of Psychology, Human Relations, Socio-Analysis*, and *Organisational and Social Dynamics*.

Thinking through Crisis

IMPROVING TEAMWORK AND LEADERSHIP
IN HIGH-RISK FIELDS

Amy L. Fraher

CAMBRIDGE
UNIVERSITY PRESS

CAMBRIDGE UNIVERSITY PRESS
Cambridge, New York, Melbourne, Madrid, Cape Town,
Singapore, São Paulo, Delhi, Tokyo, Mexico City

Cambridge University Press
32 Avenue of the Americas, New York, NY 10013-2473, USA

www.cambridge.org
Information on this title: www.cambridge.org/9780521757539

First published 2011

Printed in the United States of America

A catalog record for this publication is available from the British Library.

Library of Congress Cataloging in Publication data
Fraher, Amy Louise.
    Thinking through crisis : improving teamwork and leadership in high-risk fields /
Amy L. Fraher.
        p.   cm.
    Includes bibliographical references and index.
    ISBN 978-0-521-76420-9 – ISBN 978-0-521-75753-9 (pbk.)
    1. Crisis management.   2. Teams in the workplace.   3. Leadership.   I. Title.
    HD49.F73   2011
    658.4'056–dc22   2010050330

ISBN 978-0-521-76420-9 Hardback
ISBN 978-0-521-75753-9 Paperback

For KATHY

CONTENTS

FIGURES AND TABLES

FIGURES

TABLE

PREFACE AND ACKNOWLEDGMENT

In the fall of 1979, I was the starting right halfback on Old Saybrook High School's varsity field hockey team. The year before had been a season of high expectations but ultimately low achievement for our team, and in the spring most of the starters graduated, moving on to other places. In response, the '79 season was dubbed a 'rebuilding year' by our small-town newspaper, as nearly the entire varsity team was replaced by our less-experienced junior varsity members. Admittedly, we were a pretty motley crew: jocks, hippies, preppies, and nerds. No one player really excelled; we were all about equal in skill. Yet, what we lacked in the flashy talent of the previous year's team, we made up for in shear grit and determination. A mongrel team of underdogs, motivated by what we felt was a general 'dis' to our potential. Of course this never got articulated; it simply got enacted.

In the end, our motley crew turned a 'rebuilding year' into the best school record ever achieved, including winning the Connecticut State Championship. I graduated that spring and moved on myself, participating in college athletics and then years later, the All-Navy basketball team. Although I often played with much better *individuals* on those teams, I never played on a better *team* than that high school hockey squad. What was different in the *team chemistry* of that group that allowed us to achieve so much with so little? And what caused subsequent teams with more talent and potential to ultimately fall short?

I wondered, are teams good because they have chemistry, or do they have chemistry because they are good? I have been intrigued by this question for thirty years. Over that time, I continued to work in teams: first as an enlisted U.S. Marine, then as a Naval Officer and Naval Aviator, commercial airline pilot, and now, college professor and organizational consultant. Over the course of this career, I was exposed to numerous leadership theories, team-building strategies, and training programs, leading me to develop my own *Team Resource Management* (TRM) model.

This book is a by-product of my exploration to understand better the influence of team chemistry, the role of team learning in organizational errors and their prevention, and the impact of the environment on team performance during the critical period in which a disaster unfolds. Understanding these dynamics is important for everyone who is interested in working more effectively in teams and organizations. But, it is essential for those of us in high-risk fields.

As with any project of this magnitude, many people and organizations have been influential in its creation. Some, such as colleagues at the *International Society for the Psychoanalytic Study of Organizations* (ISPSO) provided me with intellectual stimulation and a forum to exchange ideas and test my theories through scholarly activities. Others such as the Parliamentary Archives and The Stationery Office (TSO) in the UK, U.S. Navy and COMPACFLT Public Affairs Office, National Air and Space Museum, National Transportation Safety Board, and U.S. Department of Transportation provided invaluable research materials. I would like to thank them all for their contributions to this book.

I would also like to thank Dougie Brimson, Benjamin Chesluk, Matthieu Daum, Phil Edwards, Kathleen B. Jones, Sarah H. Kagan, Susan Long, Will McMahon, Ian Poynton, Phil Scranton, my editors Ed Parsons and Simina Calin, and the anonymous reviewers at Cambridge University Press for their feedback, suggestions, support, and encouragement. Thanks also to my friends and family, Coach Splain and the 1979 hockey team, and students and colleagues at San Diego Miramar College. Finally, thanks to my fellow yogis at Ginseng Yoga for the reminder to breathe every once in a while. Namaste.

ACRONYMS AND ABBREVIATIONS

AAMP   Advanced Aircraft Maneuvering Program
BRI   Bristol Royal Infirmary
CO   Commanding Officer
COI   Court of Inquiry
CRM   Crew Resource Management
FAA   Federal Aviation Administration
MBPS   Munchausen-By-Proxy Syndrome
NASA   National Aeronautics and Space Administration
NDM   Naturalistic Decision Making
NHS   National Health Service
NTSB   National Transportation Safety Board
OMBP   Organizational-Munchausen-By-Proxy
OOD   Officer of the Deck
ORM   Operational Risk Management
PCU   Pediatric Cardiology Unit
TEM   Threat and Error Management
TET   Tribal Engagement Teams
TGA   Transposition of the Great Arteries
TMI   Three Mile Island
TRM   Team Resource Management
UK   United Kingdom
US   United States of America
USS   United States Ship
XO   Executive Officer

Introduction: How Teamwork Is More Important than Technical Prowess

In 2001 during a routine training mission off the Hawaiian Islands, a U.S. Navy fast-attack nuclear submarine surfaced into a Japanese fishing trawler, severing the boat in half, killing nine people, and creating an international incident. The submarine was known as one of the best in the fleet, expertly operated by a hand-selected crew and led by a talented and charismatic captain.

That same year, a modern Airbus airliner broke apart in flight, crashing into a New York City suburb, and killing all 260 people aboard and 5 people on the ground. This jet used some of the aerospace industry's most advanced technologies and was flown by one of the best trained air crews in the world, yet resulted in the second deadliest aviation accident on U.S. soil to date.

In 1989, a fatal human crush occurred during a British football match in Sheffield, England, killing ninety-six spectators, injuring hundreds more, and traumatizing thousands. People had been packed so tightly in the stadium's 'pens,' or open viewing areas, that many died standing up while oblivious security officials actually pushed escaping fans back into the mayhem.

Finally, a pediatric cardiology unit at a well-reputed hospital in the United Kingdom continued to attempt a risky new surgical operation over a seven-year period even though the procedure was resulting in dozens of infants' deaths. Although doctors arguably possessed the technical skills, teamwork broke down as thirty to thirty-five more babies died than might be expected had the standard of care been equal to that at other hospitals.

In contrast to these examples of performance breakdown, there is the successful rescue of 155 people from the icy waters of the Hudson River in New York City in January 2009, when their airliner experienced a dual engine failure after multiple bird strikes. What enabled this heroic team to succeed – effectively making sense of their challenges in a technologically complex and dynamically evolving environment – while these other teams failed? These five case studies – the USS Greeneville submarine collision, Hillsborough Stadium football crush, American Airlines Flight 587 in-flight breakup, Bristol Hospital pediatric cardiology deaths, and US Airways Flight 1549's Hudson River landing – provide data to understand better the dynamics that impact team performance in high-risk fields. In different ways, each case illustrates how teamwork can be more important than technical prowess in preventing disaster in high-risk fields.

For our purposes, a high-risk team is two or more people working together in an environment where there is significant risk of injury or death to the team or to others as a result of the team's performance. Professionals in fields such as aviation, military, law enforcement, and firefighting risk their own personal safety at work every day, making these excellent examples of high-risk professions. Other fields such as automotive technology, emergency planning, engineering, medicine, nuclear power, or off-shore drilling, among others, may not seem as risky for individuals working within them, yet decisions and actions made by people in these fields can greatly affect the safety of others. Just imagine yourself on the operating table – the surgeon and his or her team's safety may not be directly at risk, but your health certainly is. Therefore, we will consider these high-risk teams as well.

All groups and organizations have subtle, and not so subtle, dynamics that influence team behavior. Yet, teams operating in high-risk fields have unique, often covert, characteristics influenced by the nature of their tasks, their hazardous and unforgiving operating environments, and the ambiguous ways clues to a crisis often emerge. Factors such as time urgency, peer pressure, exposure to personal risk, professional competitiveness, fear of malpractice suits or other forms of retribution, inter- and intra-team conflicts, reputation management, shifting tasks, conflicting goals, uncertainty, dealing with casualties, handling media pressures, and otherwise living with the weighty repercussions of one's decisions often combine to make decision making in high-risk teams an exceptionally stressful activity.[1]

In addition to high-risk professionals managing these stressors, recent disasters have illuminated a surprising range of individuals required to act as key decision makers during a crisis, especially during the initial onset of a problem when it may not yet be clear what the issue is. For instance, actions taken by principals, teachers, and university administrators during school shootings; hospital employees during hurricane evacuation; hotel managers during natural disasters; plant supervisors during industrial accidents; and chief executives during product recalls play central roles in determining when, and if, a situation escalates to full-blown crisis. As a result, it is evident that a wide range of professionals require the ability to think through crisis and manage anxiety, sifting through ambiguous and often conflicting information in order to determine a course of action.[2]

Social science researchers call this process naturalistic decision *making* (NDM), when knowledgeable individuals are operating in dynamic environments with ill-defined goals and ill-structured tasks that require real-time decisions in reaction to continuous change.[3] Developed about twenty years ago, we are only starting to understand the variety of factors that come to play in such scenarios. Yet several NDM studies[4] found that the difference between expert and novice decisions was more often related to the decision-making process itself, not the rank or experience of the individual. How teams gather and share information, developing a 'mental model' of the situation as it unfolds, proves pivotal.

Military studies found that Army commanders store memories of lessons learned in tactical situations as 'war stories' available for retrieval when required. In aviation, we call this hangar flying. These stories become stored templates of knowledge, resources that experienced commanders can draw on when faced with a new challenge.[5] However, this information acquisition process can take years. How can we help teams accelerate their learning process?

Airline pilot Chesley "Sully" Sullenberger, captain of US Airways Flight 1549, provides some guidance: "In addition to learning fundamental skills well," he notes, professionals in high-risk fields "need to learn the important lessons that have been paid for at such great cost over generations" – the teamwork and leadership failures, written in blood, which have provided key lessons learned in the past. Captain Sullenberger emphasizes:

> We need to know about the seminal accidents, and what came out of each of them. In other words, we need to know not only what to do but why we do it. So that in the case when there's no time to consult every written guidance, we can set clear priorities, and follow through with them, and execute them well.[6]

One way to accomplish this is to examine case studies of leadership and teamwork challenges as we do in this book. Like war stories and hangar flying, this approach is an invaluable tool to consider 'what if' scenarios in a controlled setting before people become challenged in high-tempo operations. Although technical training approaches have worked adequately in the past, the complexity of new operating systems, expansion in automation, and pace of technological developments demand new thinking as accidents increasingly result – not from individual error – but from dysfunctional interactions at the interface of human and machine.[7]

As a result, we need new models of accident causality based on socio-technical systems theory that can address the complex interrelatedness of operations in today's high-tech systems. *Socio-technical* theory emphasizes that to improve teamwork, organizations must balance social, or *socio*, factors – such as organizational culture; group norms; values and identity; psychological expectations; and emotions like trust, fear, and anxiety – with *technical* factors – such as modern, well-designed equipment; accurate operating manuals and checklists; relevant standard operating procedures; and effective training methods. Until socio-technical factors are in balance, optimum team performance will not be achieved.

To explore teamwork within these complex socio-technical systems, a *systems psychodynamics* perspective proves helpful. Systems psychodynamics integrates psychoanalytic theory, group study, and open systems perspectives as a way to understand the collective psychological behavior within and between teams and organizations.[8] The advantage of this approach is that it provides a way to consider the motivating forces resulting from the interconnection between various subunits of a social system.[9] As systems become increasingly complex, we can no longer accurately predict the ways things might fail. Therefore, teams must learn to think through crisis, considering the myriad of possibilities that might be occurring.

As a result, we find that team chemistry, the challenge of collaboration, the influence of the system, and the impact of the environment during the critical incubation period while a disaster unfolds prove pivotal to the outcome. As the case studies in this book demonstrate, ultimately a team's ability to learn and adapt spontaneously to the evolving situation, manage individual and group anxiety, and make proper sense of emerging events increases the likelihood of preventing or surviving an organizational disaster. This suggests that teamwork is more important than technical prowess in mitigating organizational disaster. Intended for both frontline operators as well as a wide variety of academic programs – from business management and organizational psychology to educational leadership and public administration – this book bridges the span between practitioner training guide and NDM research report and addresses gaps in our thinking about *crisis decision making*, a relatively new field of management.[10] Understanding the internal dynamics of groups and the stressors teams must manage in order to succeed, will allow people to become more effective leaders, followers and teammates in all kinds of situations.

Rethinking Normal Accidents and Human Error – A New View of Crisis Management

In 1984, Charles Perrow published *Normal Accidents*, one of the first texts to consider the impact of our increasing use of technology in high-risk fields, analyzing the implications on everyday life. Because risk can never be entirely eliminated, Perrow argued, system designers can neither predict every possible failure scenario nor create perfect contingency plans for front-line operators. In other words, no matter how effectively conventional safety devices such as warning systems, overflow valves, or automatic shutdown features perform, some accidents are unpredictable because some failures are simply not 'conventional.' Particularly challenging is the fact that as one unexpected failure stresses different parts of the system in unusual ways, compound failures emerge with increasingly unanticipated results. In fact, these types of unpredictable, compound failures are so inevitable, Perrow argues, we should call them 'normal accidents,' not because of their frequency, but because these accidents are the 'normal' consequence of ever-evolving technologies generating increasingly complex operating systems that stress team operations and sense making in unpredictable ways.[1]

As a result, one of the major factors precipitating compound failures in complex systems is the inability of operators, trained to respond 'by the book,' to evolve their mental picture of the system failure as new data emerge. Such a failure is either so catastrophic or so complex that it shocks people's sense-making capacities. It becomes literally incomprehensible.

Examples of this lack of imagination and flawed sense making abound. In 1977, a Southern Airways DC-9, Flight 242, departed Huntsville, Alabama, en route to Atlanta. Descending from 17,000 feet, the jet entered a thunderstorm, sustained a lightning strike that shattered the cockpit windscreen, and ingested massive amounts of water and hail, flaming out both engines. As the pilots attempted unsuccessfully to restart the engines, the jet glided toward the ground unpowered. Breaking out of the clouds minutes before impact, the aircraft crashed on a rural highway, colliding with a gas station and killing sixty-two people on board and eight people on the ground. Miraculously, nineteen passengers and both flight attendants survived.[2] No turbojet in history had ever experienced a similar failure. It was unimaginable.

The probability of this compound failure was considered so remote, the Federal Aviation Administration (FAA) did not mandate pilots' training for this type of emergency, and the aircraft manufacturer's flight manual provided no guidance.[3] As the incident unfolded, the captain alerted Atlanta air traffic controllers (ATC) about their predicament, demanding, "Get us a vector to a clear area, Atlanta."[4] Yet, ATC was so dumbfounded by the jet's emergency, they repeatedly requested the struggling crew to switch radio frequencies and check their transponder code, minor concerns in the midst of this chaos.

In addition, more than eight minutes before the DC-9's dual engine flameout, another commercial jet had also reported "heavy moderate turbulence and quite a bit of precip"[5] as they flew through the same storm.[6] However, when they complained, rather than consider the danger, ATC defensively responded that there was another aircraft in the area and "He'd be a lot harder than the cloud."[7] Had the FAA, aircraft designers, airline company policies, and ATC training been better able to prepare this aviation team to think through crisis and make sense of the severity of the emergency as it unfolded, this scenario might have ended differently.

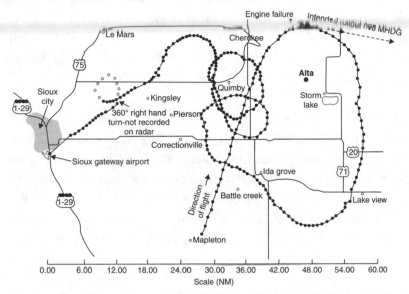

FIGURE 1.1. United Airlines Flight 232 ground track as the team learned the parameters of their emergency and developed proper response measures.[8]

Similarly, the much-publicized crash of United Airlines Flight 232 in 1989 also resulted from compound system failures, unpredictable in their cascading effects. Yet, unlike the Southern Airways example, United Flight 232's team adapted in the moment, allowing for better sense making and team learning as the crisis unfolded, enabling a relatively successful landing given the circumstances.

About one hour after departing Denver en route to Chicago O'Hare Airport, United Flight 232, a DC-10, suffered a catastrophic failure of its number two engine mounted in the tail. As engine components broke away from the airplane, pieces severed hydraulic lines pressuring the flight control systems. With all controllability lost, the aircrew had to relearn how to fly the airplane, working together to use asymmetrical thrust on the two remaining wing-mounted engines to steer the jet to an emergency landing at Sioux Gateway Airport, Iowa (see Figure 1.1). One hundred ten passengers and one crewmember died.

Yet, astonishingly, 165 passengers and 10 crewmembers lived. Once again, no one had ever trained for this type of emergency, and aircraft manuals provided no guidance for the failure of all three hydraulic systems in flight. It was considered an inconceivable scenario.[9]

Driven in part by the increasing occurrence of 'normal accidents' – such as the KLM and Pan Am 747 collision in Tenerife in 1977, Three Mile Island nuclear accident in 1979, National Aeronautics and Space Administration's (NASA) Challenger crash and Russia's Chernobyl nuclear accident in 1986, the London underground's Kings Cross fire in 1987, and Piper Alpha oilrig explosion in 1988 – James Reason published *Human Error* in 1990, another significant text in the burgeoning field of *crisis decision making*. Reason's *Swiss Cheese* model broke failures down into *active* errors, associated with frontline operators like pilots, nuclear control room crew, and medical teams, and *latent* errors, associated with system designers, high-level decision makers, and managers.[10] Rather than blame accidents on individual workers' active errors, Reason argued frontline operators were often just one link in the chain inheriting defective systems full of latent errors – accidents waiting to happen – such as poor system designs, incorrect installations, faulty maintenance, poor training, inaccurate operating manuals, and bad management decisions driven by overly economic considerations. These insidious latent errors lay dormant in the system, waiting for opportunities to emerge and link with operators' active failures, in a "window of accident opportunity."[11]

Building on Perrow and Reason's contributions, new frameworks based on the psychoanalytic study of disasters have emerged with a particular focus on sense making, analyzing factors leading to team performance breakdown, accident, and death in high-risk industries. Examples include studies of nuclear power plants,[12] Mount Everest climbing expeditions,[13] medical operating rooms,[14] NASA explorations,[15] wildfire fighting,[16] oil platforms,[17] and Post-9/11 airlines.[18] Previously, most research explained disasters as resulting from a single flawed decision by an individual operator, an example of Reason's *active* error. In this view, a disaster was "an aberration, an unfortunate accident – as much a tragedy for the well-meaning and generally competent *individuals* who made the decision as for its more direct victims."[19] Analysis focused almost exclusively on operator errors while training aimed to mitigate the recurrence of these individual failures through technical repetition, for instance more time in the flight simulator or on the firing range. Few leaders considered the influence of group dynamics or systemic factors like regulatory oversight, licensing criteria, financial concerns, or organizational culture on team performance prior to or during the disaster period. Yet as our increasingly complex systems produce more and more unimaginable latent errors, it becomes clear that a new vision of teamwork is required: one that considers the system as well as the team in which individuals are operating.

Applying a psychodynamically informed perspective, recent research[20] suggests that errors often result from a breakdown in sense-making team learning in response to anxieties created by changes in the environment.[21] In other words, disasters often result from a team's failure to sense the severity of an impending problem, ask questions, surface conflicts, and discuss errors in a timely fashion. In contrast, team learning is fostered when team members: effectively identify and integrate resources; authorize themselves to speak up, ask questions, investigate points of conflict, and identify errors; resist jumping to conclusions by tolerating ambiguity and a state of *not knowing* as information unfolds over time; and actively analyze the situation in order continue to evolve their mental model. United Flight 232 is an excellent example.

What was exemplary about United Airlines Flight 232 was the calm, controlled sense making that led to an extensive use of resources and high level of team learning by all involved under unprecedented conditions. For example, the captain directed an off-duty DC-10 pilot, who just happened to be a passenger on the flight, to manipulate the throttles, using engine power to control pitch and roll, which freed the captain and first officer to wrestle together with the flight controls. ATC immediately recognized the extent of the problem, only asking for essential information while vectoring the jet toward the airport and organizing ground emergency services. Although the airplane touched down slightly left of runway centerline and skidded, rolling inverted into a cornfield, firefighting and rescue operations began immediately because ATC's early warning allowed emergency responders and local hospitals nearly thirty minutes to prepare. In addition, the airport had an established emergency plan, a National Guard unit on site, and recently had conducted a full-scale disaster drill. As a result, the entire team – pilots, flight attendants, passengers, ATC, medical personnel, firefighters, emergency responders, and National Guard – worked together effectively using resources and making sense of the unfolding situation, minimizing the accident's catastrophic potential. Had Southern Airways Flight 242 had that level of systemic support, results might have been different.

Joining Perrow and Reason, psychoanalytic researchers have contributed importantly to understanding the complexity of interrelated factors leading to modern disasters, analyzing the changed and charged environment of our increasingly technologically sophisticated systems. Yet, the question remains: How should we respond to these changes in the short and long term? Perrow rightly challenges the dominance of technological elites in the determination of which risks we should all bear. This long-term solution begs the question of whether there are better team-building strategies to help make the difference between success and failure in both the short and long term.

To offset the potential for latent errors to combine with active errors with devastating results in our increasingly complex systems, high-risk organizations must cultivate a special form of attentiveness or "mindfulness" in their individuals and teams. Focusing on technical training is no longer sufficient. Teams must develop the ability to

think through crisis, sustaining a vigilant curiosity about their operating environment, a proactive concern for safety, and attentiveness
to the possibility for failure – preparing for the unprecedented – even
when events are proceeding well. Teams must develop the ability to
concentrate on a specific task while also holding the bigger picture in
mind and a resilience to adapt to the unexpected. Finally, teams must
foster a flexible leadership hierarchy that values expertise regardless
of rank and can flow easily from *centralized* to *decentralized* climates
depending on the demands of the situation.[22] As we will see in the
following chapters, how teams in general and leaders in particular
manage this process and respond to anxiety as a disaster unfolds is
critical to the situation's outcome.

2

USS *Greeneville* – The Downside
of Charismatic Leadership

Commanding Officers have a lot of presence onboard submarines
... and for the most part, their judgments are unquestioned. Their
decisions are unquestioned. They are the authority at sea. If the CO
says it is safe, who is going to question that is it not safe?
Lieutenant Junior Grade Michael John Coen,
Officer of the Deck during USS *Greeneville*'s
collision with *Ehime Maru*[1]

On February 9, 2001, the USS *Greeneville*, an American fast-attack
nuclear submarine, collided with a Japanese fishing trawler, the *Ehime
Maru*, during a routine training mission off the Hawaiian Islands. The
accident occurred when the submarine, embarked for a community
relations day, ascended like a rocket during an emergency surfacing
demonstration for sixteen civilian dignitaries and a visiting admiral.
The *Greeneville*'s powerful steel rudder, designed to surface through
thick ice, destroyed the fishing boat, sinking it in less than ten minutes
and killing nine crewmembers (see Figure 2.1).[2]

Two extensive federal investigations, one by the National
Transportation Safety Board and the other by a U.S. Navy *Court of
Inquiry*, concluded that "the responsibility for collision avoidance rests
solely on the submerged submarine."[3] Moreover, the Navy blamed the
Greeneville captain, Commander Scott D. Waddle, for "the failure
of the ship's watch team to work together" to avoid the collision.[4]
Immediately following the accident, the embarked admiral began a
preliminary investigation, later reporting: "There's no question that

FIGURE 2.1. The fast-attack nuclear submarine USS *Greeneville*. Note the reinforced sail (forward) and rudder (aft) designed to break through ice.[5]

the visitors' presence, although perhaps a passive deterrent," influenced the watch team's performance. Yet, the passengers "were not the only reason" for this accident. "There was *something else* going on," the admiral observed. "And I'm still not sure in my own mind what that something else was."[6]

Greeneville's crew was well rested, expertly trained, and widely regarded as one of "the best on the waterfront."[7] The submarine was a marvel of modern technology. And Captain Waddle was charismatic, confident, and popular with his crew – a highly decorated officer with a distinguished record of achievement, an excellent reputation, and a 'go-Navy' attitude. They were exactly the right crew in the right submarine to take distinguished visitors on a public affairs outing and put on a good show. Or were they?

About a month before the collision, the *Ehime Maru* departed Japan and the Uwajima Fisheries School, steering for Hawaii where the weather was warm, fish were plentiful, and waters thought to be safe. A floating classroom, the ship trained high school students in engineering, preparing them for the professional fishing trade. On the day of the accident, the *Ehime Maru*, a gleaming white vessel, exited

FIGURE 2.2. The Japanese fishing vessel *Ehime Maru*.[8]

Honolulu Harbor at noon en route to fishing grounds about 300 nautical miles south of Oahu for the day's lessons (see Figure 2.2). Once outside the harbor, the captain, a forty-year maritime veteran, increased the trawler's speed to eleven knots and engaged the ship's autopilot, steady on course 166 degrees. The autopilot maintained this exact configuration until the *Greeneville* collision twenty-eight minutes later (see Figure 2.3).

That same morning, the *Greeneville* departed Pearl Harbor on schedule at 8 A.M. to conduct their public relations cruise, transiting out of the harbor on the water's surface so guests could visit the bridge and observe the captain and his team in operation. Lieutenant Keith A. Sloan, the navigator, noted there was "a high choppy sea state" and a "hazy, off-white sky," which was "probably the worst I've seen" for identifying vessels through the periscope. "You could actually see a long, long distance, but not see *clearly* very far at all."[9] Sloan recalled viewing two trawlers through the periscope about equal distance away. "One was dark-hulled, the other white." As the ships came closer, he noted no problem acquiring the "dark-hulled vessel during periscope

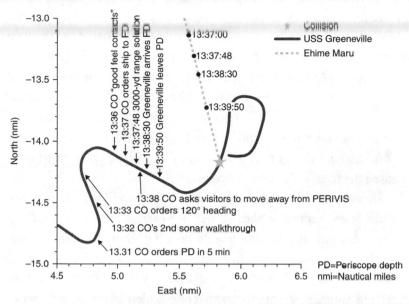

FIGURE 2.3. USS *Greeneville* and *Ehime Maru* collision track. Plot shows the actions of the Commanding Officer (CO) Captain Waddle and the track of the USS *Greeneville* and *Ehime Maru* prior to their collision on February 9, 2001.[10]

sweeps, but concerted effort was required to relocate the white-hulled vessel." Yet, none of this information was passed on to the captain or other watchstanders.[11]

As the submarine left Pearl Harbor, a new young officer, Lieutenant Junior Grade Michael J. Coen, was busy below decks readying the submarine to dive. With a reputation for being "methodical to a fault,"[12] Coen was one of the last to finalize preparations to dive, a delay that "did not go unnoticed" by senior officers. "I got some very high tension from the captain" about that delay, Coen recalled.[13] Once outside the harbor, the *Greeneville* submerged and events proceeded as planned. Guests toured the submarine, driving the ship in the control room and listening to water noises and whale recordings in the sonar room. But around 11 A.M., things began to go awry.

To his crew's surprise, Captain Waddle decided to demonstrate the ship's capabilities by taking the submarine to 'test depth,' a classified maneuver not normally done in civilian company, and the *Greeneville* submerged to 700 feet. His reasoning for this unorthodox decision was that he thought the visitors would be impressed and enjoy having a "special story" to tell their friends. He also wanted to "obtain deep seawater samples at test depth" to package as mementos for his guests to take home.[14] This unplanned event, along with delays during lunch, caused the team to fall behind schedule.

Meanwhile, the watch team changed over, and Lieutenant Junior Grade Coen and Petty Office Patrick T. Seacrest came on duty. Coen only recently qualified as *officer of the deck* (OOD) and had about three months' experience at sea. In contrast, Petty Officer Seacrest was a senior enlisted watchstander with fourteen years of service on three previous submarines, highly trained and widely experienced operating the submarine's sophisticated sonar equipment.

Together, the watch team collaborated to maintain the 'big picture'. Listening for vessel noise, they developed an image of obstacles in the area in order to collectively build a mental model of threats. At the time, only two boats had been identified, both of which were assumed to be a safe distance away. One was the *Ehime Maru*, mistakenly placed at 14,000 yards heading away from the *Greeneville* when she was actually 10,000 yards away and converging – autopilot still steady on course and speed.

After lunch, *Greeneville*'s plan was to complete four training maneuvers, demonstrating the crew's technical prowess and the submarine's tactical capabilities, then return to Pearl Harbor by 2 P.M. Yet at 1 P.M., the watch team still had not started the training evolutions.

Lieutenant Sloan went to the captain's stateroom to alert him that they were falling behind schedule and might be late returning to port. He found Captain Waddle autographing photographs for the visitors to take home. Sloan recalled, the captain "did not want to be late.

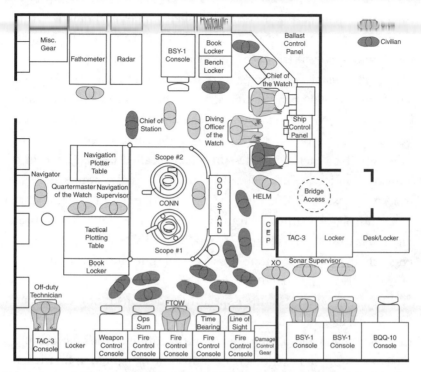

FIGURE 2.4. Approximate location of thirty-three civilians and crew in the USS *Greeneville*'s control room and sonar room when the submarine executed the emergency ballast blow maneuver, colliding with the *Ehime Maru*.[15]

He wanted to get going," and this concerned him because he knew Lieutenant Junior Grade Coen was on watch. Although Coen had observed the training maneuvers scheduled, he had never completed them in the role of OOD.[16] Sloan knew Coen was "not the fastest guy in the world" and had a reputation for being "meticulous" and "not easily pushed."[17] Yet, "as Captain Waddle left his stateroom," Sloan heard him say "he was going 'to push the OOD.'"[18]

Around 1:10 P.M., the civilian guests were invited to the control room to observe the maneuvers, and in response thirty-three people crowded into a space about twenty by twenty feet (see Figure 2.4). Forty-five minutes behind schedule, the *Greeneville* finally commenced the first event. Called 'angles and dangles,' this maneuver demonstrated the submarine's ability to rapidly change depth and speed like an airplane evading threats. As OOD, Coen was in charge of executing the maneuvers. Yet, Captain Waddle stood immediately behind him "driving the whole evolution" while describing events for the civilian guests crowded around him. Coen became just "a mouthpiece,"[19] parroting the captain's commands to other watchstanders.[20] Lieutenant Sloan recalled he had been in a similar situation before. He said Captain Waddle "wants it done quickly. He wants it done his way. I didn't like it and I'm sure that Coen didn't like it either."[21] Would Coen resist the captain's pressure? Sloan was unsure: "I have seen" Coen "stand up" to other senior officers before. "I would assume" that "would translate over to the captain as well. Maybe, maybe not."[22]

The next event was a high-speed turn demonstration displaying the submarine's maneuverability evading torpedoes in a tactical setting. "As it had been during angles, the attention of the" captain and OOD "was focused exclusively on ship control," so much that when Coen attempted to leave the immediate area – as he should to keep abreast of the sonar picture and obstacles in the area – Captain Waddle "stopped him," "placing a hand on his shoulder accompanied by words about how his attention needed to be on ship control."[23] Meanwhile, Captain Waddle continued to narrate the evolution, proudly boasting he "would challenge any other boat to perform these maneuvers so well."[24] The visitors agreed: "It was a very professional job," the admiral recalled.[25]

Yet high-speed turns disturb the water, creating what sonar operators describe as "spaghetti noodles moving all over" their viewing screens.[26] As a result, contact with the *Ehime Maru* was lost for two minutes at 1:33 P.M. To update the data, Seacrest needed the submarine steady on course, speed, and depth for *at least two*, three- to five-minute legs in order to triangulate the boat's position, developing an accurate picture of obstacles in the area.[27] Yet for a series of reasons, this steady state was not forthcoming, unbeknownst to the team, the *Ehime Maru* – still steady on course 166 at eleven knots – had now closed to within 6,000 yards.

The final, fateful series of events began with an ascent to periscope depth, a visual search for surface obstacles, a quick evasive dive, and the emergency surfacing maneuver. To accomplish this safely, the *Greeneville* still needed to reacquire reliable sonar data and update their picture of surface obstacles in the area. However, rather than provide the crew the time they needed, Captain Waddle surprised his team with another unusual action. He ordered Lieutenant Junior Grade Coen to "get to periscope depth in five minutes," an impossible order to accomplish legally and safely.[28]

Although other officers heard the captain's order and later testified that they thought it to be overly aggressive, they nonetheless did and said nothing to intervene. Coen recalled, "I believed it was rapid and rushed" to execute the captain's order. "And I was tense and excited basically to be challenged like this" with everyone "watching me," but "I believed it was achievable." Relying on the experience of his captain, he stated, "At no time did I feel that it could not be done or that if we did it, it would be unsafe."[29]

Ten minutes before collision, Petty Officer Seacrest reacquired contact with the boats in their area. Mistakenly satisfied that he had an accurate picture on the two previously held vessels, Seacrest began to concentrate on identifying the new contact. It was highly unusual, if not dangerously unsafe, for a submarine to ascend to periscope depth without a clear picture of surface obstacles. This risk concerned and distracted Seacrest from recognizing the *Ehime Maru*'s position now just 2,510 yards away and still closing. Yet, rushed by the captain, crowded by observers, and distracted by his new contact, Seacrest failed to notice. The team proceeded to periscope depth – the charismatic captain eager to demonstrate his submarine's power and crew's tactical skills, and the fledgling OOD too new to know better.

As the *Greeneville* periscope broke the surface, Coen completed three quick visual sweeps as waves slapped against the viewer. Just as he reported "no close contacts," Captain Waddle took the periscope, raised the ship a few feet to clear the waves, and began conducting his own scan of the hazy horizon, looking for surface obstacles. Intending to take the crew by surprise, the captain abruptly ordered 'emergency deep' after just sixty-six seconds at periscope depth, a third unconventional maneuver, and the crew responded, quickly diving the submarine.

At 1:40 P.M. – five minutes before impact – Petty Officer Seacrest finally noticed the *Ehime Maru*'s new position north of the submarine and closing. Yet, once again, he failed to inform his team about this new information.

As the watch team prepared for the last training event, the captain invited three guests to man submarine controls to assist in the maneuver under the supervision of qualified watchstanders. "The ultimate roller coaster ride,"[30] the *emergency main ballast blow* shoots 4,500 psi air into the submarine's main ballast tanks, creating positive buoyancy that forces the 7,000-ton submarine to the surface. Once initiated, surfacing is unstoppable.[31] As a sign of his comfort and confidence, the captain once again narrated the crew's activities for the visitors, as the submarine shot toward the surface. Less than a minute later, there was "a shudder," "two loud thumps," and the captain exclaimed "What the hell was that?" The submarine had collided with the *Ehime Maru*, slicing the trawler in half from starboard to port.[32]

Focusing on team chemistry, the challenge of collaboration in complex and dynamically evolving high-risk environments, and the role of team learning in high-risk team operations, we will now examine individual behaviors, group dynamics, and systemic factors that contributed to this mishap – all forces shaping what that "*something else*" was that influenced *Greeneville*'s team performance that day. Let's start with the *Greeneville*'s captain.

In many ways, Captain Waddle was a model naval officer, known to be one of the strongest commanding officers in the submarine force.[33] A second generation career military man, Waddle attended the U.S. Naval Academy, majoring in chemistry, and he described himself as "part Boy Scout and part rebel."[34] Although he excelled as president of his high school National Honor Society, Eagle Scout, and captain of the football team, at the Academy he participated in the cheerleading squad because he was too small for college sports. "Years later, as captain of the *Greeneville*," Captain Waddle recalled "I'd often find that my cheerleading skills came in handy, especially when motivating my men, speaking to civic groups and colleges on behalf of the Navy, or conducting public relations cruises."[35] Initially focused on becoming a pilot like his father, Captain Waddle's poor eye sight forced him to select another career path. After a summer cruise on the USS *Skipjack* in 1978, he "was hooked" on submarines, not "just the amazing machine" but "the amazing crewmen." In particular, he was fascinated by the captain's authority: "*I want that guy's job,*" he wrote in his autobiography.[36]

After graduating from the Naval Academy in 1981, he rose quickly through the submarine officer ranks, receiving the coveted dolphin warfare specialty pin in 1986 and passing the notoriously difficult engineering exam on his first attempt. Waddle claimed to have found his "niche" when he discovered that what he "really enjoyed was motivating men, bringing out the best in them, training them, instilling in them standards of excellence, and then turning out an exceptional product for the Navy."[37] The future seemed bright for this young officer until personality clashes put him at odds with some of his supervisors. It became apparent that Captain Waddle had issues with conservative leaders who lacked flexibility, "stickler[s] for the rules and regulations," and he was not afraid to say so. One captain even issued him a *Nonpunitive Letter of Caution* warning: "You need to harness your energy and apply it in areas that would be more productive."[38]

When Captain Waddle took command of the USS *Greeneville*, his first goal was to develop a command climate in which his crew could ask "a question," "challenge a decision," or speak up if "they thought it was unsafe or if we were overlooking something."[39] To accomplish this he removed the "fear factor" and created a "more relaxed atmosphere" of "mutual respect and trust," developing "three tenets" that he felt "summed up our working conditions aboard the *Greeneville*: safety, efficiency, and backup."[40] He tried other ways to make "life aboard ship as pleasant as possible" too, improving the food, providing video games for relaxation, and increasing the crews' time off with their families. He also had a sense of humor. In 1999 at the annual Submarine Birthday Ball, the *Greeneville* entered a contest for 'best table center-piece.' Their entry was a rotating periscope popping out of a toilet commode as a recorded voice boomed, "We're closer than you think." They won first prize.[41]

Whereas Captain Waddle's 'part-rebel' persona might have caused consternation with his seniors, it endeared him to the young men under his tutelage. In many ways a 'man's man' and a 'sailor's captain', Waddle's team responded to his wholesome good looks, concern for families, sense of humor, and machismo. "If we go to war," he was known to say, "you want to go to war with me!"[42] He pushed his submarine to its operational limits, and his men responded with eager enthusiasm, just like the Navy wanted. All of this makes the causes of *Greeneville*'s teamwork breakdown on February 9, 2001, so difficult to discern.

How can we reconcile the inconsistencies between the outstanding reputations and accolades the *Greeneville* captain and crew enjoyed prior to the collision and the team's performance that fateful day? As one admiral noted, the "'superficial' indicators of readiness all looked good. The boat was clean, the crewmembers were 'positive' … happy with their leadership … and proud of their organization."[43] Moreover, retention of *Greeneville* sailors was exemplary; double the navy-wide rate. All signs of a satisfied and productive Navy submarine. Yet everyone concedes, "Something was different" that day.[44]

"The crew was complacent," Captain Waddle reflected, "including me to some degree." Our mission was to "take these VIPs out on a lazy Friday and it was just another VIP cruise." That lackadaisical attitude "was wrong."[45] "One of the root causes" of the accident, the captain noted, was overconfidence. Even when a submarine crew is great, "they sometimes take for granted their expertise, and they become complacent. And that's what happened on that day."[46]

Yet accident investigators found the explanation much more complicated than simply overconfidence and complacency. The National Transportation Safety Board (NTSB) concluded, "The teamwork problems demonstrated on the day of the collision were due in part" to Captain Waddle's "overly directive style," particularly in relationship to the OOD on duty, Lieutenant Junior Grade Coen.[47] The failure of key watchstanders to effectively perform their duties and speak up, providing the vital information their team needed, resulted in the crew's inadequate analysis of surface obstacles in the area. In particular, the rushed ascent to periscope depth, the inadequate visual search, and the emergency surfacing maneuver resulted in collision with the misidentified contact, the *Ehime Maru*.

These team failures were not errors in technical proficiency but inadequacies in leadership, communication, teamwork, and sense making. This is especially disconcerting when one considers the captain's proclaimed efforts to develop a climate of trust and openness in which the crew could ask questions without fear of reprisal. It would be reasonable to expect that the *Greeneville*'s three tenets of safety, efficiency, and backup would mitigate any tendency toward the overconfidence and complacency Captain Waddle believed caused this accident. Yet, this did not happen.

One of the advantages of working in a team in a high-risk environment is using one's teammates to cross-check and compare 'mental models' to discern what is really going on. To accomplish this, the team must not be afraid to speak up or to risk conflict as a way to discover new information and manage errors. Yet, in the *Greeneville* example there are numerous instances during which crew members noted information or observed teammates' actions that caused them concern, and then failed to communicate these concerns to their teammates. For instance, Lieutenant Sloan did not inform his team about his difficulties viewing ships through the periscope due to the haze. Petty Officer Seacrest did not share his difficulty tracking contacts. In addition, although senior officers noticed the watch team's struggles, they failed to intervene as the submarine fell further behind schedule.

One of the most glaring deficiencies in team performance was an inadequate concern for safety, a lack of backup, and a loss of situational awareness by key personnel of the submarine's watch team. For example, Lieutenant Junior Grade Coen testified that shortly before 1 P.M. he realized, given the submarine's position and the remaining schedule of activities, that they either needed to cancel some of the training maneuvers or return late to port. Although he "did not formally discuss this" with anyone, he felt it was clear "we had to do one or the other."[48] This confusion may have also led Petty Officer Seacrest to be less than diligent about tracking surface contacts and Coen to be less inquiring. Coen admits he was "aware" that Seacrest "did not have a great picture" of obstacles in the area. But he wasn't overly concerned because he "assumed that some evolutions would be cancelled" and "that a senior officer would brief him about the changes."[49] Although others within the team were similarly confused, few people spoke up. In fact, when Lieutenant Commander Gerald Pfeiffer, the submarine's executive officer (XO), tried to remind the captain about their time constraints by politely inferring – although never directly recommending – that the captain cancel the last event and return to port, Captain Waddle snapped, "I know what I'm doing."[50] This does not sound like a climate of safety, efficiency, and backup.

Such communication failures directly contributed to this maritime accident. Numerous 'red flags' can be identified throughout the day, signaling the possibility of errors and impending team breakdown: for instance, the crew falling behind schedule then rushing to complete maneuvers in order to return to port on time, trying something new under pressure with VIPs watching, imprecise communications, confusion about the sequence and plan of evolutions, and role ambiguity such as when Captain Waddle drove the submarine through the OOD.

Particularly troubling is that little effort was made to clear up these inconsistencies, thus providing the safety and backup their tenet allegedly supported. The crew seemed to just trust that the captain would take care of things. Yet this still does not completely explain the impact of Captain Waddle's "overly directive style" on teamwork that day. For that analysis, we must now examine the systemic factors contributing to this accident as a way to reconcile the inconsistencies between *Greeneville*'s reputation and its performance on the day of the accident.

Although some military analysts observed that the submarine force, or 'silent service', did more to protect American soil and win the Cold War than any other branch of the U.S. military, by the late 1990s severe budget cuts were impacting operations and the construction of new submarines. "Suddenly," Captain Waddle observed, "the Navy was in the awkward position of having to validate the peacetime need for its expensive, secretive, silent service."[51] Without Cold War enemies to justify their existence, the nuclear-powered submarine program had a new mission: "To survive."[52] Public relations cruises, like the one on February 9, 2001, helped accomplish this task. Although some captains avoided these events because they believed they were an interruption, Captain Waddle "loved it," taking personal pride in supporting "requests from his senior officers" and showing off his ship and team of sailors.[53] This promotion was an important systemic dynamic on the day of the accident.

In many ways, Captain Waddle was exactly the kind of 'go-Navy' cheerleader the post–Cold War, all-volunteer armed services needed. He had the attitude, charisma, and confidence that a submarine commander needed to help the 'silent service' survive in the challenging peacetime environment. Yet, ironically the same skills that the *political system* required from Captain Waddle actually undermined the *social system* and his ability to build his team on board the *Greeneville*. His competence 'crowded out' the space needed for his team members to learn and grow into their own leadership roles. In other words, Captain Waddle's impressive persona contributed to the atrophy of his crew's ability to act independently, speak up, ask questions, and authorize themselves to work collaboratively to execute the submarine's mission.

As psychodynamic researcher Debbie Bing noted, "strong leaders can 'steal' talent, ambition and thinking power from others simply by acting singularly on their own instincts and knowledge while undertending to others' ideas, strengths and the dialogue of a good team."[54] Unless the leader can be exceptionally reflective in the moment about the impact of his or her behavior on others – for instance, stepping back at times when instincts would ordinarily urge him or her to take action – it is difficult for the team to achieve the level of mindfulness and resilience needed to succeed in today's complex high-risk operating environments. This accident is an unfortunate example of the downside of charismatic leadership at work.

Although it is easy to blame this team dysfunction on the charismatic leader – just as the Navy's *Court of Inquiry* blamed Captain Waddle for "the failure of the ship's watch team to work together" to avoid the collision – the dysfunctional dynamic is actually co-created by pressures from the wider system, such as the Navy's fiscal challenges in the peacetime environment and the internal dynamics of the team itself.

As Captain Waddle's capabilities grew in response to the system's escalating demands, his team's confidence in their own skills and opinions
diminished, increasing their dependency on him. It was a slow, steady
spiral into team breakdown.

For example, on the day of the collision many people reported being
troubled by activities on board the *Greeneville*, but few spoke up, asked
questions, or intervened. Lieutenant Sloan noticed how the hazy visibility made viewing light-colored boats like the *Ehime Maru* through
the periscope difficult; senior officers thought the captain's pressure
on the watch team, in particular his order to get to periscope depth
in five minutes, was overly aggressive; and Petty Officer Seacrest felt
rushed, crowded, and lacked confidence in the accuracy of his surface
picture. Yet all failed to authorize themselves to act on this information,
speak up, or share it with their team in any meaningful way. One has
to wonder if they were intimidated, intentionally withholding information, or just being lackadaisical, as Captain Waddle suggested.

Perhaps Lieutenant Junior Grade Coen best describes the roots of
the team's befuddlement: "The commanding officer has many years of
experience, many years of training." He is "the authority at sea." His
"decisions are unquestioned." Coen said he thought, "Here's a man"
who can "much more rapidly assess and evaluate information" than
we can; if the captain "says it is safe, who is going to question that is it
not safe?"[55]

These observations are particularly revealing. It seemed that the
captain's competency and ability to rapidly assimilate new information
led the team to feel that it could not ask questions or provide input to
help in the decision making. They seemed to feel like they were per-
petually a step behind, and every piece of information they might have
offered was already outdated, useless, or unneeded. "Surely, the captain must already know this," they began to unconsciously assume. It
was a progressive cycle of team breakdown.

Contributing to this dynamic was Captain Waddle's habit of improvising without discussing his intentions with the team: for instance,

taking the submarine to 'test depth', driving the submarine through junior officers, only spending sixty-six seconds at periscope depth, and allowing civilians to man the submarine's controls. One could argue that as the submarine's commander, it was Captain Waddle's prerogative to exercise these privileges. However, one cannot ignore the implications of this improvisation, coupled with his charismatic leadership style, on the team's ability to function effectively.

These types of impromptu changes kept the team off balance, not sure what to expect next or how they could contribute. The submarine XO, Lieutenant Commander Pfeiffer, described the impact: "The first time we" exceeded "classified depths and speeds" with civilians onboard "I may have said, 'Hey, is this really' what we are 'going to do?'" Is this really "what your intentions are"? "And then it became the norm and I kind of accepted it as that's how we're going to" operate here.[56] Devaluing their own skills, the team unconsciously colluded with the captain by putting all their strengths into him as the omnipotent leader. Just like Pfeiffer, the team stopped asking questions and resigned themselves that this was 'how we're going to operate', further encouraging dependency on the charismatic leader, their captain.

Over time the team's dependency and growing inefficiency caused the captain to become increasingly frustrated. For instance, Captain Waddle admits that he pressured Lieutenant Junior Grade Coen because he was "so fricking slow." It took "forever for me to get information out of him," he complained. "So I tried to teach him."[57] By pushing him and "giving him an 'artificial time constraint,'" Captain Waddle believed he could get him to be more efficient. Exasperated by Coen's methodical nature, Captain Waddle became drawn even further into the team's operations. Lieutenant Commander Pfeiffer recalled being alarmed when Captain Waddle "got in the middle" of operations: On "all submarines you should be a little concerned when the captain" is driving the ship "instead of standing back and watching things," keeping the big picture. Yet once again, Pfeiffer failed to intervene.[58]

A final repercussion of Captain Waddle's leadership style had to do with special relationships developed within his team. As the captain's competency overwhelmed the team's ability to function independently, space disappeared for the productive exploration of differences between team members. People refrained from questioning one another in public – especially challenging the captain – as an instinctive move to protect themselves from exposure and embarrassment. Meanwhile, special relationships blossomed in private.

For example, Lieutenant Commander Pfeiffer talked about how his adjoining stateroom afforded him "proximity to the captain" so that he could provide the captain "some private criticism or feedback that wouldn't be appropriate publicly."[59] Lieutenant Sloan said that, although other officers like Lieutenant Junior Grade Coen struggled with the captain's leadership style, he "had a very good working relationship" with Commander Waddle. "I knew if it was really important, I felt he would listen to me. I really felt that."[60] And Petty Officer Seacrest, who had been hand-selected to be the *command career counselor* with the important task of reenlisting the highly trained nuclear sailors, said he had "very frequent" exchanges with the captain, who took a personal interest in retaining his submarine's sailors.[61] These special relationships encouraged the team to work conflicts out in private, not process issues in public as a routine aspect of team operations.

CONCLUSION

As Commander Waddle's team became more and more enamored with him, their perceptions of his omnipotence grew, 'crowding out' the team's sense of competence and self-authorization. His habit of employing unorthodox approaches and improvising without warning further pulled the team off balance. To compensate, an informal network emerged in which individuals sought connection and special relationships with the captain in private as a way to avoid conflict and the risk involved in developing public solutions. Contrary to the open command climate the captain intended, in which the team could challenge a decision or speak up if they thought something was unsafe, a dependency dynamic emerged in which few people questioned anything.

In the absence of an explicit effort by Captain Waddle to give authority back to his team so that others could experience both the risk and the responsibility of taking it – in their own way, at their own pace – the team lost touch with their own competency and leadership skills. In an effort to please their charismatic leader, the team learned to spend an inordinate amount of energy orienting actions around the captain, rather than developing their own authority and leadership skills. In other words, rather than thinking and acting on their own, they often tried to guess what the captain would want, even in areas where they had more knowledge or expertise. Their overwhelming faith in his abilities diminished their own capacities.

A 'fictitious truth' developed in which Captain Waddle's team assumed the charismatic captain knew all – the hazy visibility, poor tracking of boats in the area, the location of obstacles – while simultaneously training the OOD, driving the submarine, narrating events, and playing public relations tour guide: A herculean task, no human could achieve. Yet, the Navy as a 'system' had grown to expect this level of performance. This powerful, covert dynamic is the 'something else' that was going on aboard the USS *Greeneville*. This 'fictitious truth' explains the inconsistency between the outstanding reputation the USS *Greeneville* enjoyed, in general, and its performance that fateful day in February, and why the system of safety, efficiency, and backup failed to work.

In sum, the demands of the peacetime military for charismatic leaders like Captain Waddle and his resultant popularity with his crew actually put the USS *Greeneville* at risk for this team performance breakdown and "window of accident opportunity."[62] This potential is particularly acute in high-risk fields where the repercussions of human error can be so devastating. When leaders are extremely competent and team members trust and respect them – like Captain Waddle and his crew aboard the USS *Greeneville* – team leaders must be ever vigilant to keep a dependent group dynamic from emerging. In a dependent team, individuals develop an almost irrational respect for their charismatic leader as all-knowing to defend against their anxieties provoked by the work environment. As in the *Greeneville* accident, team members can withhold important information, not from technical incompetence or fear of the leader's reprisal, but because the individuals unconsciously believe these impressive leaders already know the information because they 'know everything'.

The *Greeneville*'s watch team's failure was to succumb to this dangerous dependency dynamic, not seeing Captain Waddle as a man with limitations but rather a deity with supreme powers. Captain Waddle's leadership failure was to not guard against the potential that his charisma might create this dependency. Finally, the Navy's failure was to expect so much. Until high-risk organizations, and leaders and teams within them, understand the need to balance these parameters, they risk falling prey to the seductive power of charismatic leadership.

3

The Hillsborough Football Disaster – Explosive Team Chemistry

The thing that sticks in my mind ... is the state of panic that ... overcame the senior officers. The command structure of the force totally broke down for several minutes and no one appeared to grasp the severity of the situation.[1]
    Police Constable S. Smith on duty during
    the Hillsborough football disaster.

On April 15, 1989, the Liverpool and Nottingham Forrest football clubs prepared for their semifinal match at Hillsborough's Sheffield Wednesday Stadium, a neutral venue in the north of England. The game was stopped only six minutes after kickoff when spectators standing in the stadium's terraced 'pens' behind the Liverpool goal began staggering onto the field and collapsing; ninety-six Liverpool fans were killed, many suffocating to death while standing up. More than seven hundred people were injured, four hundred received hospital treatment, and thousands more were traumatized by that day's events. Fearing a riot or outbreak of *hooliganism*, police actually pushed escaping fans back into the crush amidst the confusion. How could officers trained to 'protect and serve' have contributed to such a devastating tragedy? What happened to their sense-making capacities when the situation began to go awry?

By all accounts that Saturday began as a beautiful spring morning: The sun was shining; players were excited to be in the semifinals; and fans were exhilarated to have secured a ticket, "quietly confident of a good game."[2] The match was a sellout. Therefore, police expected 54,000 ticket holders along with the usual gate crashers hoping to get in some way. One detective recalled, "It was like a party really. We were all like fans, all excited and bubbling over." Most of the police "are football fans anyway and probably a lot of them would have worked it for nothing!"[3]

Coincidentally, Liverpool had played Nottingham Forrest in the same match and stadium the previous year, so fans and law enforcement were familiar with the setup. Most of the 1,133 police on duty had significant experience working football matches at Hillsborough and elsewhere.[4] Several hundred stadium security employees were also on duty, backed up by closed-circuit television throughout the stadium and a computerized ticket counting system that issued an alert if any area reached max capacity.[5] Chief Superintendent David Duckenfield was the match commander. He was assisted by Superintendent Greenwood inside the stadium, Marshall at Liverpool's entrance, Chapman at Nottingham Forrest's entrance, and Murray inside the stadium in the police control box. All of these veteran officers had extensive experience policing football, in general, and semifinals at Hillsborough, in particular – *except Chief Duckenfield.*

Chief Duckenfield had taken command of his police division *just twenty-one days* before the match and had no experience as match commander. When he arrived, the pre-planning was already in progress under the leadership of his predecessor, Chief Superintendent Brian Mole, who oversaw both the 1987 and 1988 semifinal matches. Given Chief Duckenfield's limited experience, making major changes to Chief Mole's plans at that late date would have only led to confusion. Therefore, Chief Duckenfield inherited Chief Mole's policing plan, which had worked adequately in previous years, a leadership team with experienced senior officers, and a support network of motivated junior officers, all happy to be attending the football game. It seemed like a perfect opportunity for Chief Duckenfield to gain experience with little risk, or so they thought.

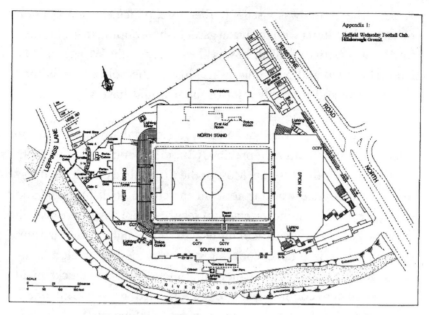

FIGURE 3.1. Hillsborough's Sheffield Wednesday Stadium layout (from a report presented to Parliament by the Secretary of State for the Home Department by Command of Her Majesty).[6]

Fans began to arrive early on game day. Although the Hillsborough gates opened at noon and police tried to persuade the spectators to enter, most were reluctant, choosing instead to sit by the river in the sunshine picnicking, drinking beer, or visiting local pubs.[7] Not a surprising response since there was no pregame entertainment, limited food options, no alcohol, and no seats inside for those with tickets on the terraces.

As a policy, rivaling teams' supporters are 'segregated' to avoid fighting at British football matches. Therefore, Liverpool fans were allocated the north and west sides of the stadium entering via Leppings Lane, whereas Nottingham Forest fans were assigned the south and east sides entering via Penistone Road (see Figure 3.1). Unfortunately for Liverpool fans, the Leppings Lane entry was awkwardly pinned between village shops and a bridge over the river, making access difficult. Once past a bend in the lane, Liverpool fans squeezed through metal perimeter gates to find they had three poorly marked options for entry: north-stand fans needed to move left, west-stand fans entered straight, and the largest majority – 10,100 terrace ticket holders – needed to move right. This created considerable chaos.

One Liverpool fan recalled: "We had not anticipated the confusion that greeted us as we approached" Leppings Lane. It wasn't until we were already inside the gates that we realized we must move right "to our allocated turnstiles" but "even this slight change of direction" was difficult in the crowd. "People were colliding" as they "tried to get to the correct place."[8] I was "particularly surprised to see so few policemen actually near the turnstiles … There was just a single mass of people," he recalled.[9] In previous years, police ejected ticketless fans and organized the queue before fans approached the stadium. Yet to save money this year, 127 fewer police officers were on duty, a 14 percent reduction overall and a 20 percent reduction to Leppings Lane manning levels.[10]

By 2 P.M., it became apparent that, although Nottingham Forrest fans were filling their end of the stadium, Liverpool fans were slow to arrive. In fact, only 12,000 had entered so far compared to 20,000 by this time the previous year. In addition, Liverpool's center terraces or 'pens' behind the goal – pens 3 and 4 – were filling rapidly while the wing pens 1 and 2 on the south side and 6 and 7 on the north were nearly empty (see Figure 3.1). Experienced football fan Jenni Hicks, who lost her two daughters in the crush, recalled: "When you have been to a lot of matches, your instinct tells you when something is not right." Observing the Leppings Lane terraces where her family was standing, she recalled thinking, "This is not how it should be on a semifinal day … This is a big game." This crowd pattern just "wasn't right."[11] Another spectator agreed, noting: "A regular fan" can "tell what a crowd looks like. You know when it's full, you know when there are gaps." I "couldn't see gaps between the heads in Leppings Lane"; it was "this mass of humanity that wasn't swaying and moving" in the center. Yet, "the three wing sections were empty."[12]

The overcrowding in pens 3 and 4 behind the Liverpool goal caught Chief Duckenfield's attention as well. Seated in the police control box elevated above pen 1, he had a commanding view of the field and stands. At 2:15 P.M., he ordered a PA announcement directing "fans in pens 3 and 4 to move forward and make room for others."[13] Yet, he did little else to assist. In previous matches, such as the 1988 Hillsborough semifinal, police actively funneled fans toward less full pens, monitoring the overcrowding. On this occasion, Chief Duckenfield directed that all pens would be available and "fans should find their own level" without assistance – a fatal decision.[14]

Outside the stadium, Liverpool fans "were converging on the grounds in vast numbers"[15] as people previously stuck in traffic or enjoying the spring day now became eager to enter the stadium. Chief Duckenfield recalled he "was aware" of the "increasing number of supporters in Leppings Lane" waiting to enter the ground. Yet Superintendent Murray, the more experienced officer, advised, "With half an hour to kickoff we should get them all in on time."[16] As per police protocol, Murray noted, unless "there was an identifiable problem" that prevented people from "arriving on time," they would not delay the start.[17]

As urgency to enter before kickoff built, the impending danger was obvious to police and fans alike outside the gates. One spectator observed, the crowds "were becoming uncontrollably large" and "the turnstiles choked with people. Police had made no attempt to isolate and filter out" spectators "without tickets. There were no identifiable queues to the entrances, just a claustrophobic free-for-all of fans fighting for access."[18] Similarly, a doctor arrived with his family just after 2:30 P.M. and withdrew to wait rather than fight the crowd at the turnstiles. Concerned, he warned police: "You've got to get a grip of this situation, it is out of control, there is going to be a tragedy."[19] Yet little was done to effect any change.

By 2:45 P.M., the carnival atmosphere gave way to aggression and chaos[20] as the crowd swelled to more than 5,000 outside the Liverpool gates.[21] The situation was approaching intolerable. Police officers on foot were pinned, in danger of being crushed themselves. Mounted officers were surrounded and ineffective.[22] And the antiquated turnstiles could not rotate fast enough to allow people through as quickly as they were arriving. "The mood was a mixture of panic and anger."[23] A big part of the problem, Police Sergeant Robert Burns noted, was that many Liverpool fans arrived without tickets and were nonetheless attempting to enter, taking advantage of the chaos. Each "had to be manhandled and forcibly ejected."[24]

Inspector Paul Hand-Davis, mounted section commander and an eleven-year veteran policing football, radioed for backup assistance[25] as police attempted to gain control. Whatever tactics they tried, he recalled, "the crowd simply ignored us." Eventually it "became so overcrowded that my horse," who "weighs well over ½ ton" began "to lose his footing" and we were both lifted off the ground "by the crowd."[26] Answering the call for backup, Police Constable Michael Buxton arrived in his Land Rover to direct people "by loudspeaker not to push."[27] He recalled, "I was amazed at what I found." Liverpool fans "were simply pouring down Leppings Lane towards the ground." The turnstiles were overwhelmed. The crowd was "fanatical" to enter,[28] the "pressure at the front of the queue was tremendous, and I became very concerned" people would be hurt.[29] "It seemed as if *something more important than a football match* was taking place."[30]

It was obvious action needed to be taken. With fifteen minutes until the start, Police Constable Buxton radioed Chief Duckenfield from the Land Rover requesting the kickoff be delayed. There was still sufficient time to accomplish this request. Yet, Chief Duckenfield told him "it was too late" – a second fatal decision.[31]

Superintendent Marshall, commander of the Liverpool entrances, shared his officers' concerns. Unprecedented in his twenty-seven years of policing football, he recalled, the stadium was "under siege"; "this was no ordinary crowd" of football fans; "it had outgrown our capacity to manage it effectively."[32] Fearing the worst, he radioed Chief Duckenfield at 2:47 P.M. and requested that the stadium gates be opened to relieve the crowd pressure on the turnstiles. He radioed again and again, begging for permission as his voice escalated. However, Chief Duckenfield remained indecisive.[33] In the police control room, Superintendent Murray began to apply pressure as well: "Mr. Duckenfield, are you going to open the gates?" he demanded.[34]

Finally, the Chief authorized the gate opening allowing fans – with and without tickets – to quickly flow into the pens. With little direction from police or stadium officials and kickoff imminent, most spectators headed straight into the already overcrowded terraces behind the Liverpool goal. This third fatal decision became the inciting incident to disaster.

Inside the stadium, things were not faring much better on the Liverpool terraces. One fan who arrived early recalled that everyone was "having a good time," singing and batting a beach ball around until "suddenly, I realised that I couldn't really move that well" and "it started to get uncomfortable. I discovered I was pinned, sandwiched in place."[35] Another fan noted that as early as 2:30 P.M., things "started to look naughty" behind the Liverpool goal. Then, "about twenty to three, I really started to get concerned" because "I saw this old chap" in "his sixties" and "he was pressed against the fence slightly twisted, and he wasn't moving. His face looked pale." He looked "like a dead man pinned up against the railings" with "his tongue hanging out."[36]

By this time, the Leppings Lane gates had been opened, and fans surged straight ahead into the grounds, intensifying the crushing. People were forced forward, toward the barriers, while people in front "were screaming to push the crowd back." But no one could move.[37] "It was absolute bedlam," a fan recalled. Eddie Spearritt and his 14-year-old son Adam were in pen 3: "It was just like a vice which was getting slowly tighter and tighter," and then Adam fainted. "There was a policeman on the track, only five or six feet away from me, and I was screaming and begging him to open the perimeter gate. You can scream your head off when you're screaming for your son's life … I must have been like a lunatic." But "the policeman didn't open the gate."[38]

Trevor Hicks, whose two daughters died, also described fans' desperation vis-à-vis police officers' disconnection prior to kick-off: "There was a young lad trying to come over" the perimeter fence to escape the crush, he recalled, "and a policeman literally put his hand on his forehead and shoved him back" into the crowd. "We were actually pleading with these two officers on the steps" outside the police control box. "I'm shouting out 'Can't you see what's going on, for Christ's sake? There's a problem!' Rather than help, the police officer told me, 'Shut your fucking prattle.'"[39]

Another fan described, "There was a woman in front of me in pen 4. She started screaming, she was shouting out 'let me out.'" After awhile "this plea for help turned into a full wrenched scream, one long continuous scream." She wasn't the only one. "Everyone it seemed was shouting at anyone who walked past." But "nobody took any notice."[40] Suddenly "a couple of photographers" started focusing their cameras "towards pen 4 taking pictures." Ignoring pleas for help, photographers "crouched moving their cameras to get a better picture." "Surely if they had noticed that something" so "drastic was happening" that "it was worth taking pictures of, why had no one else noticed and helped?"[41]

At 2:54 P.M., the football players ran onto the field and the crowd eagerly surged forward in anticipation, oblivious to the crush that was already occurring down front. One fan recalled, "Even before the teams were on the pitch, people all around me" were "calling out for someone to help them.[42] When I heard the teams arriving I remember thinking 'God, no. Please don't bring them out now. Things will only get worse.'" Unfortunately, "my fears" were "realised"; "What happened" next "was a nightmare."[43]

For all their efforts to get into the stadium on time, the 3 P.M. kick-off was a blur for many Liverpool fans as they struggled just to stay alive. Already, many spectators were weakened to collapse, overcome by asphyxia, unable to breathe.[44] Yet they remained upright, held in place by the crowd's intense pressure. "If no relief came in four minutes there would be irreversible brain damage; if longer, death."[45] In desperation, some fans began climbing the side-fences to move laterally toward open areas on either side of the crush. Others were hoisted up from above, out of the pens to higher seating areas. While this slightly helped to relieve the crush, and ultimately saved escaping fans' lives, climbing on the fences escalated police officers' fear that spectators were getting out of control.

At 3:04 P.M., Liverpool's star midfielder Peter Beardsley narrowly missed a score, causing fans to surge forward once again in excitement and further crushing spectators at the front against the perimeter fencing. In pen 3, the crowd force became so powerful it broke spans of crush barrier – a hip-height metal railing specifically designed to dampen crowd surges – with deadly results for dozens of Liverpool fans who toppled on top of one another. Ironically, this lethal pileup is the incident that finally got police attention, and the match was paused at 3:05 P.M. and 30 seconds.[46]

What happened once the game was stopped is confusing and not well documented. Police and fans alike were in shock. What they were seeing was incomprehensible. Yet one thing is clear: Initially, no senior police officer took charge of the rescue effort or attempted to organize the mayhem that ensued. There was no leadership, communication, or teamwork of any kind. "Everything rested on the initiative of individual police officers," their personal awareness of the situation, and their motivation to be of service.[47]

Police Constable S. Smith recalled, "The thing that sticks in my mind [was] the state of panic [that] overcame the senior officers. The command structure of the force totally broke down for several minutes, and no one appeared to grasp the severity of the situation." Still primarily concerned about public disorder and fearing an outbreak of hooliganism, Chief Duckenfield issued a call over the police radio: "All officers on to perimeter track."[48] And police officers immediately began to arrive, assuming there was a fight or some other crowd disorder.[49] Once on site, "they were told their objective was to stem a pitch invasion" in which rowdy fans run onto the field to disrupt the game.[50] The reality was quite different.

One officer recalled that they ran toward the stadium entrance in response to Chief Duckenfield's radio call and down onto the field. "To my horror I then saw the reality of what was taking place," he said. It wasn't a fight at all. "The first 4 or 5 rows of supporters" standing behind the "fencing had all been crushed." Mentally unprepared, the spectacle was shocking and "truly gruesome." It "was a horrific scene of carnage." The victims were blue from cyanosis, vomiting, and incontinent. Their mouths were open, tongues hanging out, their eyes staring – a pile of dead bodies.[51] Panicking "supporters from the back were climbing over bodies to get out, thereby hindering the rescue attempts," and the uninformed "crowds were still pushing forward and chanting at the police," waiting for the game to resume.[52] "I was unaware if" Chief Duckenfield even "realised the seriousness of the situation," he noted.[53]

Another officer recalled, "We urgently required cutting equipment, bullhorns, or the public address system to let the crowd know what was happening." He expected a call for medical professionals to come forward to assist and "a fleet of ambulances." But none of these resources was initially forthcoming.[54] In the absence of cutting tools, police and fans pulled together, working the perimeter fence's wire mesh with bare hands and brute force in order to breach the enclosure. Without stretchers, fans pulled advertising billboards down to carry the dead and injured out to safety. As a result of the crush barrier failure, there was a pile of approximately fifty intertwined bodies, six or seven deep, as far as twelve feet back from the fence. There was "no way to select the living from the dead in the pile," so police and fans simply worked as a chain, passing people out on to the pitch as efficiently as possible. "Who lived, who died was a matter of luck."[55]

What remains amazing is that all of these distressing scenes occurred within clear view of senior officers in the police control box who did little to assist or organize. The crowd was left in ignorance until Liverpool manager Kenny Dalgish broadcast an appeal for calm at 3:45 P.M. and then finally cancelled the game at 4 P.M. Fans left the stadium quietly and without incident.

Two days later, England's home secretary appointed Lord Justice Peter Taylor to conduct a parliamentary inquiry into the deaths at Hillsborough stadium. Calling police actions "a blunder of the first magnitude,"[56] Lord Taylor concluded that the main cause of the disaster was "the failure of police control."[57] In particular, he cites the lack of "effective leadership"[58] by senior officers who "froze" under pressure, unable to "face the enormity" of their decisions.[59]

Adding insult to injury, Chief Duckenfield even initially lied, claiming hysterical Liverpool fans forced open the gates and rushed the field in a pitch invasion, causing the fatal crush. "This was not only untruthful," Lord Taylor observed, but "it set off a widely reported allegation against the supporters which caused grave offence and distress" to Liverpool fans and grieving families already mourning lost loved ones.[60]

Aside from these criticisms, little more was specifically done to understand this breakdown in leadership and teamwork that day until now. Applying Reason's theory that disasters can be broken down into *latent* errors, which I call systemic factors, and *active* errors, which I consider individual behaviors and group dynamics factors, we can analyze further the events surrounding the Hillsborough football disaster. Investigating, for instance, how a complex set of systemic influences – such as post–World War II English culture and the design of football stadiums – interacted with *active* police mistakes, such as poor situational awareness, a fixated mind-set, and rigid application of policies, we can uncover individual and group dynamics that under-mined teamwork in this high-risk situation, resulting in the death of ninety-six spectators.

These factors aligned into a 'window of accident opportunity' when another failure linked with the chain of events that day: the fail-ure of *team learning*. When senior police officers failed to sense the severity of the impending problem, or to surface conflicts and dis-cuss errors in a timely manner, evolving their mental model as facts emerged and adapting to the environmental challenges, *team learning* broke down. As mayhem ensued, senior police froze, further exacer-bating the chaos and hampering the rescue effort. By examining some of the individual behaviors, group dynamics, and systemic factors that contributed to these errors, it becomes clear why this "blunder of the first magnitude" occurred and could happen again unless teams learn to think through crisis.[61]

"Frederick Boas, the distinguished American anthropologist, once remarked that to have an understanding of a complex phenomenon, it is necessary not only to know what it is, but how it came into being."[62] This philosophy seems particularly helpful when considering the history of crowd violence and hooliganism at British soccer matches – and its impact on policing at Hillsborough on April 15, 1989 – because the story starts long ago.

Not unlike Roman gladiators in the first few centuries, football has been associated with crowd violence from its earliest beginnings. The roots of the modern game can be traced to a folk form played with an inflated pig's bladder in thirteenth-century England between youths of neighboring villages. With hundreds of players to a side and few rules, football matches provided an opportunity to engage in manly displays of tribal aggression and settle old scores, regularly resulting in serious injury and even death. At least fifteen attempts were made to control the sport via royal proclamation beginning as early as 1314 when King Edward II banned football. All were largely ineffective.[63]

Warring groups enjoyed the competition, spontaneous aggression, and open physical violence, often with a secondary purpose. In seventeenth-century Scotland, for example, a football match was often a prelude to a raid across the English border because the same pugnacious young men were game for both.[64] Let us remember that for centuries public executions in England, not outlawed until 1868, were one of the most popular 'spectator sports.' Violence was a way of life, stimulating aggression in football players and inciting passion in football fans.[65]

The transformation of football from an unregulated war on an ill-defined battlefield to a civil, rule-governed, profit-making sport came largely as a result of urbanization, industrialization, and capitalism. Steady urban development encroached on the traditional battlefield game, relegating it to smaller and smaller spaces. Industrialization demanded employees work longer hours, and matches were bad for business as they distracted customers from the marketplace, thus reducing profits. A more formal form of football emerged in the mid-1800s when English public schools adopted the game, developing written rules that required players to exercise self-control and display gentlemanly conduct. By the end of the nineteenth century, football was organized at a national level, generating income for wealthy owners and stable employment for talented players.[66]

Yet despite middle-class efforts to refine, manage, and claim ownership over the game, football remained a central feature of the working man's life with most grounds built within working-class communities like Hillsborough. Football was a way for England's working class to bond, enduring the hardship, poverty, and frustration of their lives when few other distractions were affordable. Supporting the local club was practically a civic duty, and the advent of the Saturday half-workday and improvements in public transportation further stimulated match attendance. By 1950, football was indisputably England's number one sport.

As football evolved, so did football fans. Football-related violence dou-bled between 1960 and 1965 as a new phenomenon emerged: Groups of young men called *hooligans*[67] attended matches – not just to watch football – but to engage in violence both inside and outside the sta-dium. Fighting, stalking rival fans, infiltrating one another's terraces, drinking, vandalizing, and harassing innocent bystanders were some of their pastimes. Charging the field in a 'pitch invasion' and throwing 'missiles' such as bottles, rocks, bricks, darts, and sharpened coins at one another, players, referees, and police were just some of their tactics to disrupt the game.[68]

During the 1970s and 1980s, hooliganism formalized into a complex network of 'firms' with clear communication channels to coordinate violence. Initially consisting of young, white working-class males decked out in their teams' regalia, firms now expanded to include 'lads' from middle-class backgrounds, older men with families, and football *casuals* who flaunted money and expensive designer clothes as a way to one-up rival firms. By not sporting their team colors, casuals made it impossible for police to identify their club affiliation and enforce fan segregation, thus allowing them to infiltrate rival fans' terraces to provoke confrontation.[69]

Called the "English Disease,"[70] hooliganism contained all the ele-ments of an urban gang. It had become an autonomous self-sustaining force with its own vocabulary, codes, rules, leaders, structures, and uniforms. These new forms of crowd violence demanded a new model of policing. No longer was the sight of a single officer sufficient to calm a disorderly crowd. Advances in hooliganism demanded large-scale police interventions akin to tactical military operations, often at the expense of fan safety and comfort. Challenged to differentiate the ordi-nary football fan from the prospective hooligan, police responded by simply considering all supporters potential offenders. To limit oppor-tunities for fighting, fans traveled in segregated trains and buses and were herded to and from the station by mounted police officers and dogs. In retaliation, destruction of trains and buses became a favorite hooligan pastime. As every fan became a potential suspect, police became the natural enemy. In response, some police officers confessed to "throwing people out of the ground simply to show who was 'in charge,'" escalating the confrontation.[71]

One aspect of the evolving hooligan culture that becomes central in our analysis of events at Hillsborough is the term '*blag*'. To blag is to gain entrance to a restricted area or obtain some material goods for free through confidence, trickery, or cheekiness.[72] Journalist Bill Buford followed Manchester United supporters and observed this hooligan strategy firsthand. Buford recalled how English fans quickly overwhelmed Italian security personnel unaccustomed to such a large, drunk, and disorderly crowd, as they moved toward the airport terminal gate with singular purpose. Initially confused, Buford eventually realized fans were pushy and aggressive for a reason: At least ten had boarded the airplane without payment, tickets, or boarding passes, hiding under seats and in the lavatory for a free flight home.[73]

You might reasonably ask, could some Liverpool supporters have been attempting a blag when about 5,000 fans – many ticketless – arrived in force outside the Leppings Lane turnstiles about 2:30 P.M.? Acting pushy and aggressive, were they trying to overwhelm police and stadium officials as a way to enter without a ticket and watch the match from the open terraces? I suspect the answer is yes. To explore this possibility and examine how this strategy backfired on April 15, 1989, contributing to the death of ninety-six of their fellow fans, it is important to understand a bit more about the stadium itself and the terrace culture that emerged over time.

Hillsborough's Sheffield Wednesday stadium was designed more than one hundred years ago.[74] Boxed in on all sides by the surrounding working-class community, the ground was never intended to accommodate the crowd size or vehicle parking required in 1989 because in 1899 fans typically walked to the match from the local area. Over time, parts of the football ground, such as high-cost executive boxes, were improved. Yet, the uncovered terraces where generations of working-class fans enjoyed the game changed little over the years.[75]

As Lord Taylor reported, Hillsborough's terrace facilities were "squalid," lavatories primitive, and refreshments unhealthy. With no place to sit, fans ate on the run or standing on the terraces in all types of weather, dropping trash where they stood. Most troubling, Lord Taylor noted, was that the loss of dignity, respect, and minimal comfort for spectators in this environment bred "bad manners and poor behavior."[76] One has to wonder why terrace spectators did not demand better accommodations.

To understand the answer to this question, it is important to realize the enormous symbolic value football stadiums have for their fans. Generations of working-class men feel ownership over certain sections of a football ground, strongly attached to inexplicable idiosyncrasies that carry memories of a collective experience, linking them to previous generations. The terraces, in particular, are a unique and passionate environment. The emotion and camaraderie of standing where their forefathers stood, cheering the same team colors, and swaying in unison amongst an amorphous crowd are integral to their match experience. Quite simply, they do not want a seat. In fact, for some fans increasing standards of comfort and safety reflects a 'feminizing' of football and adoption of middle-class values,[77] indicating further erosion of their working-class heritage and the 'terrace culture' so central to their enjoyment of the game.[78]

As a result, when changes were made to the stadium terraces at Hillsborough, it was typically for security reasons, not for spectator comfort or safety. Piecemeal modification of exits, entrances, and fences were sporadically instituted – much of it in response to hooliganism with little consideration of the wider safety implications such as fan flow or emergency egress. This became a critical factor during the 1989 crush. Over the years, the terraces became enclosed with eight-foot-high perimeter fencing, angled back at the top to prohibit rowdy fans from throwing debris or climbing over. Crush barriers were added to dampen the crowds' surge forward, running parallel to the goal line about three feet high and ten feet long, yet often blocking egress. Radial fencing, about eight feet high, was installed at right angles dividing the open standing area into seven separate 'pens', prohibiting fighting crowds from surging side to side and hooligans from evading police grasp. Each pen had one small gate along the perimeter fence, locked from the outside, allowing police to remove unruly fans from the pitch-side but preventing spectators from exiting onto the field. Yet, as was evident on that disastrous day in April, these piecemeal modifications contributed to the fatalities. Radial fencing prohibited fans from expanding sideways during overcrowding, crush barriers pinned spectators in place then created a pileup when they gave way, and locked gates and high perimeter fencing hindered emergency escape.

As one might predict, increasingly militant police strategies, escalating hooligan violence, and the generally inhospitable stadium environment drove many fans away. Previously, generations of working men – fathers, sons, brothers, and uncles – stood shoulder to shoulder with neighbors on the terraces, cheering the home team.[79] By the late 1980s, attendance had plummeted from it its peak of 77 million fans in 1950 to about 20 million spectators.[80] Of these fans, many had inherited previous generations' loyalty to their community team, yet they failed to inherit the self-discipline or tacit social control family and neighbor supervision would have provided. As a result, hooligans surrounded by their 'mates' effectively monopolized certain sections of the football grounds – typically the terrace pens behind the goal – driving out fans who were uncomfortable with their overly aggressive and generally offensive behavior.[81]

Media coverage, especially British tabloid press, sensationalized football violence with headlines such as "SAVAGES!" and "ANIMALS!" that escalated the public's fears.[82] This media attention encouraged football supporters of all kinds, not just hooligans, to amplify their presentation. Fans carefully selected clothing, scarfs, banners, body painting, slogans, noisemakers, and chants to represent their cause. Many chants, although twinged with humor, were extremely racist and highly inflammatory, intentionally designed to insult the opposing team and interfere with the game itself. Yet some were also self-deprecating, such as the infamous southeast London Millwall chant: 'No one likes us, we don't care.' Other songs, such as Liverpool's anthem *You'll Never Walk Alone* from the 1945 Rodgers and Hammerstein musical *Carousel*, invariably sung by fans moments before kickoff, or West Ham United's anthem, a popular 1919 song *I'm Forever Blowing Bubbles*, reflect an awareness of, and commitment to, their longstanding club history.

In sum, how English football and its fans came into being reveals that the character of the football supporter is a complex mix of loyalty, commitment, respect, cunning, good humor, resilience, and aggression. Although hooliganism attracts all kinds of people, its roots can be found in English working-class culture in which frustration and hardship are facts of life and violence with a 'secondary purpose,' like a border raid or blag, is common. Not always negative, these working-class characteristics can be directed toward positive goal achievement such as during England's national defense in World War II. Yet, at other moments, these individual behaviors and group dynamics can cross the line toward disorderly conduct, lewd behavior, assault, vandalism, racism, and destruction. To more clearly understand how hooliganism became a factor during the Hillsborough disaster, we need to investigate what motivates people to behave in this way.

Social scientists began studying hooliganism in the 1970s, attempting to make sense of this antisocial behavior. At the risk of oversimplification, research concluded that hooliganism is rooted in some young men's complex reactions to the English class structure, a post-modern identity crisis, and the seductive euphoria produced by crowd violence.

Basically, hooligans commit offenses because it feels good and gains them respect among their peers.[83]

At the individual and group level of analysis, being a hooligan enables some young white Englishmen, who have little prospect of success in school or career, to 'belong', fostering a sense of self-worth, camaraderie, and identity through peer recognition. Hooliganism provides an opportunity to vent frustrations and collectively establish a reversal of the power struggle of modern society in a masculinity ritual of their own design. As one Manchester United hooligan describes it: "We look forward to Saturday's" football match "all week long. It's the most meaningful thing in our lives. It's a religion really. That's how important it is to us. Saturday is our day of worship."[84]

In their world, drinking, fighting, and violence are one of the few sources of excitement, emotional arousal, and status that make progression up a 'career ladder' – even if it is a hooligan hierarchy – seem possible. Similar to joy riding in a stolen car, tagging walls with graffiti, or other forms of youthful risk taking, hooligans seek emotionally arousing experiences to offset the boredom and monotony of their everyday lives. "Violence is their antisocial kick, their mind-altering experience, an adrenaline-induced euphoria" with the same addictive qualities of drugs or alcohol. Yet it is made all the more powerful because it is generated organically by the body itself and amplified by a collective of bodies intensifying the experience in shared space.[85]

At a systemic level, one cause of the escalation of violence in the postwar period could be that as professional football became increasingly commercialized, the role of the local club became less community based. During this "embourgeoisement of football,"[86] players, managers, and owners were no longer locals. Yet they increasingly profited at the community's expense. Football-related violence was one effort to reclaim control over the game from the middle class, reestablishing the traditional working-class weekend with its community connection and distinctly male rituals.[87]

Another systemic factor is that as England lost prestige as a world power in the postwar period, football-related violence provided young Englishmen an opportunity to act out frustrated feelings of nationalism and resolve feelings of subordination. Unwilling to accept their country's diminished international stature, World War II imagery provided hooligans with the symbols to affix their patriotism and justify their racism. Fighting the war all over again, using football as a metaphoric battlefield, hooligans returned England to its moment of triumph, at least in their minds.[88]

Given these motivational forces, it becomes clear that many hooligans seek out opportunities to rage against perceived class-based injustices as a way to reverse modern society's power structure and resolve feelings of subordination. Using football-related violence to stimulate an emotional high, they attempt to reclaim control over the game from the middle class while providing an identity and earning respect within their firms.

Just such an opportunity to rage against injustice was provided at Hillsborough when, for the second straight year, match organizers only allocated Liverpool, a team known for substantially higher attendance rates than their competitors, 44 percent of the available 54,000 tickets and twenty-three turnstiles for entry. This equates to more than 5,500 fewer tickets and nearly one-third less entry points than their opponent, Nottingham Forrest.[89] In addition, Nottingham Forest fans were allocated 21,000 of the coveted terrace tickets compared with Liverpool's 10,100. Therefore, at £6 per terrace ticket compared with £12 for a stadium seat, Liverpool's allocation was not only smaller but twice as expensive. This injustice did not go unrecognized or unaccounted for by Liverpool fans.

Similar to Buford's description of Manchester United hooligans, the mass arrival of 5,000 Liverpool fans does not appear to be a coincidence. It seems people had been organizing at designated spots and, at a pre-established time, departed en route for Leppings Lane with the goal to arrive *en force*. Emulating the Liverpool team itself bursting on to the field prior to kickoff, fans seemed eager to arrive organized and united, feeling the high energy and jubilant authority of suddenly sharing a singular purpose with their team: raging against the system, winning the match, and restoring their community's honor.

At about 2:33 P.M., police closed-circuit television (CCTV) footage shows Liverpool supporters swarming outside Leppings Lane gates as officers on horseback attempt to step the crowd back from the turnstiles with little success. By 2:36 P.M., the crowd swells and the morning's carnival-like atmosphere gives way to aggression, chaos, and desperation. Young men lean their full body weight into the crowd, pushing with their elbows. The mass condenses into a tight circle around the gates and turnstiles while the asphalt of Leppings Lane is clearly visible just yards behind. The scene is surreal: A desperately tight clump of humanity surrounded by open pavement. If only the outer ring of fans would step back, the pressure would be relieved. But they do not step back, they push in further.

In addition to arriving *en force*, many experienced police officers reported an unprecedented, nearly fanatical mood had come over the crowd as fans pushed to enter the stadium. "It seemed as if something more important than a football match was taking place," Police Constable Buxton succinctly noted. My hypothesis is that a secondary purpose for this aggression – this 'more important' thing that Constable Buxton sensed – was for Liverpool fans to attempt a 'blag', overwhelming the turnstiles and forcing police to open the gates and let ticketless fans enter as compensation for the unequal ticket allocations. As we know, they were successful in this mission as hundreds entered without tickets when police opened the gates at 2:52 P.M. Once inside the ground with no police direction, and euphoric from their success, the 'blaggers' continued to push straight into pens 3 and 4 behind the Liverpool goal, an area of the terraces over which they felt ownership, resulting in the crush that killed ninety-six people.

Of the eighty-nine male and seven female Liverpool fans who died that day, less than 20 percent had come through the open gates around

2:52 P.M. This suggests that the overwhelming majority of the fatalities were fans like 19-year-old Sarah Hicks, 15-year-old Victoria Hicks, or 14-year-old Adam Spearritt: people who entered the ground early with family and friends to enjoy the carnival-like environment of their team's semifinal match. As Sarah and Victoria's father, Trevor Hicks, suggested, this final crush was a symbolic confrontation between traditional football supporters who relied on police to 'protect and serve', calling out to them for assistance, and organized hooligan firms who viewed police as 'the enemy'. Fueling this confrontation were police officer's assumptions about fan behavior.

People "don't realise how important [football] was to us as a family," Mr. Hicks stated. "It was the one thing that we shared totally." Every other Saturday, driving to the match "was the family trip together." As events on the terraces escalated, Mr. Hicks noted, he tried to tell a policeman, "Can't you see what's going on, for Christ's sake? There's a problem!" But "because I was a football fan my opinions didn't matter."[90]

In sum, it is clear that systemic influences such as English culture, working-class values, the history of football, football-related violence and hooliganism, and the design, maintenance, and symbolism of football stadiums significantly contributed to the Hillsborough disaster. However, there were individual behaviors and group dynamic factors that became influential as well, particularly within the police force. One point repeatedly emphasized was the breakdown in police leadership, communication, and teamwork.

As Lord Taylor concluded, "Realisation came at different moments to different officers in different places."[91] Police Constable Smith recalled how a "state of panic" overcame senior officers like Chief Duckenfield as they struggled to grasp the severity of the situation. As the command structure broke down, communication became garbled and confusion reigned. The ensuing chaos caused senior officers to freeze and the police force to individualize. As Officer Smith succinctly summarized: "Everyone was busy doing his 'own thing' and that didn't help anyone or anything." Contributing to this breakdown were the match commander's inexperience, poor leadership and communication within the police team, and police assumptions about hooliganism. The impact of these factors caused police to poorly prepare for the Hillsborough match and, as the situation exploded, to delay in adjusting their mental model as facts emerged, critically impacting the rescue effort.

Chief Superintendent Duckenfield took command of F-unit, which polices Hillsborough, just three weeks prior to the 1989 semifinal match. With little experience policing football matches and no familiarity with capacity football crowds at Hillsborough, Chief Duckenfield was in many ways the least prepared to be match commander. Yet what he lacked in experience, his veteran management team more than made up for with extensive backgrounds in football policing, including previous Hillsborough matches. So why did this teamwork break down?

First, there were communication failures within the police team. It was made clear during pregame briefings that if a police officer needed to deviate from normal procedures, such as opening a gate or exit, senior officer approval was required. Yet, obtaining permission was difficult. The loud crowd noise, shortage of radios, garbled overlapping transmissions, and periodic equipment failures made communication a challenge. Because there were no specific policies directing the management of late or congested arrivals, the monitoring of overcrowding on the terraces, or the manning of perimeter gates, police were forced to be even more reliant on communication with senior officers in the police control box. This hampered team coordination at critical times. Valuable minutes were lost in the rescue effort as officers struggled to communicate with Chief Duckenfield to obtain permission, rather than authorize themselves to take appropriate action.

Second, senior police officers' fixation on defending against hooliganism significantly contributed to the disaster. For instance, as events evolved, senior officers' misinterpretation of spectators' attempts to escape the crush and junior officers efforts to begin the rescue – clues that could have been used to reframe their flawed mental model – were instead distorted to confirm assumptions about hooliganism. To get a sense of these events, let us relive them by weaving together excerpts of eyewitness accounts provided by several police officers.

As the crush intensified behind the Liverpool goal, some fans attempted to escape by climbing fences or being hoisted up from above, to second-level seating areas. Police Constable Bichard in the control box recalled senior officers assumed this was hooliganism. Fearing a 'pitch invasion', Chief Duckenfield ordered police to the Liverpool end to stop this apparent disorder. Particularly frustrating to the Chief, notes PC Bichard, was a Woman Police Constable on the "perimeter track just below the control box" who did "not appear to be moving people off the track" as the Chief had just directed, but was actually opening "the perimeter gate" to let people out.[92]

In reality, CCTV video footage revealed that the Woman Police Constable, Fiona Richardson, was actually one of the first officers to realize something fatal was occurring on the terraces and had the courage to act. At 2:53 P.M., Constable Richardson began repositioning "sweating and distressed" fans to the wing pens. Assisting thirty-two fans to relocate, some in obvious physical discomfort with broken bones and difficulty breathing, Constable Richardson recalled the confusion: "I didn't know what was happening" but as I looked through the open gate" I "saw a man's face" in "terror" and "I began to pull people out fast." At the same time Richardson began the rescue effort, "a club official in a suit" sent by Chief Duckenfield[93] "was trying to push people back in the gate and shouting and swearing at the fans."[94]

Another officer stated he also saw "a lot of pushing" in the crowded central pens, "the noise was terrible and people were screaming, a different type of scream." Yet he nonetheless "followed his strictly written orders and radioed for permission" before opening the gate to offer assistance.[95] "This is serious, people are dying here," he radioed. Yet he received no direction.[96] Taking up his own authority, he opened the gate. This was most likely the policeman who Eddie Spearritt recalled freed his son Adam from the pen 3 crush about 2:59 P.M., telling him, "If I'm wrong I'm going to get a right rollicking over this."[97]

It was only through the awareness and initiative of individual officers like these that police began to make proper sense of the unfolding situation. Throwing caution, procedures, and fixated paradigms to the wind, these young officers trusted their own instincts and took action, thinking through the crisis. Working frantically, side by side with distraught fans, they freed trapped spectators, providing whatever medical assistance they were able and saved people's lives.

In isolation, these factors may not seem overwhelmingly significant, but considered collectively, they contribute to the complex 'window of accident opportunity' that led to the Hillsborough disaster. If police had a plan for turning ticketless fans away and managing large, late-arriving crowds, the Liverpool hooligans' 'blag' never would have gained momentum at the Leppings Lane turnstiles. Once it started, police had little choice but to open the three west stadium gates to quell the dangerously escalating pressure at the turnstiles. Yet this action, in itself, did not have to lead to disaster. If senior police had communicated with stadium officials, stewards, or other police inside the ground, directing them to close off the overcrowded center pens and guide fans toward the open outer wing pens – as was done to control overcrowding in previous years – this would have averted further crushing and broken the accident chain that fateful day. Instead, senior officers provided little leadership or coordination of subsequent activities surprising officers inside the stadium with the inrush of fans when the gates were opened.

Through the gift of hindsight it may seem easy, and perhaps even unfair, to level criticism at police about what could or should have happened at Hillsborough more than twenty years ago. It is not my intent to blame and criticize. My goal is to consider how we might collectively learn by considering how leadership might have been exercised differently, increasing our understanding of the dynamics of teamwork as a way to avoid accidents in the future. This is important because, similar to Chief Duckenfield's challenge as division commander, it is not uncommon for new leaders in all fields to find themselves tested beyond their expertise. As a consequence of ever-evolving technologies generating increasingly complex operating systems, even experienced leaders can find themselves leading teams in unfamiliar scenarios. One of the biggest leadership challenges then is to create a more open, decentralized environment where operators can work together, innovating as required and adapting their mental model of the system failure as new data emerges.

Under these circumstances, stabilizing measures such as increased communication and collaboration as a way to improve teamwork and facilitate team learning and adaption to the environment need to be added to ensure team success. For example, to add stability to police leadership at Hillsborough, Chief Duckenfield could have worked collaboratively with his team, harnessing their extensive experience thereby compensating for his own inadequacies, creating a more open, decentralized environment. He could have invited another officer to actively mentor him in his match commander role, providing a sort of 'on-the-job' training; avoided role changes from previous matches; declined to reduce police numbers from previous years; and, most importantly, investigated some of the informal policing strategies that had proven successful in previous events but never made it into the formal written *Operational Order*. Informal strategies such as separating out ticketless fans before they approached the turnstiles, guiding fans to open terraces and closing off full ones, were all important factors that disastrous day.

Without these leadership stabilizing forces, Chief Duckenfield created a centralized leadership climate that he could not sustain when things began to go awry. Akin to a military command-and-control hierarchy, the success of a centralized leadership model relies on clear direction and the exchange of respect and trust between a strong, knowledgeable leader and his loyal team. A lack of trust, often present when the leader is new, inexperienced, or yet unproven, can undermine teamwork in a centralized environment, leaving the leader and team vulnerable to breakdown.

The positive aspects of centralized leadership, when effectively implemented, are that the centralized leader can quickly get people organized, motivated, and on task because communication is predominantly directed from the top down. A centralized leadership strategy is often essential to success in high-stake, fast-paced, time-critical emergencies in unforgiving environments and could have been effectively implemented at Hillsborough, particularly during the rescue effort, if the proper sense making had occurred. Yet there are tradeoffs. Some of the negative aspects of centralized leadership are that innovation can be squelched and the loss of the leader – either due to death or incompetence – is often cataclysmic to team performance. In the absence of the strong, clear leadership the team has come to depend on, people cannot function, do not know who to follow, and become conflicted about self-authorization. This is what happened to police at Hillsborough.

Rather than consciously raising the issue of his inexperience, collaborating with his team to develop a solution through a more decentralized leadership structure while there was time, Chief Duckenfield attempted to hide his inadequacies behind his authority and role as chief and match commander. Once this façade gave way around 2:52 P.M. and the severity of the situation became clear, Chief Duckenfield froze, denying the direction the centralized leadership climate needed to function efficiently. Without this clarity, the police command structure folded and the force individualized.

The lack of clear roles, tasks, and mental framing seniors leaders should have provided caused many police to become emotionally overwrought when they arrived on scene. Many reported that the day felt blurred,[98] "a sort of unreal feeling of disbelief and numbness" that "soon gave way to a situation of almost total panic."[99] Believing they were responding to a call for crowd control assistance, officers instead found death and chaos. One officer recalled, "After realising the enormity of the disaster, I appeared to be drifting in and out of reality."[100] Many police reported feeling "confused" about what to do, the "radio was garbled," and it was total "mayhem."[101]

Dependent on the centralized leadership structure for direction, but lacking clear means of communication, many officers became overcome with emotion, shock, and anger, unable to think or contribute effectively. For instance, twelve-year veteran Police Constable Roy Green reported he was "used to the feelings of the crowd" at football matches and considered himself "to be extremely experienced in crowd control."[102] Yet as events unfolded that day, he recalled, "Even I was becoming emotionally upset and in fear of my own safety. I will be honest; I did not think I was going to get away from that location alive."[103] I encountered "a close colleague wandering around, crying." He "was in some distress and I ushered him to a location behind the first aid room to hide him from view." I "was shaking, sweating, and totally exhausted" and "his distress was distressing me." So I left him there because "I did not know how much more I could take." I felt "if I had stayed with him, I honestly think I would have broken down."[104] Other officers reported a sense of helplessness, feeling powerless to render assistance.[105] Police Constable Alan Ramsden recalled, "People were crying for help and we could do nothing." Police Constable Iain Alastair Paterson was on patrol outside the stadium without a radio. Never notified about the crisis, he reported "I felt and still do very angry that I was unable to assist the injured and my colleagues in the ground" because there was no clear communication. "I felt that I had been left out as a spare part."[106]

In sum, the inability of senior officers to think, make proper sense of the unfolding situation, adapt their mental model, and lead their team in the rescue effort in a timely manner was, as Lord Taylor concluded, "a blunder of the first magnitude."[107] After the initial blag outside the Liverpool gates, it was clear that the site of crowd congestion was simply transferred from one bottleneck – outside the Leppings Lane turnstiles at 2:52 P.M. – to a final stopgap – pens 3 and 4 at 3:06 P.M. Clues provided by Liverpool spectators and police officers during those fourteen minutes could have been considered differently by senior officers as a way to reframe their fixation on hooliganism, making better sense of what was actually occurring rather than reinforcing their inaccurate paradigm. Yet, instead they "froze," unable to "face the enormity" of their decisions and the repercussions of their actions.[108] Even as information emerged to support a different hypothesis and individual police attempted to take corrective action, the centralized leadership structure caused officers to remain fearful of superior's retaliation if they self-authorized the initiation of the rescue effort.

One could argue that the history of hooliganism in English football might justifiably lead police to assume that curious crowd behavior could escalate to football-related violence and hooliganism. Yet, senior officers' inability to think through the crisis and adapt their mental model as new information emerged ultimately caused this disaster. Police fixation on rigid policies and a centralized hierarchy as a means to ensure team discipline and crowd control escalated the chaos and delayed the emergency response. If police had begun the rescue effort sooner, in a more organized fashion with correct tools and emergency medical support services, many people might have been saved. Instead, ninety-six football fans – many of them children – needlessly lost their lives.

4

American Airlines Flight 587 – Latent Failures Align

An improperly trained pilot can break any airplane.[1]
Captain John Lauber, Vice President of
Safety and Technical Affairs, Airbus

On November 12, 2001, American Airlines Flight 587 departed New York City's John F. Kennedy International Airport at 9:14 A.M. en route to Santo Domingo, Dominican Republic. The beautiful, clear fall morning was jarringly transformed when, less than two minutes after takeoff, the Airbus A300–605R encountered wake turbulence from a previously departing Boeing 747 and broke apart in flight. All 260 people onboard as well as 5 people on the ground were killed, making this accident the second deadliest single aircraft crash on U.S. soil to date. Similarities between the tragic events of 9/11 just two months prior and this disaster, such as the airline, size airplane, time, and location of the crash just fifteen miles from New York City's World Trade Center, led many people to initially suspect terrorism. However, this fear proved unfounded when investigators quickly eliminated sabotage as a factor.[2]

The morning prior to the accident proceeded uneventfully. The pilots arrived early and conducted their normal routines. The airplane was inspected, fueled, loaded, and 'weight and balance' calculations were within limits. The weather was clear, and winds were light out of the northwest. The boarding process took a little longer than usual due to the recently adopted changes in post-9/11 security procedures. This resulted in the aircraft pushing back from the terminal gate about an hour late. Then Flight 587 taxied for takeoff from Runway 31L, oriented to 310 degrees magnetic, behind Japan Airlines (JAL) Flight 47, a heavy 747.

While completing their standard checklists, the captain and first officer chatted amicably. At 9:11 A.M., JAL was cleared for takeoff but did not actually lift off for about another minute. Meanwhile Flight 587's captain, Ed States, transferred aircraft control to First Officer Sten Molin to fly this first leg. An experienced and conscientious copilot, First Officer Molin recognized the potential to encounter turbulence behind the departing heavy 747 and asked the captain: "You happy with that distance?"[3]

Captain States replied, "We'll be all right once we get rollin'. He's supposed to be five miles by the time we're airborne, that's the idea."

"So you're happy," the copilot inquired again.

"Yeah."

"Takeoff check's complete, I'm on the roll. Thank you, sir."

Flight 587 lifted off the runway about one minute and forty seconds behind the JAL jet, following the aircraft on a climbing left turn for departure. Yet the larger, heavier 747 scribed a wider turning radius, causing the smaller, more nimble Airbus to remain inside – and most critically, downwind from – the 747's turn (See Figure 4.1). Meanwhile, the American pilots ran through their 'after takeoff checklist' and checked in with New York Departure air traffic controllers (ATC) on the radio. ATC reported Flight 587 in radar contact and instructed them to continue their departure route. Captain States acknowledged. This was the last radio transmission from Flight 587.

Immediately after beginning their left turn, Flight 587 hit a pocket of disturbed air as the northwesterly winds drove JAL's wake into the climbing Airbus's departure path.

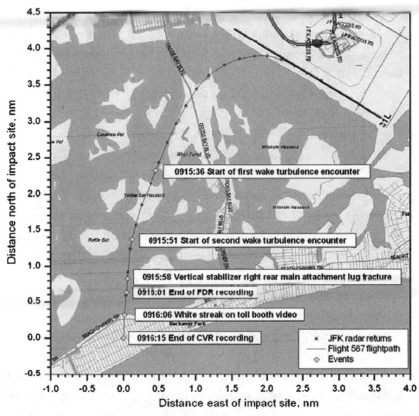

FIGURE 4.1. Flight path of American Airlines Flight 587 and key events.[4]

"Little wake turbulence, huh?" Captain States inquired to his copilot flying the airplane.

"Yeah," increase speed to "two fifty, thank you."

Fifteen seconds later, Flight 587 had a second encounter with JAL's wake.

"Max power!" First Officer Molin called in a strained voice.

"You all right?" the captain inquired, tension beginning to rise.

"Yeah, I'm fine."

"Hang on to it, hang on to it!"

Sound of a snap.

"Let's go for power, please," the first officer pleaded.

Sound of a loud thump, a bang, and a human grunt. A roaring noise started, increasing in amplitude. The Airbus tail had just separated from the jet.

"Holy [expletive]!" the first officer screamed. "What the hell are we into? We're stuck in it!"

"Get out of it, get out of it!" the captain demanded.

The airliner impacted the ground moments later.

The fatal accident sequence started when the second wake turbulence encounter rolled the Airbus, already in a moderately banked turn, steeper. The first officer sensed this roll acceleration and reacted, but with increasingly aggressive flight control inputs, slamming the yoke from left to right while simultaneously jamming rudder pedals to their limits.

What both pilots failed to recognize was that the first officer's erratic flight control inputs were causing the airplane's motion, not the wake turbulence.

Although the jet was flying well below the airplane's *maximum maneuvering speed*, the first officer's abrupt control inputs exceeded the airplane's designed aerodynamic load limits. As a result, the aircraft's tail, called a vertical stabilizer, fractured, causing a nearly instantaneous separation from the airplane body. Figure 4.2 depicts Flight 587's amazingly intact vertical stabilizer being recovered from Jamaica Bay about three-quarters of a mile from the main wreckage area. Figure 4.3 shows the right rear main attachment fitting's fracture at the lughole, shredding like a sheet of notebook paper torn from a three-ring binder.

The accident airplane was purchased new by American Airlines in 1988, had 37,550 flight hours, and was current with all FAA airworthiness directives and other maintenance inspections. ATC who handled the flight were properly trained and certified and complied with

FIGURE 4.2. Recovery of American Airlines Flight 587's vertical stabilizer.[5]

FIGURE 4.3. Fracture point of Flight 587's vertical stabilizer.[6]

requisite wake turbulence spacing regulations.[7] The accident pilots were fully trained and current in all applicable certifications, were well rested, and had flown together often, reportedly enjoying one another's company. Data collected from the airplane's *cockpit voice recorder*, which taped thirty minutes of audio, and *flight data recorder*, which monitors dozens of engine, flight control, and onboard system parameters, proved particularly helpful in the postcrash analysis.

The main wreckage of Flight 587 was found about four miles south-west of JFK airport, confined to an area about 500 by 300 feet, signify-ing a near-vertical ground impact. The tail section was recovered from Jamaica Bay, north of the main wreckage; and left and right engines were found about 800 feet northeast, indicating all had separated from the airplane body, or fuselage, in flight. Commercial airliners, especially those with wing-mounted jet engines like the Airbus A300, require large and powerful rudders to maintain coordinated flight, compensate for engine failure, and offset crosswinds during takeoff and landing. The rudder is attached to the aft portion of the vertical stabilizer and is moved via cockpit foot pedals when force is applied by either pilot.

The A300–600's vertical stabilizer and rudder are constructed from composite materials. Similar to super-strong plastics, composite materials consist primarily of long carbon or glass fibers held together by an epoxy polymer. The materials are manufactured in 'plies', or sheets of fibers, that are premixed with flexible epoxy, then stacked and shaped in a mold and cured under heat and pressure to form aircraft components. Lighter, more flexible, and easier to maintain than metal, composites have become popular in all types of manufacturing, not just airplanes. With no industry standards for rudder pedal sensitivity, Airbus was free to design their own flight control system.

Responding to pilot requests to improve aircraft handling, Airbus's A300–600 model incorporated new features designed to assist pilots, making it easier to move the rudder pedals at higher airspeeds while protecting the airplane by limiting the amount of rudder the pilot can deflect. Ironically, these two changes substantially increased flight control sensitivity, making the A300–600 *twice as responsive* to rudder pedal inputs at 250 knots than at 165 knots. This becomes a very impor-tant factor in the accident analysis, so let's explore this topic further.

At slower airspeeds, the A300–600 pilot can only deflect the rud-der to its maximum point by exerting significant force on the rudder pedals. However, at moderate speeds such as that of Flight 587 during the in-flight breakup, the pilot can deflect the rudder to maximum

TABLE 4.1. *Airbus A300–600 rudder control system design characteristics compared with the Boeing 727 (adapted by author from NTSB research data)*[8]

Airplane	Breakout force	Speed	Rudder pedal force	Rudder pedal travel	Resultant rudder deflection
A300–600	22 lbs	135 knots	65 lbs	4 inches	30 degrees
		250 knots	32 lbs	1.2 inches	9.3 degrees
Boeing 727	17 lbs	135 knots	80 lbs	3 inches	18 degrees
		250 knots	50 lbs	1.3 inches	7 degrees

using half that force, hitting the stops by moving pedals just 1.2 inches – nearly imperceptible inputs made during an adrenaline-pumping wake encounter like First Office Molin believed he was experiencing (See Table 4.1).

Although First Officer Molin's background flying the Boeing 727 – which requires substantially more rudder pedal force (50 pounds versus 32 pounds) to deflect the rudder fewer degrees (7 degrees versus 9.3 degrees) at 250 knots – may have had some influence, it does not entirely explain his aggressive reaction. We are still left with the fundamental question – what happened?

The crash of American Airlines Flight 587 alarmed the aviation industry and presented the National Transportation Safety Board (NTSB) with an unprecedented challenge: This was the first aircraft accident in history involving the in-flight failure of a major structural component manufactured using advanced composite materials. What if, the aerospace industry feared, this advanced new technology was unsafe?

The concept of 'composite' materials – a combination of two or more materials bonded together, which differ in form or composition and act in concert to improve specific characteristics not found in either original element alone – is actually not new. Egyptians discovered that huts built with mud and straw bricks were stronger than mud bricks alone as far back as 4,000 B.C. Mongolian warriors increased their archery performance by coating silk bowstrings with pine resin, and Roman artists improved fresco durability by adding ground marble to their plaster. Perhaps the most applicable historical example is found when indigenous cultures added goat hair to clay, which converted to carbon during the firing process, greatly increasing the strength of pottery in a manner similar to today's carbon fiber composites.

In the aviation industry, airplane structures were first built from wood and fabric. Aluminum construction began in the 1930s, and innovations in carbon and glass composites gradually evolved after World War II. The first commercial passenger jet built with composite materials was the Boeing 707, designed using about 2 percent fiberglass, and the U.S. military followed with composites on the F-14 Tom Cat and the AV-8B Harrier. Today, composite materials comprise about 10 percent of a Boeing 777 and about 24 percent of the U.S. Air Force's advanced tactical fighter, the F-22 Raptor. The advantages of using advanced composites in airplane design is that they weigh about 20 percent less than aluminum components resulting in better aircraft performance and fuel efficiency while being strong, durable, and corrosion resistant. The only real disadvantage, or so the aerospace industry thought until Flight 587, is the relatively high cost of material production.[9]

After extensive testing of the Airbus A300–600's composite components, the NTSB concluded that Flight 587's vertical stabilizer was designed and manufactured properly, had no preexisting damage, and failed within predictable design specifications. To contextualize these findings, consider that for certification an airplane's vertical stabilizer must support aerodynamic loads up to 1.5 times the 'limit load' – the maximum aerodynamic load a structural element is expected to experience at least once during its service life – without catastrophic failure. Flight 587's vertical stabilizer was subjected to *two times the limit load*, far exceeding design specifications.[10] It is no surprise that it failed.

To determine how much the previously departing 747's wake turbulence contributed to this excessive aerodynamic load, the NTSB conducted three computer re-creations. Results confirmed that Flight 587 did encounter about 80 percent of the 747's initial vortex strength, causing some lateral forces on the tail. Yet, investigators classified this wake as "typical" turbulence and reported that the high aerodynamic loads that led to structural failure were pilot induced. Therefore, the NTSB concluded, the probable cause of Flight 587's in-flight breakup was not flawed composite materials or JAL's wake turbulence but "the first officer's unnecessary and excessive rudder pedal inputs."[11] If the first officer had stopped his flight control inputs, the natural stability of the aircraft would have neutralized the motion, similar to a boat rocking through waves, and this disaster would have been averted.

How could an experienced airline pilot like First Officer Sten Molin, with nearly 8,000 flight hours and no history of accidents, have made such a tragic mistake? To investigate this question, we must broaden the analysis, considering the U.S. airline industry as a 'system' prior to this accident and focusing, in particular, on factors influencing pilot employment and training in the 1980s and 1990s, the era when First Officer Molin began his commercial pilot career.

The U.S. Airline Deregulation Act of 1978 changed commercial aviation forever. The purpose of this legislation was to withdraw government control from civil aviation, allowing airlines to compete over routes, schedules, and fares in a free market. A leaner, more competitive aviation industry emerged in the 1980s in which airlines such as Southwest and ValuJet thrived using a simple business model – flying one type of aircraft on short-haul, point-to-point routes – while many previous behemoths died on the funeral pyre of the hub-and-spoke system, which required a variety of aircraft to meet the demands of its complex networks. Since deregulation, at least a dozen large U.S. airlines and more than one hundred smaller air carriers declared bankruptcy, some

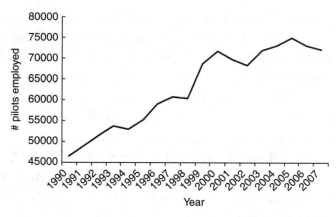

FIGURE 4.4. U.S. commercial pilot employment.[12]

numerous times. Examples include America West Airlines, Braniff International Airways, Continental Airlines, Delta Air Lines, Eastern Air Lines, Midway Airlines, Northwest Airlines, Pan American World Airways (PanAm), Trans World Airlines (TWA), United Airlines, US Airways, and ValuJet Airlines. Some did not survive.

Many airlines' struggles to stay solvent in the post-9/11 period originated with decisions made during this initial phase of deregulation when intense competition and unfettered expansion required the extensive purchase of new airplanes and record hiring of employees. Between 1985 and 1988 alone, nearly 30,000 commercial pilots were hired in the United States. To contextualize this information, consider the fact that there are only about 70,000 commercial pilots currently employed in the aviation industry (See Figure 4.4). In 1989, *Future Aviation Professionals of America* estimated U.S. airlines would hire another 32,000 pilots by the year 2000, and the FAA estimated airline fleets would increase by 25 percent, or nearly 4,200 additional commercial aircraft.[13]

The rapid aviation industry expansion exhausted the available labor supply and put younger, less-experienced pilots in the cockpit of nearly every U.S. air carrier. As Captain Vern Laursen, vice president of flight training at TWA, cautioned, by 1999 "every airline in the country will have 30-year-old captains."[14] Contributing to the pilot shortage was the mandatory retirement of large numbers of experienced Vietnam-era pilots at age 60, competitive bonuses paid to keep military pilots in the service, and the high cost of civilian flight training. To overcome this pilot paucity, airline executives negotiated with aviation universities to promote professional pilot educational programs while simultaneously reducing previous standards for age, vision, height, weight, and experience. For example, in 1986 most major airlines only hired college graduates. By 1989, one new-hire pilot in ten had no college diploma, just like First Officer Molin.

Sten Molin was hired by American Airlines at the age of 24, ten years prior to the accident. Growing up in an aviation family, he dropped out of college after only one year to follow in his father's footsteps, pursuing a career as an airline pilot. In 1987, his father began to teach him to fly in small single-engine, propeller-driven airplanes like the Cessna-152; and in June, Sten earned his Private Pilot Certificate, crossing the first hurdle to commercial employment. As Sten accumulated flight experience, his father, an Eastern Airlines pilot, researched flight schools. In the fall of 1987, he sent Sten to an accelerated training program at Tennessee's Bolivar Flight Academy, where Sten earned his instrument, commercial, flight instructor, and multi-engine certificates after just ninety days of training.

Returning home to Connecticut, Sten worked as a civilian flight instructor until he was hired by a series of commuter airlines over the next three years.[15] In 1991, just four years after his first flight, he was hired by American Airlines and assigned the three-engine turbojet Boeing 727 – a huge step up from the small single-engine airplanes and commuter airplanes he was accustomed to flying.

First Officer Molin's rapid career progression was not atypical for the industry at the time. Employment challenges caused many major airlines accustomed to hiring military pilots with thousands of operational hours flying high-powered equipment to increasingly rely on less-experienced flight instructors, commuter pilots, and other civilian sources for employees. Although many of these civilian pilots possessed comparable *amounts of flight time* to military pilots, often the *type of aircraft* – light single-engine and small multi-engine airplanes – and *flying environment* – often visual or simulated instrument flight in familiar, local areas – limited their exposure to the fast-paced pressures of scheduled air service flying complex aircraft in inclement weather, unfamiliar airspace, and nonroutine operations. Aviation industry analysts worried about the safety implications of this rapid industry expansion, in general, and the ramifications of putting less-experienced pilots in control of large powerful passenger jets, in particular. In response the FAA, the federal regulatory body tasked with enforcing aviation safety, began reviewing the rigor of its pilot certification process – the first such review in thirty-three years.[16]

Was the crash of Flight 587 an anomaly caused solely by pilot error, or did the factors of airline deregulation, rapid industry expansion, and antiquated governmental oversight also contribute significantly to the creation of this scenario? Four aviation accidents that occurred in the late 1980s and early 1990s provide clues to answer this question. Although – like Flight 587 – each crash was attributed to 'pilot error' by NTSB accident investigators, each also contained 'systemic' failures that aligned with individual errors and team mistakes in a "window of accident opportunity" that resulted in disaster. By analyzing these examples, perhaps we can understand more clearly First Officer Molin's actions and the crash of Flight 587.

CASE 1: CONTINENTAL AIRLINES FLIGHT 1713

On November 15, 1987, Continental Airlines Flight 1713 was delayed leaving Denver's Stapleton Airport by almost two hours due to snow, fog, freezing temperatures, and reduced visibility. Once cleared, the airplane deiced and awaited takeoff clearance for another twenty-seven minutes as snow continued to fall. The takeoff roll was initially uneventful until the first officer over-rotated on liftoff, stalling the jet, which impacted the runway and rolled inverted, killing twenty-eight of the eighty-two occupants onboard.[17]

Both pilots were inexperienced in their crew positions and unaccustomed to their required duties during cold weather operations: The 43-year-old captain had just 166 total hours in the DC-9, of which only 33 were as captain. The 26-year-old first officer was hired by Continental Airlines just four months before the accident and had only 36 flight hours in the DC-9. He was assigned the accident flight, only his second as a Continental first officer, because he had not flown in twenty-four days and needed to gain proficiency.

Yet, unbeknownst to the captain, the first officer had a documented history of poor performance and problems during training. A previous employer's chief pilot described him as "tense and unable to cope with deviations from the routine."[18] At Continental, his DC-9 instructor also voiced concerns during training: "Completely lost control of the airplane"; "Pitch control jerky"; "Altitude control when pressure is on is somewhat sloppy"; and "Airspeed control generally way out of limits";[19] all piloting deficiencies that became a factor on the day of the accident.

The NTSB determined the probable cause of this accident was 'pilot error.' Yet, in their final report, the NTSB included an unusual systemic indictment:

> The rapid growth of the aviation industry at a time when fewer experienced pilots are in the workforce has reduced the opportunity for a pilot to accumulate experience before progressing to a position of greater responsibility. This loss of 'seasoning' has led to the assignment of pilots who may not be operationally mature to positions previously occupied by highly experience pilots.[20]

Although specific ways to address these deficiencies were not offered, the NTSB suggested "the time has come for the FAA to establish and the industry to accept" operational safeguards to compensate for this 'loss of seasoning.'[21]

CASE 2: GP EXPRESS AIRLINES FLIGHT 861

In 1992, a second example of a fatal aviation accident involving unseasoned airline pilots, new to their flight-deck roles and over their heads in a challenging situation, occurred. GP Express Airlines Flight 861, a Beech C-99, impacted terrain and killed three people when the inexperienced crew lost situational awareness while maneuvering in clouds to land in Anniston, Alabama. It was the 29-year-old captain's *first day* as an airline pilot and his 24-year-old copilot's second month as a first officer. Like Sten Molin, both pilots had logged a large percentage of their flight experience in small single-engine airplanes and had minimal actual instrument flight experience flying in clouds.[22]

One unusual company cost-saving strategy central in this accident was GP Express's policy to provide only one aeronautical approach chart to each crew, which was held by the first officer during this accident. As pressure built, the new captain became disoriented, overwhelmed, and increasingly reliant on the first officer's erroneous flight guidance. Yet without a chart for verification, the captain had no way to identify the copilot's mistakes or reorient himself.

Approximately three minutes prior to impact, the first officer joked sarcastically about the captain's obvious task saturation: "Didn't realize that you're going to get this much on your first day did ya?"

"Well, it's all kind of ganged up here on me a little fast," the captain confessed.[23]

Two minutes later, the captain discussed executing a missed approach – akin to going around for another try – but the first officer convinced him to continue the landing.

They crashed one minute later.

The NTSB determined that both 'pilot error' and 'organizational failures' contributed to this accident. The pilots failed to use approved instrument approach procedures, and GP Express senior management failed to provide adequate training and operational support by paling an inadequately trained captain with an inexperienced first officer without sufficient airport charts. In addition, neither pilot completed a formal *Crew Resource Management* (CRM) program, a teambuilding and resource management training program standard at most airlines, which would have enhanced their workload management skills, perhaps even preventing this accident.

CASE 3: SCENIC AIR TOURS FLIGHT 22

A third example of a fatal aviation accident caused by oversight failures and a young pilot who lacked 'seasoning' involved a commercial sightseeing company on the Island of Maui in Hawaii. The 26-year-old captain had been employed by Scenic Air Tours for about eight months prior to the accident and took off on April 22, 1992, in a 1957 Beech-18 on the 'Volcano Special' sightseeing tour. Although the flight was single-pilot visual operations, not certified for instrument conditions, the pilot entered the clouds over Mount Haleakala and became disoriented, colliding with the rising terrain and killing all nine people on board.[24]

Particularly disturbing was the postaccident discovery that the young captain, eager to advance his commercial aviation career, falsified his employment application, stating that he had accumulated 3,200 flight hours when in fact he only had about 1,600 – well below Scenic Air Tours 2,500 minimum. Over the previous four years, he had worked for at least nine different aviation employers, five of whom dismissed him for cause such as "below standard work," "failure to report for duty," "poor training performance," and "misrepresentation of qualifications."[25] Yet this information was not made available to Scenic Air Tours.

In the ten years prior to this disaster, the NTSB investigated twelve sightseeing company accidents resulting in ninety-six fatalities of which six crashes were caused when, similar to Scenic Air, a fully functioning aircraft was mistakenly flown into the ground. These commonalities prompted more questions about safety, training, and oversight in the aviation industry; in particular, the FAA's failure to require that commercial operators conduct a substantive background screening of pilots before employment. In at least three accident investigations between 1987 and 1992, the NTSB urged the FAA to require aviation employers to screen pilots more thoroughly. However, the FAA dismissed these recommendations believing that the benefits of these requirements would not outweigh the cost of promulgating and enforcing the new regulations.

CASE 4: GP EXPRESS PROFICIENCY CHECKFLIGHT

Our fourth example of a fatal airplane crash involving young pilots, like First Officer Molin, who had quickly worked their way up the commercial aviation ranks during the rapid expansion of the post-deregulation period, occurred at 11:50 P.M. on April 28, 1993, in Shelton, Nebraska. The official purpose of this flight was for a company check airman, age 28, to administer a required proficiency check to another check airman, age 29, both commuter airline captains at GP Express Airlines. Yet the actual goal of the flight emerged to be a late night opportunity for the two young pilots, known to be good friends who liked to joke around, to conduct unauthorized aerobatic maneuvers in their Beech C-99, a fifteen-seat turboprop airplane.[26]

The flight started with the accident pilot asking the check airman if he was "up for a 'vertical thing'" on takeoff as he radioed company ground personnel at the airport to "look out the window" and watch.[27] Once airborne, they continued with other stunts, including a lethal 'aileron roll' maneuver that, moments prior to ground impact, both pilots confessed never attempting before. Postcrash investigation revealed that an *Airmen Competency/Proficiency Check Grade Sheet*, the FAA paperwork required to document completion of the required flight maneuvers, was found in the check airman's company mailbox – already completed and signed. Clearly, the pilots never intended to conduct a proper FAA checkride.

Based on this evidence, the NTSB determined that both pilots were willing participants in the unauthorized, hazardous aerobatic maneuvers violating company policies, FAA regulations, and the tenants of prudent airmanship. They also cited the failure of GP Express management to establish and maintain a corporate culture committed to pilot professionalism and safety and noting, for instance, the lack of a company training department and *Crew Resource Management* program as delinquencies.

Evaluating the commonalities between these four accidents and American Airlines Flight 587 reveals some compelling 'systemic' similarities highlighting industry-wide problems with pilot training, FAA oversight, and the ways airlines screen and hire new employees, schedule inexperienced crews, and measure competency in this new generation of pilots. For the moment, let's exclude 42-year-old American Airlines Captain Ed States and 43-year-old Continental Airlines Captain Frank B. Zvonek Jr. from the analysis. Each of the remaining seven accident pilots were less than 30 years old, had acquired initial airplane experience as a civilian pilot flying small single-engine airplanes, and were hired with minimal flight experience between 1987 and 1991, the rapid post-deregulation expansion period. Progressing quickly up the commercial ranks, 57 percent of these young pilots found themselves in the captain seat within months of initial employment just as TWA training Captain Laursen had cautioned. Four of the accident pilots crashed within their first eight months of employment – one on his *very first day as an airline pilot*. Moreover, almost half of the seven accident pilots (43%) had a documented history of serious performance problems with previous aviation employers.

Of course, this is a small sample, and thousands of airline pilots successfully traversed this same civilian career path during this period without incident. Rising up through the commercial ranks, they are flying safely on the flight decks of every airline in America today. Yet, something was different in these examples. Underlying all five crash scenarios – American Flight 587, Continental Flight 1713, GP Express

Flight 861, Scenic Air Tours Flight 22, and the GP Express Proficiency Checkride – is evidence that these pilots failed to develop some important *basic skills* during their early training that proved essential to safe flight in the complex commercial aviation operating environment.

Examples of these basic skill deficiencies include flaws in *technical* prowess such as inadequate instrument flight procedures, deficient basic flying techniques, and weak knowledge of aerodynamics, aircraft systems, and nonroutine operations such as during American Flight 587, Continental Flight 1713, GP Express Flight 861, and Scenic Air Tours Flight 22. Other flaws were *human factors skill* deficiencies such as the failure to develop an honest, professional work ethic, which led to 'errors of commission' or the intentional disregard for established rules, regulations, and procedures such as in Scenic Air Tours Flight 22 and the GP Express Proficiency Checkride examples. Other human factors failures led to 'errors of omission' or mistakes made due to unintentional negligence, faulty mental functioning, poor situational awareness, or flawed sense making, which contributed to deficient team performance. Examples include the weak leadership, chaotic teamwork, unbalanced workload management, ineffective resource management, and vague communication found in all five accidents.

These examples of basic skill deficiencies – both technical and teamwork – become particularly disconcerting at the commercial pilot level because, as Captain Larry Rockliff, Vice President of Training at Airbus, observed: "Once you're already in the profession" employed as a commercial pilot "and simply transferring or transitioning from one aircraft type to the next, it's very, very late to be teaching basic skills that were missed."[28]

Now, let's add American Flight 587's Captain States and Continental Flight 1713's Captain Zvonek back into our analysis and consider the NTSB findings regarding these captain's actions and responsibilities on the day of their accidents. For example, on conclusion of Flight 1713's accident investigation in 1988, the NTSB found that although the flight lasted less than one minute, the Continental captain displayed "several decision making deficiencies." These deficiencies included "inadequate supervision" of his copilot, "poor judgment in allowing an inexperienced first officer to attempt a takeoff" in inclement weather, and not arresting "the first officer's rapid rotation" on takeoff.[29] In sum, the NTSB sent an unambiguous message that airline captains have both the authority and the responsibility to divide the cockpit workload according to pilot skill level and then actively intervene if things do not proceed safely. Despite advances in *Crew Resource Management* training at the time that urged more integrated concepts of leadership and teamwork, the NTSB advocated that captains adopt a more *centralized* leadership model or risk criticism for inadequately supervising their crew.

Fifteen years later, when the NTSB released Flight 587's accident investigation, a different perspective emerged regarding an airline captain's responsibility. Of the 196-page, 86,000 word final NTSB accident report, only one paragraph or 136 words, discussed Captain States's actions and responsibilities during Flight 587. This section noted that the captain questioned First Officer Molin about the "little turbulence," asked if he was "all right," and then coached and encouraged by stating "hang on to it" and "get out of it." Although "the captain did not intervene or take control of the airplane, which would have been within his authority as pilot-in-command," the NTSB deduced this was because he "believed that the wake was causing the airplane motion," not the first officer.[30]

In contrast to their 1988 conclusions regarding Continental Flight 1713, this NTSB report appears to support captains who exercise a more *decentralized* leadership model in which 'inquiry' and 'coaching' are acceptable alternatives to more aggressive interventions. Satisfied Captain States had done his best, the NTSB concluded that "given the captain's limited knowledge of the circumstances and the short duration of the accident sequence," his "response to the situation was *understandable*."[31]

Understandable? Flight 1713's flight was almost half the time of Flight 587 – fifty-three seconds versus one hundred seconds – and Continental Captain Zvonek had even less knowledge of the copilot's actions, employment history, and flying skills than Captain States who had flown with First Officer Molin thirty-six times prior to the accident. How could two such similar fatal aviation disasters – both large commercial swept-wing airliner crashes flown by young first officers hired with minimal experience acquired by flying small civilian airplanes – have such glaringly different NTSB accident investigation results?

To understand these incongruities, we need to move now from analyzing the post-deregulated aviation industry 'system' through a socioeconomic lens to a sociopolitical one. Through this shift we will find that, in response to political pressures and the overwhelming pace of industry expansion and technological advances, the aviation industry as a whole developed a laissez-faire approach to safety. During the 1990s and early 2000s, a series of latent failures emerged yet lay dormant until November 12, 2001, when individual, group, and systemic failures aligned, causing the crash of Flight 587 (See Figure 4.5).

In the early 1990s, safety analysts predicted that even if aviation industry accident rates remained constant, the anticipated 3 to 4 percent annual industry growth would result in a near doubling of U.S. air crashes by the turn of the twenty-first century. In global terms, this meant an airline crash every week worldwide by 2015. Alarmed by these statistics, U.S. government researchers identified two types of aircrew error as factors in more than 70 percent of all airline fatalities: *Controlled Flight into Terrain* (CFIT) and *Loss of Control in Flight*. CFIT is when a fully functioning aircraft is inadvertently flown into the ground, such as GP Express Flight 861, Scenic Air Tours Flight 22, and the GP Express Proficiency Checkride. Loss of Control in Flight is when pilots unintentionally exceed safe maneuvering parameters in what is termed an *airplane upset*, such as American Flight 587 and Continental Flight 1713.

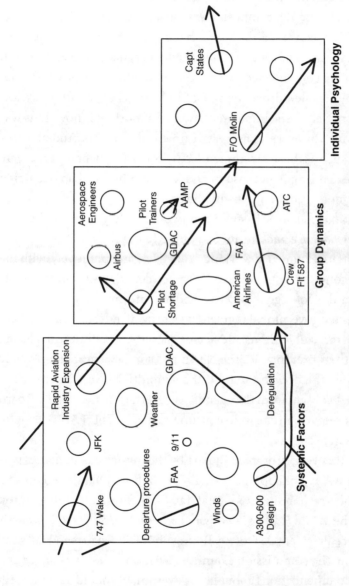

FIGURE 4.5. American Airlines Flight 587 – individual, group, and systemic factors align.

This information, among other sobering insights, caused the FAA to slowly awaken to their daunting challenge: how to enforce aviation safety during the rapid industry expansion caused by airline deregulation. They conceded they were having difficulty keeping up. For instance, the average time to produce a new regulation, even one with urgent safety consequences, was three to four years. Motivated aviation lobbyists often drove the rate of industry change through select personal projects. The implementation of important innovations was often stymied by overly conservative financial concerns. And new regulations, such as those recommended by NTSB accident reports, were often rejected simply because the odds of another mishap occurring was so remote it could not justify the costs.

After an extensive self-study and two-day safety summit, the FAA adopted *Challenge 2000* in 1996, a guide to development of aviation safety initiatives aimed at working proactively, not punitively, with the aviation community to achieve "zero accidents."[32] Although a noble aim, even this lofty goal of zero accidents in some ways shows how disconnected government regulators were from industry reality where human error is ubiquitous and accidents, although diminishable, are never entirely preventable. The NTSB had similar sentiments. "While I applauded the decision to hold the summit," NTSB Chairman Jim Hall stated, "absent from the agenda were certain critical Safety Board concerns requiring reform like airline management, FAA oversight, and corporate culture."[33]

Later that year, prompted in part by the mysterious midair explosion of TWA Flight 800, the in-flight fire onboard ValuJet Flight 592, and the corresponding 340 total fatalities, President Bill Clinton created the *White House Commission on Aviation Safety and Security* led by Vice President Al Gore.[34] Taking up NTSB Chairman Hall's call for reform, the commission examined aviation industry changes and made recommendations about how government should adapt its regulation. Citing *Challenge 2000* as important first steps, the commission recommended a more realistic reduction in aviation accidents by a "factor of five within a decade" and a reengineering of the FAA's regulatory and certification programs. "The FAA," Stuart Matthews, president of Flight Safety Foundation, succinctly noted, "was simply never created to deal with the environment that has been produced by deregulation of the air transport industry."

Eager to address the high number of *airplane upset* accidents identified by industry researchers – a critical key to meeting Vice President Gore's challenge to reduce aviation accidents five-fold or by 80 percent by 2007 – many U.S. airlines proactively modified their training ahead of the FAA's stalled regulatory process. They found that although some pilots received aerobatic training early in their careers, few had received upset training in the large, multi-engine transport jets they currently flew. Taking the lead, American Airlines instituted the *Advanced Aircraft Maneuvering Program* (AAMP) as mandatory annual training for all its pilots. During AAMP, pilots read materials, watched videos, and discussed hazardous in-flight situations in the classroom, and then practiced recognition and recovery techniques in the flight simulator. Pilots were instructed that the rudder could be used to assist in controlling the airplane's roll angle during airplane upset recovery and, in certain extreme situations, even full rudder inputs are appropriate. This seemingly mundane training point became pivotal in the accident analysis of Flight 587.

One simulator event, particularly relevant when considering First Officer Molin's actions, was the *Excessive Bank Angle Exercise*. This flight simulator scenario began with the instructor informing the crew that "they were following a heavy jet (some instructors specifically stated that the airplane was a Boeing 747)." As the instructor issued "wake turbulence warnings," the simulator momentarily rolled ten degrees in one direction then past ninety degrees in the opposite direction while inhibiting the pilots' flight control inputs for ten seconds or until the aircraft exceeded fifty degrees of bank. In other words, as the pilot fought to regain control of the aircraft, the flight simulator intentionally blocked the inputs until an airplane upset condition was established.

The simulator instructor who provided First Officer Molin's most recent training taught that recovery was "better when the pilots got on the flight controls earlier." If they just used bank angle without rudder to recover, "they would put themselves in a sideslip," he noted. Therefore, "a little bit" of rudder was necessary to recover properly in the flight simulator. Yet, by inhibiting pilots' flight controls, the exercise encouraged aggressive inputs that would not necessarily match those required in a real airplane in flight. As a result, requiring immediate and aggressive responses using both aileron and rudder to overcome the simulated 'wake encounter' behind a '747', this training primed First Officer Molin's response during Flight 587. One has to wonder if these tendencies had surfaced before.

Most pilots reportedly liked flying with First Officer Molin. Captain David M. Lander thought he was "nice, polite, courteous, and very cooperative in every way." Captain Louis J. Merz recalled he was "always in a good mood, and got along with everybody." He was "a very competent pilot who flew the airplane well," an "8.5 out of 10" compared to other first officers. Captain Robert Marinaro described how First Officer Molin "loved aviation" and "felt very lucky being able to fly for American Airlines." He was "a very bright guy, always ahead of the airplane, thorough, and paid attention to detail."

Similarly, Captain John Lavelle reported First Officer Molin was "a real gentleman" with "excellent" flying skills; "a perfectionist who worked hard" and did "everything by the book." "However," Captain Lavelle added, "he had one strange tendency: to be very aggressive on the rudder pedals." During one flight, Captain Lavelle recalled, First Officer Molin encountered some wake turbulence and over responded, pushing the rudder "to full stops," which dangerously yawed the jet side to side. Captain Lavelle noted "it is typical" for him to fly with his "feet on the pedals at critical times when the copilot is flying." Therefore, he felt Molin's rudder inputs. "It was a very aggressive maneuver," and he "had never seen any other pilot do this." He thought they "had lost an engine."

"On two subsequent occasions," Captain Lavelle recalled, Molin overreacted on the rudders, and when he inquired Sten "said he was leveling the wings due to wake turbulence" as instructed during AAMP training. Once on the ground, they discussed the incident further. Captain Lavelle explained that Sten's control inputs were "quite aggressive" and did not level the wings but rather created "heavy side-loads" that could damage the airplane. Yet, First Officer Molin was "adamant that he was complying with AAMP." He "insisted that AAMP gave him directions to use rudder pedals in that fashion." In sum, Captain Lavelle noted, First Officer Molin "was a great pilot in all aspects except the one quirk: his use of the rudder pedals."

So how was AAMP developed? In 1996, eighty aviation industry representatives met to improve safety and discuss pilot training strategies in light of recent industry developments and Vice President Gore's challenge to reduce accidents. Yet "right from the beginning," Captain William Wainwright, chief test pilot at Airbus, recalled, there were conflicts between the airlines' pilot trainers and the manufacturers' test pilots. Because many major airlines, like American, were already running large numbers of pilots through their flight simulator training programs, the airlines "naturally considered themselves to be the experts" and were therefore reluctant to accept "the technical advice given by the manufacturers," Captain Wainwright recalled. Three areas of differing opinions quickly emerged, foreshadowing the crash of Flight 587.

First, because American Airlines flew eight different types of airliners, pilot trainers wanted simple, reproducible procedures that were easy to teach in all models. Yet, given the infinite aerodynamic possibilities presented by the varying airplane designs, the manufacturers were uncomfortable with the trainers' one-size-fits-all approach. They felt it encouraged rote, procedural-based pilot responses to complex unpredictable scenarios and preferred instead a more cognitive learning approach.

Second, there was a difference of opinion regarding the emphasis of rudder during upset recovery. "Based on our experience as test pilots," Captain Wainwright cautioned, "we are very wary of using the rudder" in recovery because "it is the best way to provoke a loss of control" situation. However, the test pilots had great difficulty convincing the airlines of this danger because pilot trainers always responded that their techniques "work in the simulator." This techno-logic squelched further critical inquiry, stalling the debate and leading manufactures to their third concern: the role of flight simulators in teaching upset recovery at all.

The manufacturers doubted the fidelity of the simulators when flying outside the normal parameters of everyday operations. As computerized systems, simulators are only as realistic as the data programmed into them. "We discovered," Captain Larry Rockliff, vice president of training for Airbus, noted, "that the simulators in some fairly simple maneuvers were not representative of what the airplane should actually be doing." Therefore, manufacturers recommended that flight simulators *not* be used in AAMP because of the risk that these inaccuracies could foster negative training, just as had occurred with First Officer Molin. Believing they knew best, however, the airlines disagreed and proceeded with their training programs.

Four 'red flags' surfaced the following year – a full four years before the crash of Flight 587 – that should have alerted safety regulators like the FAA, industry leaders, airline executives, and airplane manufactures to the brewing trouble aboard the Airbus A300–600. The first incident involved rudder pedal excursions on jets in flight that resulted, in some cases, in vertical stabilizer damage just like Flight 587.

The most severe example occurred when another American Airlines jet, Flight 903, experienced an airplane upset on a trip from

Boston to Miami, injuring one passenger and one flight attendant. The Airbus, on autopilot, entered a stall and rolled right during its level-off from descent for landing because the flight crew did not maintain adequate airspeed. The pilots lost control when they used full left rudder in an effort to arrest the roll but luckily recovered the aircraft in time for a safe landing.

Referencing this incident, the second red flag was a letter sent to American's Chief Pilot Cecil Ewell by Captain Paul Railsback, American's manager of flight operations-technical. In it, he voiced "grave concerns about some flawed aerodynamic theory and flying techniques" presented during AAMP when "pilots are told to use rudders as the primary means of roll control in unusual attitude recoveries." "This is not only wrong, it is exceptionally dangerous" because the rolling moment caused by the Airbus rudder "is slow to take effect, then rapidly becomes uncontrollable," Captain Railsback stated. The Flight 903 incident occurred as the result of "excessive rudder inputs by the crew, which is exactly what they were taught." In an eerie foreshadowing of Flight 587, Captain Railsback concluded "American Airlines is at grave risk of a catastrophic upset because AAMP is teaching" techniques that are "wrong, dangerous, and directly contrary to the stated concern" of the airplane manufacturers.

American Airlines Captain David Tribout, A300 technical pilot, waived a third red flag by sending Captain Wainwright at Airbus a letter stating: "I am very concerned that one aspect of" AAMP "is inaccurate and potentially hazardous," that is "in the event of a wake turbulence encounter" instructors teach that "THE RUDDER should be used to control roll." Captain Wainwright faxed his response the next day: "I share your concern over the use of rudder" and "will be pleased to talk." A few months later, the fourth alert surfaced when industry representatives from the FAA, Airbus, Boeing, and Boeing-Douglas submitted a joint memo to American's Chief Pilot Ewell. In an effort to collaborate "as part of a growing industry-wide effort of working together on common training and flight safety issues," they once again voiced "concern" about AAMP's "excessive emphasis on the superior effectiveness of the rudder for roll control" and the fidelity of flight simulators in upset training. In closing they stated, "AAMP is an excellent program and we applaud American Airlines for expending the time and money in developing and implementing it." Yet, "we recommend you review" our suggestions "and work with the manufacturers" in order "to maintain correct information in your program."

Six weeks after receiving the manufacturers' memo, Chief Pilot Ewell responded defensively: "Let me say this one more time," he emphasized, "we do not advocate the introduction of large sideslip angles" using the rudder in AAMP. Disregarding his own pilot's feedback, he stated the proper use of rudder "is very clearly explained" in training and "we have come a long way toward representing realistic scenarios" in our flight simulators. In closing, Captain Ewell inferred that manufacturers should mind their own business by emphasizing that American Airlines is "charged" with "real life" responsibilities, unlike Airbus "which is technically and optimally controlled" like "academia."

This certainly seems a curious response to an offer of collaboration about a potentially life-threatening issue. During the postcrash investigation of Flight 587, NTSB investigators delved into this unusual communication exchange between engineers and frontline operators. Inquiring whether the manufacturers found American Chief Pilot Ewell's response to their offer of collaboration "an open invitation for further dialogue," Airbus Captain Rockliff replied wryly: "We did not." Little more seems to have occurred on the subject until the crash in 2001.

In hindsight, it is hard to believe that these clear points of conflict could be so blatantly ignored by American's Chief Pilot and industry safety monitors. American's A300 fleet standards manager, Captain Delvin Young, stated prior to Flight 587 that he thought commercial pilots knew "quite a bit" about large airplane rudder systems. Yet after Flight 587, he realized that the airline industry as a whole "didn't know much" and "In fact possibly had wrong perceptions" about rudder designs.[35] Most pilots believed as long as the airplane is below *maximum maneuvering speed* "the rudder limiter will protect the aircraft structurally" from *any combination of pilot flight control inputs.* If parameters were being exceeded, "there would be a limitation or a warning."[36] Yet, Captain John Lauber, vice president of safety and technical affairs at Airbus, disagreed. Inferring that aerospace engineers never planned to provide this level of protection, he noted, "An improperly trained pilot can break any airplane."[37]

Let us now consider how these systemic and group dynamics intertwined with the individual factors present during Flight 587. In other words, why did *this* high-risk team's dynamics align with *these* systemic failures resulting in *this disaster on this day*?

Numerous captains reported that First Officer Molin was a "bright guy" with "excellent flying skills," a "perfectionist" who "worked hard" and did "everything by the book." A "competent pilot" who was thorough and "paid attention to detail."[38] Yet, as Captain Lavelle noted, he had this "one quirk; his use of the rudder pedals."[39] First Officer Molin's initial ninety-day training program at Bolivar Flight Academy may have contributed to this rudder "quirk" or basic skill deficiency. At Bolivar, First Officer Molin would have had limited exposure to aerobatic flight, unusual altitude flying, or upset recovery in powerful, complex aircraft. Yet, he would have practiced 'spins' and 'spin recovery' in his small single-engine airplane. A spin is an aggravated stall in which one airplane wing is more stalled than the other, causing the plane to corkscrew in a spiral toward the ground. To successfully recover, the pilot neutralizes the control wheel, *applies and holds full opposite rudder*, then briskly moves the control wheel forward.[40] In the panic and disorientation of Flight 587's accident sequence, could First Officer Molin have reverted back to some of these early basic skills? – in particular, *applying and holding full opposite rudder*? According to the FAA's *Flight Instructor Handbook*, the "principle of primacy" supports that those things learned first are retained deepest, creating a strong, almost unconscious physical response.[41]

Consider, for instance, the 2002 crash of a Cessna-310 in La Verne California.[42] After takeoff, the small twin-engine airplane experienced an engine failure and, while attempting to turn back toward the airport, impacted trees, terrain, and pedestrians, resulting in four fatalities and nine injuries. Postcrash analysis confirmed that the accident pilot – who had several thousand flight hours – had configured the airplane exactly as his instructor did during their 'practice' engine failures, not as the real emergency procedures dictated. In his panic, he mimicked what he learned first rather than thinking through the crisis and evaluating the complex situation as it unfolded. Could this have happened to First Officer Molin as well?

First Officer Molin clearly took his career and training seriously. As he quickly progressed up the commercial pilot career ladder, his perfectionism probably helped compensate for his youth and inexperience causing him to faithfully follow manuals, checklists, and training procedures to the letter. He was, for example, influenced enough by AAMP to confidently refer back to the procedures he learned when challenged by Captain Lavelle. Ironically, his conscientious nature and detail-oriented personality combined with his basic skills deficiencies unwittingly made Molin the perfect candidate for the AAMP training inconsistencies 'red flagged' by Captains Wainwright, Rockliff, Railsback, and Tribout. These captains' concerns about flight simulators encouraging rote, procedural-based pilot responses, training scenarios such as the *Excessive Bank Angle Exercise* resulting in negative training, and the risk of full rudder deflection provoking "loss of control" in the actual airplane all come to fruition during Flight 587. First Officer Molin's aggressive flight control responses reflect those procedures learned in AAMP, particularly during the *Excessive Bank Angle Exercise* in which quick responses with both control wheel and rudder pedals were required when following a heavy 747.[43]

Of course, it is impossible to unequivocally determine what elements broke down to undermine this flight crew's teamwork. But the cockpit voice recorder showed that First Officer Molin twice called for maximum power, yet postcrash evidence revealed that Captain States did not comply. This indicates that the two pilots had a different 'mental model', or impression of what was occurring. First Officer Molin believed they were encountering severe wake turbulence or perhaps windshear, and wanted power. Yet by not complying with his request, Captain States appears to sense something else is occurring; a situation in which more power might be detrimental. Yet, he did not voice his concerns.

Although the accident sequence lasted less than two minutes, this breakdown in communication is an important factor. If Captain States had voiced his reasons for not complying with the copilot's "max power" requests, perhaps their mental models could have converged, helping them make better sense of the unfolding situation. In addition, Captain States' laid back leadership style and the familiarity of flying together thirty-six times prior to the crash may have further undermined their teamwork. A less familiar or more aggressive captain might have had his or her feet on the rudder pedals and, noticing the copilot's overcorrection, taken control during the wake encounter in a more centralized leadership fashion, possibly averting the disaster. It is important to be cautious about generalizations when reflecting about these possibilities. However, we can nonetheless learn about breakdowns in teamwork and potentially thwart future disasters through this studied analysis.

Where are we now? In 2007, a decade after Vice President Gore's commission issued its challenge, the U.S. aviation industry reported a 65 percent drop in fatal accidents nearly achieving the 80 percent goal. This decrease prompted FAA administrator Marion C. Blakey to state: "This is the golden age of safety, the safest period in the safest mode, in the history of the world."[44] Advocates of the FAA's new pro-grams, such as Ms. Blakey, claim *Challenge 2000* and their efforts to work collaboratively not punitively with the airline industry proved central to this decline. Yet, critics claim that the FAA's role as the avia-tion industry's safety watchdog grew toothless over that decade.

Prior to the 1990s, the FAA was a "cop on the beat" inspecting "everything from the nuts and bolts in your tool kit to the paperwork in the cockpit," and handing out penalties to those who broke the rules.[45] After 9/11, critics note the FAA's more collaborative approach "went too far," "coddling the airlines" and drifting too far "toward over-closeness and coziness between regulator and regulated."[46] They point to the crash of Alaska Airlines Flight 261 in 2000 for mainte-nance failures, Boeing and American Airlines $3.3 million fine for vio-lating federal aviation regulations in 2004,[47] American Airlines 2008 grounding of its entire MD-80 fleet to re-inspect wire bundles found in noncompliance,[48] and the record $10.2 million fine against Southwest Airlines in 2008 after it failed to comply with a special inspection of older 737s for fuselage cracks as examples of the repercussions of the FAA's lax oversight.[49] In several cases, it took whistleblowers testifying to Congress to get appropriate FAA action.[50]

This new interpretation of the roles and responsibilities of the regulator and regulated could account for the glaring differences in levels of accountability after the Continental Flight 1713 crash in 1987 and American Flight 587 in 2001. Although this general shift away from holding captains directly responsible for all activities on their flight decks toward a more decentralized leadership approach might foster better communication in some situations, it seems some impor-tant elements of leadership and teamwork are still missing from this model for successful operations in high-risk fields. Where is the analy-sis of teamwork, not just between captain and copilot, but in the case of Flight 587, between aerospace engineers, airplane manufacturers, and airline operators?

In contrast with the FAA's "golden age of safety" viewpoint,[51] some analysts worry that the increasing rarity of fatal airline crashes may lead industry leaders to become complacent, making safety and training less of a financial and managerial priority. Mike Ambrose, director of the European Regions Airline Association, is concerned new airline managers who have no experience with aviation accidents will "tend to believe this level of safety is a given, so will more easily pass responsibility for safety down the authority chain."[52] Others note the way federal agencies quantify safety and the random nature of accidents makes some of the accident decline attributable to data manipulation and luck.

Yet, most people agree that the decline in U.S. fatal accident rates is related to enhanced human factors skills and expanded technological developments. For example, an increased prevalence of *Crew Resource Management* training programs, a more integrated philosophy of teamwork across employee workgroups, and a deeper understanding of the diverse factors influencing error making in high-risk fields has improved human factors. Improved technologies such as increasingly reliable aircraft systems, greater collision avoidance capability provided by the *Enhance Ground Proximity Warning System* (EGPWS), *Terrain Avoidance Warning System* (TAWS), and *Traffic Alert/Collision Warnings System* (TCAS), and enhanced flight and navigation systems, such as the *Flight Management system* (FMS), *Electronic Flight Instrument Systems* (EFIS), and *Global Positioning System* (GPS), all contributed. Yet, it may be too soon for congratulations.

In our increasingly globalized world, it is not enough to focus solely on reducing U.S. accidents. According to a Boeing study,[53] the decade between 1996 and 2007 may have shown an overall decline in U.S. crashes, but 2005 reported a fourfold increase in accidents and fatalities worldwide – twenty-two crashes or 'hull losses' with 805 fatalities in 2005 compared with fourteen crashes and 180 deaths in 2004. The advantage of averaging this difficult year with the rest of the decade reduces some of its statistical impact but not its overall importance, especially because the largest causal area (55%) of aviation accidents remains human error.

Meanwhile, back in the United States, NASA quietly discontinued an $11.3 million project known as the *National Aviation Operations Monitoring System* (NAOMS). This ambitious program collected critical aviation safety data directly from pilots to identify areas for improvement in air travel safety. Rather than wait and analyze an accident after it occurred, this program examined everyday operations, for example, asking pilots about airspace congestion, ATC miscommunications, crew fatigue, and passenger disturbances. More than 30,000 pilots were interviewed between 2001 and 2004 before the study was suddenly terminated. The data remained unused for two years until an anonymous NASA whistleblower informed the Associated Press, who filed a Freedom of Information Act request. Initially denied because, NASA noted, the data "could materially affect the public confidence in, and the commercial welfare of, the air carriers," a congressional inquiry finally forced its release.[54]

One has to wonder what was so troubling in this study that NASA, already on the ropes from previous leadership blunders, would risk public outrage and the implication that government agencies were prioritizing commercial aviation industry financial interests over public safety. A review of the NAOMS data, not fully released until December 2007, produced some clues. Numerous inconsistencies with other governmental statistical reports emerged, potentially tarnishing the government's "golden age of safety" image. NAOMS data reported four times the number of engine failures and twice the number of bird strikes and near midair collisions than other government monitoring systems, calling into question the appropriate way by which to measure aviation safety. When pressed about these inconsistencies, NASA administrator Michael Griffin criticized the NAOMS "reporting mechanism," stating the project was "poorly organized" and the data was "not properly peer reviewed" and likening it to "hangar talk."[55]

Yet NAOMS researchers Jon Krosnick PhD, a Stanford University professor, and Robert Dodd PhD, principal investigator, defended their work. This defense, the $11.3 million NASA spent, and the high response rate from pilots raise suspicions about the motivations behind NASA's abrupt change of heart. As Congressman Brad Miller noted, "If 80 percent of the pilots" asked agreed "to sit still for a half-hour survey, voluntarily, my conclusion is the pilots had something they wanted others to know about."[56] The question remains, why don't some people want to hear it?

Much remains unsettled about the Flight 587 disaster. Although they continue to fly the aircraft – they still own twenty-three A300–605Rs – American Airlines charges that the crash was mostly Airbus's fault because the A300–600 was designed with unusually sensitive rudder controls that few pilots were aware of. Airbus charges that the crash was mostly American's fault because AAMP did not train pilots properly about the aerodynamic theory and handling characteristics of large multi-engine airplane rudders. And both American Airlines and Airbus blame First Officer Molin for pilot error and his excessive rudder pedal inputs. Conspicuously absent from the probable cause list are the critical concerns voiced by NTSB Chairman Jim Hall regarding airline management, FAA oversight, and corporate culture failures that were central to all five aviation accidents discussed in this chapter.

Of the eighteen 'findings' and eight 'recommendations' in Flight 587's final NTSB accident report, not one directed aircraft manufacturers and frontline operators to improve their communication, work more collaboratively to develop trainings, or create new methods by which to periodically exchange information across their organizational boundaries, creating a feedback loop between designer, manufacturer, and operator. These oversights lead one to deduce that the cause of the next metaphoric 'Flight 587' will be the result of previous lessons learned and ignored as well.

5

Bristol Royal Infirmary – The Price of Organizational Overreach

Nobody exactly knew what a learning curve was except for saying that whenever you start any new operation you are bound to have unfortunately high mortality ... I do not think any surgeon wants to be seen as in a way practising with his patients but that is the definition of 'learning curve.'[1]

> Dr. Janardan Dhasmana, pediatric cardiac surgeon,
> Bristol Royal Infirmary, United Kingdom

On January 10, 1995, Amanda Evans and Robert Loveday took their sick baby, Joshua, to see cardiac surgeon Dr. Janardan Dhasmana at Bristol Royal Infirmary (BRI), a hospital in the United Kingdom. Eighteen-month-old Joshua was suffering from a rare congenital heart deformity called *Transposition of the Great Arteries* (TGA) in which his heart's aorta and pulmonary arteries were reversed, connected to the wrong sides of his heart.[2] As a result of this misplacement, oxygen-rich blood circulated back to Joshua's lungs rather than to his body, while un-oxygenated blood circulated throughout his body, often turning him blue from hypoxia.

Dr. Dhasmana recommended a relatively new procedure called an *Arterial Switch Operation* to rectify young Joshua's problem. During this open heart surgery, Joshua's heart would be stopped and his body sustained by a heart-lung bypass machine so that Dr. Dhasmana could sever his heart's arteries and 'switch' them to the correct side. Although risky, the operation was an imperative for Joshua who had a life expectancy of less than seven months without the procedure.[3]

If the surgery was successful, he had a 90 percent chance of living an active life into adulthood,[4] all excellent reasons to accept the risk and attempt the 'switch' operation.

It was a difficult and demanding medical procedure. Because the arteries of Joshua's small heart were only about one millimeter in diameter, this delicate operation demanded extensive surgical skill, recent practice, and coordinated teamwork to complete successfully.[5] Because it was often impossible to predict exactly what the team would encounter once inside, surgeons had to think on their feet, making decisions quickly so as not to delay the operation and increase the patient's risks.

Unbeknownst to Joshua's parents, an emergency meeting had been called the day prior to his operation to consider Joshua's surgery. Some of the Pediatric Cardiology Unit (PCU) doctors were concerned. Although all agreed that the benefits of the 'switch' procedure outweighed the risks, some doctors felt that Joshua might be better served at a different hospital; one with more experience conducting this unusual operation and a better track record of success. Meanwhile, Joshua's parents had no idea what was in store for their child. Joshua's mother recalled, "There were no doubts" conveyed to them about conducting the operation at Bristol. If doctors had expressed "any doubts then I would have been up and gone," taking Joshua home.[6]

Despite objections by some PCU staff, concerns by outside officials, and trepidation on the part of the surgical team, Joshua's operation proceeded as scheduled the following day. On January 12, 1995, Joshua Loveday died after eight hours on the operating table. After Joshua's death, BRI stopped conducting the difficult and risky 'switch' operation. Further research revealed that the PCU had ceased the 'switch' procedure with neonates (babies less than four weeks old) two years prior when nine of thirteen (69%) babies died during surgery. So why then did Joshua's operation go forward?

The following analysis will make clear that there was a lack of leadership and a breakdown in teamwork throughout the National Health

Service (NHS), in general, and BRI's Pediatric Cardiology Unit, in particular, on January 12, 1995. Although doctors possessed the technical skills required to conduct Joshua's operation, a lack of teamwork led to Joshua's death and many more babies like him. When compared with other hospitals between 1990 and 1995, thirty to thirty-five more babies died after open heart surgery at Bristol than might be expected had the PCU been up to the standard of care at other British hospitals.[7]

Between 1988 when the 'switch' operation was first begun at BRI and Joshua's death in 1995, there were four complex systemic factors working at odds with one another creating the 'window of accident opportunity' that led to these babies' deaths: First, there was weak regulatory oversight during the NHS's restructuring in the late 1980s and transition to 'Trust' status. Second, a new generation of managers who prioritized short-term fiscal management over long-term safety concerns entered the NHS leadership ranks from outside the health care system. Third, an inordinately long surgical 'learning curve' was permitted to perfect the 'switch' operation. And, fourth, a toxic team culture emerged within the PCU that made it impossible for teams to communicate openly and effectively without fear.

Although these four areas are discussed independently in the following chapter, they were felt by employees to be interrelated, woven within the complex fabric of the organizational climate at BRI. Unlike the other case studies already assessed in this book, this breakdown in teamwork occurred gradually over a seven-year period while different people took up different roles within the wider system. Ironically, one of the most vocal critics of the unit's *technical* competency to conduct surgical operations became one of the most influential in the *teamwork* breakdown.

TRANSITION TO 'TRUST' STATUS

The NHS was established by the British government after World War II to provide a comprehensive, government-financed health care system virtually free to all citizens. Unlike most other countries' health care systems, development of the NHS made the government ultimately responsible for the standard and quality of health care throughout the UK. Between 1948, when it was established, and the mid-1970s when a new conservative political agenda gained favor, the NHS organizational structure changed very little. By the mid-1980s when Dr. Dhasmana was first hired at BRI, however, it was a system in significant transition. The fundamental driving force behind these changes was a strong political push to control costs and reduce public spending, making government more 'efficient'.

As Prime Minister Margaret Thatcher succinctly stated, "We have gone through a period" in the UK in which too many people believe

> 'I have a problem, it is the Government's job to cope with it!' ... So they are casting their problems on society and who is society? There is no such thing! There are individual men and women and there are families and no government can do anything except through people.... Life is a reciprocal business and people have got the entitlements too much in mind without the obligations.[8]

Determined to realign this thinking, the Thatcher government commissioned an inquiry in 1983 led by Sir Roy Griffiths, deputy chairman of Sainsbury's supermarket, which had widespread implications for the NHS.

Griffiths and his team of businessmen felt that the NHS lacked a coherent system of management and precise objectives measured by clear outcomes and had no tangible form of performance evaluation defined in terms of normal business criteria. The *Griffiths Report*, as it became known, recommended replacement of the NHS's 1970s-style 'consensus management' strategies with a more formalized management hierarchy similar to that of a public corporation.[9] The result was a fundamental restructuring of the NHS to include a management board, appointment of general managers at each level, and realignment of employee duties, responsibilities, accountability, and control. In order to provide more freedom to manage their own affairs at the local level, the government created NHS 'Trusts', and fifty-seven health care providers including BRI were certified in 1991, four years before Joshua's death.

SHORT-TERM FISCAL MANAGEMENT

New hospital managers, colloquially called 'Griffiths managers', were hired under renewable contracts, providing an incentive to produce fast results in a short period of time, often at the expense of long-term planning.[10] During this rocky transition, a number of leadership challenges emerged such as keeping doctors involved in hospital management and, with so many cost-saving cutbacks, prioritizing the focus on customer service – a major shift from previous paradigms of 'doctor knows best'. Yet most new managers haled from business and industry, not from the health care field, making doctors' behaviors, hospital culture change, and quality of patient care specific areas they were reluctant to address.

As Bristol Chief Executive John Roylance noted, the widespread understanding of the manager role was "to provide and coordinate the facilities which would allow [doctors] to exercise their clinical freedom" – not to try and influence their behaviors.[11] As a physician himself, Dr. Roylance was a slightly unusual NHS manager with unique insights into the medical culture as a result of his own background and training. His hands-off managerial style was based, for instance, on his belief that physicians "are not manageable." Rather, he felt, successful hospitals should be led by doctors who are "self-teaching" and "self-correcting." To facilitate this as chief executive, Dr. Roylance preferred an informal leadership style, not writing things down unless absolutely necessary, but instead handling issues verbally.[12] Apparently adopting Mrs. Thatcher's philosophy, Dr. Roylance seemed to think that there are individual men and women doctors and there are medical units, but no hospital can manage a physician's performance except through the people managing themselves. This reliance on doctor's self-management became a critical factor in Joshua's death.

In addition to changes in the physical structure of the NHS, a shift in thinking about children's health care was also occurring. No longer viewed as simply 'little adults', children were accepted as a unique group of patients with special physiological and psychological needs. This new view prompted an increased emphasis on the pediatric health care service environment.[13] Yet, progress was slow in achieving improvements, particularly at BRI, where there were insufficient numbers of pediatrically trained staff, no specialist in pediatric cardiac surgery, and a national shortage in pediatric cardiologists and registered nurses.[14]

Despite these drawbacks, advances in pediatric cardiac treatment methods moved forward at a rapid pace. Prior to the 1950s, there were few options available for children like Joshua with congenital heart abnormalities. Development of the heart-lung bypass machine changed everything, making the first open-heart operation on a child possible in 1958. Continued advances in equipment, technology, training, and experience during the 1960s and 1970s further improved services, allowing more reliable heart repair at an earlier age with fewer surgeries. Yet, little was documented about surgical results or mortality rates at this time. Operations continued because it was generally understood that without surgery, sick babies like Joshua had very little chance of surviving. Finally, in the 1980s, a plethora of surgical reports emerged documenting results and formalizing services. In response, pediatric cardiac surgery centers like BRI were established to treat patients with more complicated abnormalities at a local level.

There were also management changes within intensive care units. In the 1980s, it was generally the surgeon who assumed primary responsibility for the patient's postoperative care. In the early 1990s, anesthetists began to be more fully involved in patient care as a new subspecialty in pediatric intensive care developed.[15] Yet this was not necessarily a smooth transition. Tensions remained between many surgeons and anesthesiologists, who were known to "have an antagonistic relationship that may have a negative impact on patient care."[16] Researchers defined this professional interface as one of surgeon as customer and anesthesiologist as service provider; not necessarily the optimal collaborative teamwork structure. A more effective model would have been an operating room team composed of surgeons, anesthetists, nurses, and support personnel, working together as professional equals, providing the best patient care and most efficient use of resources. Yet this was difficult to achieve, particularly at BRI.[17]

As one Bristol anesthetist, Dr. Stephen Bolsin, noted, "There is a particular rivalry between surgery and anaesthesia." "It is legendary," and the dynamic still "exists" today, probably because we "work so closely together," he observed. "Surgeons do not like to be told what to do by anaesthetists and anaesthetists do not like to be told what to do by surgeons."[18] Dr. Bolsin joined BRI as a cardiac anesthetist in 1988, initially working closely with PCU surgeons. The doctors got along well, maintained a professional relationship, and spoke often. Yet over time, Dr. Bolsin claimed, "a clear picture of a problem" emerged within the PCU that he felt "needed to be reviewed."

SURGICAL 'LEARNING CURVE'

In 1986, Dr. Dhasmana was hired as a cardiac surgeon in a new appointment at BRI. Although he felt welcomed, Dr. Dhasmana recalled, there was only one other cardiac surgeon on staff, Dr. James Wisheart, and not a lot of pediatric cardiology services occurring. As a result, a surgeon had "to find his own place, his own mechanism, and to ask for what he wanted" to build his practice.[19]

He called BRI's pediatric cardiology facilities "primitive"[20] – long patient waiting lists, a lack of operating room theater space, children competing with adult patients for scarce resources, a lack of trained personnel dedicated to support pediatric patients, and doctors splitting their service between operating theaters at BRI and other pediatric treatments at Children's Hospital up the hill – and he was eager to improve the hospital's services and reputation providing pediatric cardiology procedures. "The facilities were there," Dr. Dhasmana noted optimistically, "but limited; you had to really expand on it" to build the program. And expand he did.[21]

Eager to make his mark, the young surgeon began experimenting with new surgical techniques in pediatric cardiology. Dr. Dhasmana recalled, "Right from the beginning, I thought Bristol should really come on par with other" pediatric cardiology centers that I had seen, "if not better."[22] To accomplish this goal, Dr. Dhasmana stated he "was trying to bring in newer ideas" and repair babies' birth defects "at an earlier age." Previously, "a lot of foreign materials were used" in pediatric cardiology surgery "and children had problems because the heart would grow and the materials would not grow."[23] Therefore, these short-term solutions provided only a temporary fix, requiring additional operations at a later date. Basically, "you were accepting one mistake a child is born with" yet "creating another" through the surgical procedure. A much better solution, Dr. Dhasmana emphasized, was a one-time-only anatomical correction that would grow naturally as part of the body, like the *Arterial Switch Operation*. "I have been thinking about it since 1980 when I returned from America."[24]

After studying abroad, Dr. Dhasmana noted, "I got more interested in paediatric cardiac surgery and I was lucky to get an opportunity to work in Great Ormond Street Hospital, which was founded in London in 1852, specializing in the care of children.[25] "There I was exposed to arterial switch being performed" on "patients who had Transposition of Great Arteries with VSD" or ventricular septal defects: Joshua Loveday's birth defect. The presence of VSD greatly increases the risk of surgery.[26] "It was well known," Dr. Dhasmana explained, that this "group of patients" had a "very high mortality; so that is why this" risky surgical procedure was first tried with these babies. They had very little chance of living to adulthood without it.[27]

Before attempting the 'switch' operation at BRI, Dr. Dhasmana recalled, "I was going around in various meetings" and professional "conferences" and "I was hearing, 'Yes, arterial switch is a better operation, but it is better to start in this group of patients'" whose high mortality without surgery can justify doing it. "Once you have learned the art of the surgery then" the technique could be applied more widely. Although Dr. Dhasmana was eager to try the 'switch' operation because he believed it was "the operation of choice," creating the proper "anatomical correction," the other PCU doctors were not as confident. Gradually, over time they acquiesced, and in 1988 Dr. Dhasmana conducted his first 'switch' operation at Bristol. [28]

As with any new process of development, there is rarely a precise 'Eureka!' moment of skill proficiency; more often, progress is evolutionary, influenced by a number of interrelated elements, such as technological developments like new equipment and pharmaceuticals, and improved medical techniques through innovation, training, and practice. There are other more intangible influences as well, such as exploring new ideas, risking experimentation, improving teamwork, and crossing professional disciplines to integrate lessons learned from other fields. Dr. Dhasmana understood this evolutionary process of skill building and was not initially concerned about the time it would take to perfect this surgical procedure.

Although he had never tried the 'switch' procedure himself and had only assisted another physician once, five years prior, Dr. Dhasmana felt confident he was ready. "Starting a new operation," he recalled, "I did anticipate" a high mortality rate, but I expected it to be "lower a few years later."[29] "I chose this particular pathology, transposition with VSD" for the first 'switch' operations because "the mortality was high" whatever we did. "Unfortunately at that time there were no clear guidelines," he emphasized. There were no set standards and little supervision. Therefore, "almost every surgeon was really doing the best available practice" that he could, and it was deemed 'good enough.'[30]

Dr. Dhasmana recalled:

> Nobody exactly knew what a learning curve was except for saying
> that whenever you start any new operation you are bound to have
> unfortunately high mortality.... I do not think any surgeon wants
> to be seen as in a way practising with his patients but that is the
> definition of 'learning curve.'[31]

Between 1988 and 1989, Dr. Dhasmana conducted nine 'switch'
operations after which five babies died (56% mortality). Many deaths
resulted from unusual abnormalities that were difficult to detect
prior to surgery and nearly impossible to correct once the operation
was begun.

Over the next few years, Dr. Dhasmana's results improved.
Between 1990 and 1994, he conducted fifteen 'switch' operations with
three fatalities (20% mortality). These respectable results bolstered
Dr. Dhasmana's confidence that he was gaining on the surgical 'learning
curve,' and in 1990 he decided it was time to try this procedure on the
younger, more difficult babies, neonates. Over the following years, he
operated on thirteen neonates, resulting in nine deaths (69% mortality). Concerned about these results, Dr. Dhasmana instituted a
self-imposed moratorium on the neonate 'switch' operation in 1992,
in some ways validating Dr. Bolsin's sense that there was "a problem."
Yet he continued the procedure on older babies, like Joshua, where his
statistics were more encouraging.

Eager to improve his surgical techniques, Dr. Dhasmana sought
the advice of a colleague, Dr. William Brawn, at Diana Princess of
Wales Hospital in Birmingham, UK. Dr. Dhasmana recalled that he
had become "very concerned" because, he stated, "I was not able to
transfer my experience from older 'switches' to the neonatal 'switches'"
and he thought, "something is probably a little different in neonates"
that he had not yet identified.[32] Therefore, he wanted to pursue retrain-
ing with Dr. Brawn.[33]

Recognizing the value of teamwork, he also took his operating room team from Bristol to study Dr. Brawn's surgical team in

action. After observing Dr. Brawn twice, first in 1992 and then in 1993, Dr. Dhasmana noted, "As a surgeon Mr. Brawn managed to have a better team to help him in the theatre than I managed here in Bristol."[34] For instance, Dr. Brawn had dedicated specialists trained in pediatric cardiology that were accustomed to working together as a team, anticipating one another's needs, thereby shortening the length of the operation and the baby's time on the bypass machine. These improvements in teamwork proved critical to the patient's survival.

Dr. Brawn boosted Dr. Dhasmana's diminished confidence, suggesting that "this thing comes with experience." and he should just give it time "and there would be no problem."[35] Dr. Dhasmana was relieved and returned to BRI ready to start afresh. And improve he did. Between 1988 and 1994, Dr. Dhasmana operated on fifteen babies of Joshua's age with only three fatalities, an 80 percent success rate. This figure not only represents steady improvement on Dr. Dhasmana's part, but it is comparable to the UK average of approximately 84 percent.[36] With this solid track record of surgical success with the 'switch' operation in older infants, one might wonder why some PCU doctors were alarmed about Dr. Dhasmana conducting Joshua's operation in 1995. To understand this, we must now consider the broader organizational culture at Bristol and within the Pediatric Cardiology Unit itself.

TOXIC TEAM CULTURE

What *really* killed Joshua Loveday? It is undisputed that Dr. Dhasmana and his team performed the medical operation during which Joshua died. It is also clear that, given Joshua's rare birth defect, he had little chance of survival without surgery. Therefore, Joshua's death was the direct result of the failed corrective surgery for his unfortunate heart abnormality. However, this does not explain why this teamwork breakdown occurred.

In the following section, I will explore an additional contributing factor, a covert dynamic, influencing the surgical team's performance: A toxic team culture developed within BRI, in general, and the PCU, in particular, between 1988 – when Dr. Bolsin arrived and Dr. Dhasmana began the 'switch' operation – and 1995, when Joshua died.

Over those seven years, an organizational climate emerged that made it extremely difficult for pediatric cardiology surgical teams to communicate effectively or work together productively. As a result, the surgical teams fragmented into professional cliques – surgeons became defensive, nurses became skeptical, and anesthetists became uneasy – undermining team performance.

Although there were clear signs of this team performance break-down along the way – such as Dr. Bolsin's complaints, Dr. Dhasmana's unfavorable opinions about his surgical team's competence, and his self-imposed moratorium on the neonatal 'switch' operation – hospital managers' reluctance to exercise leadership, monitor doctors' behaviors, improve hospital culture, or prioritize quality of patient care stagnated systemic change efforts as well. As a result, we find that Joshua Loveday's death was actually the result of a complex interre-lated systemic breakdown.

In 1989 after a baby died during a surgery he attended, Dr. Bolsin, a BRI anesthetist, spoke to his neighbor, a senior anesthetist colleague, Professor Cedric Prys-Roberts, about a "problem" he suspected within the PCU. Dr. Prys-Roberts recalled Dr. Bolsin "was absolutely dis-traught about" the baby's death "because he did not think it was his fault" and "he wanted to unburden himself" about the fatality. He "felt that the surgery was taking so much longer in Bristol than it had been" where he trained, and he believed that this "was tolerated less well by small babies," putting them at greater risk.[37]

But one must understand, Dr. Prys-Robert was quick to empha-size, Dr. Bolsin "was not somebody who was introspective about these things."[38] He lacked social skills and "wanted to broadcast everything," making "the whole world aware" without necessarily "having the evidence to back it up." As a friend and colleague, Dr. Prys-Robert recalled his concern that Dr. Bolsin "would say something which he might later regret." So he suggested that Dr. Bolsin keep "a personal logbook" of his work and collect data, adding "I think this is proper medical practice" in any case.[39]

Disregarding Dr. Prys-Robert's advice to gather more evidence before taking action, Dr. Bolsin sent a letter to BRI Chief Executive Roylance, in 1990, igniting a series of events within the PCU. It is hard to ascertain exactly what Dr. Bolsin was attempting to accomplish with his letter or what exactly he wanted Dr. Roylance to do. First, he alluded to "two false statements" made in the PCU's application for "Trust status," then followed up with a comment about improving "patient care" and the high mortality rates "for open heart surgery" patients at BRI.[40] He concluded by stating, "I look forward to your reply which I hope will help persuade me of the benefits of Trust status for the cardiac unit," making it seem that he was really just anxious about the hospital's transition.

In retrospect, Dr. Bolsin claimed his motivation for writing the letter was out of concern "for the safety of children that were dying unnecessarily" and the desire for an open, public review of the PCU's performance.[41] Yet, he never used the word 'safety', never asked for 'data', never demanded an 'open review', or even mentioned 'unnecessary deaths' in the letter. Perhaps even more revealing about his motivations was his reflection that "the reason for bringing the chief executive in" was that "I was a member of the" PCU, and surgical data "was not being given or shared with me."[42] This sounds more like he was unhappy with his 'service' role as an anesthetist within the PCU's surgical team and was using the volatile topic of 'child safety' as way to attract attention, inflame emotions, and retaliate against the surgeons for not involving him more proactively.[43]

Dr. Roylance surmised Dr. Bolsin wrote the letter because he took exception to the fact that PCU cardiologists and cardiac surgeons provided information for the 'Trust' application without asking for his input. Considering it a simple case of professional bickering,

Dr. Roylance noted, "I was accustomed to this sort of exaggerated statement" from doctors "to support the improvements that individuals wanted" within their programs. "I rang Bolsin up and talked to him about this letter," assuring him that "Trust status would neither facilitate nor hinder our attempts to improve paediatric cardiac surgery." Then I "asked him to talk to the Chairman of the Medical Committee," Dr. Wisheart, about his other concerns. Dr. Bolsin failed to heed this advice as well.[44]

In fact, by his own admission, Dr. Bolsin conceded his letter created disharmony and mistrust within the unit. Although Dr. Roylance dismissed the letter as departmental infighting, doing little more about it, others did not react as casually. Dr. Bolsin claims Dr. Wisheart was livid, admonishing him for not speaking with him first and taking his complaints outside the PCU: "I was confronted by" Dr. Wisheart; he was "red-faced, angry, intimidating, bullying, telling me if I wanted to do this sort of thing in this unit, I did not have a future in Bristol."[45] Interestingly, Dr. Wisheart says he never saw this letter, was never told about it by Dr. Roylance, and did not meet with Dr. Bolsin to discuss it.

Dr. Bolsin's fellow anesthetists were also quite dismayed, noting there were several established avenues of communication within the unit that he could have used to voice his concerns but chose not to. They felt his actions made them all look bad and potentially impacted their working relationships with the surgeons.[46] As a result, Dr. Bolsin recalls, he felt afraid and isolated with nowhere to turn. He seemed surprised to find that when "approaching the surgeons" now – about problems that he concedes "may not have been their fault" – there "was a defensiveness or an angriness" toward him, and his efforts to collect more data about babies' deaths were met with "prickliness and sensitivity."[47]

Yet, the minutes of a 1991 "Meeting of the Paediatric Cardiac Surgical and Anaesthetic Group," which Dr. Bolsin drafted himself, indicated *surgical results were being shared and discussed openly*, and the unit's spirit seemed one of professionalism and congeniality. For example, the meeting's minutes stated that the unit's "open and closed cardiac surgery results" were discussed at length and compared against the UK averages. Data "tables demonstrated that the problem which had thought to have been reaching crisis proportions" was "actually not as serious as had been thought." A lengthy collegial dialogue ensued on numerous professional topics, and the minutes concluded with the statement: "The meeting broke up in good spirits." It is difficult to reconcile these two drastically different images of the PCU's culture – was there a 'problem' or not? Were surgical results being shared or withheld? Was Dr. Bolsin a victim of organizational backlash or did he actively participate in the organizational befuddlement that later led to a breakdown in teamwork and Joshua's death?

At the urging of Dr. Prys-Roberts, Dr. Bolsin teamed up with an experienced researcher, University of Bristol lecturer Dr. Andrew Black, to compile their own pediatric cardiology data as a means to formalize Dr. Bolsin's complaints. Dr. Black stated that he recommended they inform the surgeons, "Mr. Wisheart and Mr. Dhasmana of the intention to collect and analyse" their surgical data, but strangely, Dr. Bolsin disagreed. He argued that talking with the surgeons "would impede their task," and they should proceed without the surgeons' knowledge.[48]

Yet, Dr. Bolsin had no problem talking with others about what he perceived to be his colleagues' shortcomings. In 1992, he met with a medical reporter for *I-Spy*, a satirical magazine, providing information for a series of articles that embarrassingly referred to BRI as "The Killing Fields." When confronted, Dr. Bolsin initially denied being the magazine's source, further incensing his colleagues and diminishing their trust. Yet, he later confessed that he did meet with the reporter and provided the information because "I needed action."[49] As one might expect, this publication had a chilling effect on the PCU, in particular the surgeons' willingness to share further information with their anesthetist colleagues. Yet, Dr. Bolsin seemed oblivious to the repercussions of his actions.

Sensing things were escalating, Dr. Prys-Roberts met again with Dr. Bolsin and with his supervisor, the hospital's clinical director of anaesthesia. They confronted Dr. Bolsin, he recalled, because "we were concerned that Steve, as he frequently did, would express his frustration" inappropriately. People were listening to him and providing advice about constructive ways to move forward; he simply would not hear it. "Our view was that he did not yet have enough good evidence to go public." And they were "trying to sort of quieten him down and get him to relax and carry on with the evaluation of the data" that he did have. "My concern," Dr. Prys-Robert recalled, was that "at that stage he was likely just to have a sudden explosion of outpouring of his quite intense frustration."[50]

In 1993, after collecting data sets on 233 children who had undergone open-heart surgery at BRI in 1991 and 1992, the *Bolsin-Black data*, as Dr. Bolsin called it, was complete. Yet, it quickly became clear that the research was fundamentally flawed and largely unusable. First, because both Dr. Bolsin and Black were anesthetists and not surgeons, they asked a new pediatric cardiologist, Dr. Alison Hayes, to classify the surgical operations into recognized categories within the *UK Surgical Registry*. Dr. Hayes recalled she reviewed fifty to seventy-five pediatric cases but found the results unreliable. First, use of the Registry as "a comparative standard" was "somewhat flawed," she stated, because operations were not categorized that precisely. Second, "some of the descriptions I was provided did not give sufficient information"; therefore, "approximately fifteen to twenty cases" could not be reliably classified, a 20 percent to 40 percent inaccuracy right from the beginning.[51] Third, Dr. Black's college-aged daughter, who had no special training in statistics or medical research, categorized data over her school's summer break. Unfortunately, seven of the data fields were entered incorrectly, resulting in statistical errors as high as 500 percent in some areas.

Although the Bolsin-Black data was flawed, if introduced correctly, it still could have been a pivotal opportunity for the PCU to discuss ways to improve team performance and jointly consider the open review Dr. Bolsin allegedly desired to investigate infant safety. He had numerous opportunities to raise his concerns publically. Yet, strangely, Dr. Bolsin chose to share his data informally, chatting in corridors, in the break room, and in taxicabs, or dropping by peoples' offices unscheduled rather than raising his concerns in a formal way.

For example, a fellow BRI anesthetist, Dr. Masey, recalled discussing Dr. Bolsin's research and advising him "to share the data with the surgeons." He refused, she said, because "he thought this might limit his access."[52] Dr. Pryn, another anesthetist colleague experienced with statistics, recalled he was sitting at his desk one day when Dr. Bolsin wandered in and handed him the data. "What do you think of these?" he said vaguely. Dr. Pryn recalled, there was "a huge amount of information," and the data was "pretty raw" and had "no summary." It was "quite difficult to interpret" and needed "a lot more processing to make it intelligible" or useful in any "presentable manner."[53] Professor Vann Jones, clinical director of Cardiac Services, agreed. Immediately calling the data's validity into question, he asked Dr. Bolsin to recheck his figures and get back to him. Yet, Dr. Bolsin never returned.

At the same time Dr. Bolsin was talking with people within BRI, he was also branching outside the organization. He shared the Bolsin-Black data with a senior medical officer at the Department of Health, who urged him in writing to speak directly with his colleagues and voice his concerns through the proper communication channels established within his organization.[54] In response, Dr. Bolsin wrote back stating they have "made considerable progress" in this matter; therefore there is "little benefit from any further investigation from your end at this stage."[55] Yet less than five months later, he approached a different Department of Health official in a taxicab, handing him a brown envelope containing the audit data. He claimed the first official had given him advice he "deemed inappropriate," so he "was now justified in involving another."[56] Interestingly, this official tried to give the envelope back without opening it and, like his colleague, explained that there were "well recognized mechanisms" by "which questions of performance and/or interprofessional disputes" could be resolved. He urged Dr. Bolsin to bring his concerns to the attention of senior staff at BRI and the medical director, Dr. Wisheart. But Dr. Bolsin did not.

And the list goes on. In fact, Dr. Bolsin visited dozens of different people to share this raw and inaccurate data.[57] At times, he would be waiting for feedback from one person while continuing to reach out to others, asking them to take action on his behalf. When given advice, he rarely followed it, choosing instead to approach someone new. Most importantly, he never shared his research with either of BRI's pediatric cardiology surgeons, Dr. Dhasmana or Dr. Wisheart. This information makes it clear that although Dr. Boslin claimed to be looking for resolution, the manner in which he chose to share his concerns about babies and the PCU ensured there would be none.

A final opportunity to break the chain of events that preceded Joshua's death occurred the night before his surgery on January 11, 1995. Minutes of this meeting reported nine Bristol doctors – cardiologists, anesthetists, and surgeons – met to discuss "the results of the arterial switch programme" in light of Joshua's operation scheduled for the next day. "Reviewing the figures," the minutes noted, "it was clear that the mortality at the start of the programme was high but had improved significantly over the latter few years." A discussion ensued, and "the general feeling expressed was that there was no clinical reason for deferring the surgery."[58] Joshua's "condition merited an immediate intervention" and his cardiologist, Dr. Peter Martin, considered any further "delay inappropriate."[59]

Dr. Dhasmana recalled that he had repaired Joshua's aorta and banded his pulmonary artery when he was just a few days old, as a temporary fix. Now Joshua needed the full switch operation. "I had promised" his parents "an operation between four to six months time," Dr. Dhasmana recalled,[60] but then we were hiring "a new paediatric surgeon, moving cardiac surgery to the Children's Hospital," and somehow his operation "just slipped out of my mind."[61] During the meeting,

Dr. Dhasmana recalled, "Mr. Wisheart called me and Dr. Martin" out of the room. "Do you think this operation could be delayed?" he asked. "We have a loose cannon here," meaning Dr. Bolsin. "It could have some repercussion" if the operation did not go well. Dr. Martin and Dr. Dhasmana discussed this issue and concluded "that this was a clinical meeting to decide on the clinical course" of patient treatment. Therefore, they should not "be guided by political repercussion" but by the best interest of the child. And what was best for Joshua, they concluded, was the switch operation.[62]

To many people's surprise, Dr. Bolsin shared that he had already contacted the Department of Health to alert them about the upcoming operation, further diminishing the team's trust. In response, "it was agreed that it would be appropriate" for Medical Director Wisheart and Chief Executive Roylance to contact the Department of Health in order to clarify the situation before proceeding. The minutes reported that "the meeting dissolved with the support for the continuation of the [switch] programme but with an awareness of the political dangers" of conducting the operation given the current climate.[63]

From an outside point of view, it seems clear that the pressure of the emergency meeting, calls to the Department of Health, television and newspaper coverage depicting Bristol as the "Killing Fields," and a general lack of teamwork and collegiality within the unit, ought to have prompted a pause before Joshua's surgery. Although there may not have been a clinical reason to delay the operation, there were many social reasons. Why did this go unrecognized?

I suspect that the Bristol PCU had learned to tolerate so much tension, turmoil, and outside distractions over the years, few people recognized that waiting a few days to let things settle down was a viable option. Joshua's condition was not going to worsen significantly during that period. Yet, as Dr. Dhasmana noted, "When I am in the operating theatre, I am very focused" nothing bothers me, "I am a different person." Even when challenged, he adamantly testified that there was no way he was distracted by the stress and anxiety of the unit's escalating political situation.[64]

The medical culture in general is not prone to reflection in action. Numerous studies have found that health care professionals routinely deny the impact of outside stressors on their job performance. For instance, 70 percent of surgeons deny the effect of fatigue on their job performance compared with only 26 percent of airline pilots; 82 percent of doctors believed a true professional can leave personal problems behind when working, and 76 percent believe their decision making during emergencies was as accurate as during routine operations.[65] Another recent study found that about a third of the anesthesiologists and about a quarter of the operating room teams studied "failed to ask for help, did not accept help when it was offered, or did not work together effectively in a crisis." In particular, communication issues emerged such as "speaking into thin air, not clearly addressing a co-worker, or being imprecise about what they wanted done."[66]

Other studies found that "teamwork is in the eye of the beholder" and differs significantly by operating room role. Although surgeons rated their operating room teamwork highly 85 percent of the time, nurses only rated doctors highly 48 percent of the time. Meanwhile, all groups rated their own profession's teamwork highly, making the breakdown perennially some one else's problem.[67] Perhaps most disturbing is that one-third of intensive care responders did not acknowledge that they made errors, whereas more than half reported it was difficult to discuss mistakes in their organization or ask for help. Reasons given to account for this poor teamwork were personal reputation (76%), threat of malpractice (71%), high societal expectations (68%), fear of disciplinary action by licensing boards (64%), job security (63%), and the egos of teammates (60%).[68]

Some of the issues underlying teamwork breakdown are the nature of communication and training within these professional groups. For instance, nurses are trained to communicate holistically, often describing good collaboration as "having their input respected."

Whereas physicians are trained to communicate succinctly, describing good collaboration as working with teams who "anticipate their needs and follow instructions."[69] These differences have deep roots in educational and professional cultures and will not be easily changed. Yet successful models from other high-risk fields could be adapted.

CONCLUSION

The events surrounding the deaths of the Bristol babies became the subject of the longest medical inquiry in UK history. Written evidence from 577 witnesses, including 238 parents, medical records of more than 1,800 children, and 900,000 pages of documents were considered along with individual testimony taken over ninety-six days.[70] In sum, the inquiry found paediatric cardiac surgical services at Bristol were "frankly not up to the task."[71] Between 1988 and 1994, the mortality rate in open-heart surgery on children under one year of age at BRI was roughly double that of other hospitals. Rather than a "deterioration in standards," per se, the inquiry found a "failure to progress" in the surgical 'learning curve.'[72]

As the old NHS system transitioned to the new 'Trust status', there was confusion at a national level about who was responsible for monitoring quality. There was no protocol, nor is there now, to introduce new surgical techniques or monitor surgeons' proficiencies. As a result, a 'club culture' grew at BRI, where an imbalance of power put "too much control in the hands of too few individuals" during which "vulnerable children were not a priority."[73] Although "Bristol was awash with data," it was "often partial, confusing and unclear," with little information provided openly to parents or the general public.[74]

In response, the inquiry recommended a two-pronged strategy that had proved successful in helping to change aviation culture several decades ago. First, revise the selection criteria for future doctors to prioritize teambuilding skills over individual success. Second, develop an enhanced teambuilding curriculum for all future health care professionals – doctors, nurses, and managers – to include leadership, communication, and teamwork exercises in multidisciplinary teams throughout their undergraduate education and ongoing during their careers.[75]

A greater understanding of factors that impact teamwork might have resulted in a different ending in Joshua's story and other babies like him. Yet, it remains unclear how this dysfunctional organizational dynamic could have perpetuated over such a long period of time. In the following section, I examine the evolution of this pernicious corporate culture and how its toxicity influenced teamwork, contributing to the performance breakdowns that ensued.

CULTURAL ANALYSIS

Although the previous sections detail the leadership and teamwork failures that led to Joshua Loveday's death and many more babies like him over a seven-year period at Bristol Royal Infirmary, questions about 'why' this dysfunctional organizational dynamic emerged or 'how' it could have perpetuated over such a long period of time remain. Although it may be impossible to determine with certainty the underlying influences, actions, motivations, and behaviors that contributed to these failures, team breakdown occurred often enough over the long- and short-term that creative explanations of the possible confluence of variables leading to this failure is warranted.

To uncover 'why' this team broke down, I engage in a process of "disciplined imagination,"[76] identifying and evaluating conceptual patterns within the case by tracing the roots to what Professor Susan Long at the Royal Melbourne Institute of Technology in Australia calls an organizational *perversion*.[77] In her book, *The Perverse Organisation and its Deadly Sins*, Long instructs the reader how to search for emotions and behaviors made explicit in the roles of key players but enacted on behalf of the entire system. Indentifying five basic indicators, she notes a perverse culture: (1) reflects attainment of individual goals or pleasures at the expense of others' rights; (2) acknowledges reality, but at times denies it to facilitate "not seeing"; (3) engages others as accomplices in the perversion; (4) turns a blind eye; and (5) breeds corruption.[78]

Each of these indicators was evident at BRI, in general, and within the Pediatric Cardiology Unit, in particular. First, the organizational culture allowed individuals – such as Dr.'s Bolsin, Dhasmana, and Wisheart – to prioritize attainment of their personal goals at the expense of other people's rights and the greater organizational good. Second, the culture's mental model of functioning allowed reality and fantasy to coexist as a way to facilitate 'not seeing' the unit's problems. Third, the culture seduced dozens of people – particularly through the actions of Dr. Bolsin – to engage as accomplices in the perversion. Fourth, a culture of instrumentality thrived in which some people – such as the patients required to facilitate Dr. Dhasmana's surgical 'learning curve' and Dr. Bolsin's Bolsin-Black research – were objectified. Fifth, because of the complicity of accomplices and the self-deception required to 'not see' reality, the perverse culture bred more perversion, ultimately culminating with many babies' deaths, including Joshua.

Let's break this analysis down further in order to understand how this organizational perversion manifested itself into what I will call *Organizational-Munchausen-By-Proxy* (OMBP).

MUNCHAUSEN-BY-PROXY SYNDROME

Munchausen syndrome is a medical term applied to people who fabricate symptoms in order to gain attention, sympathy, nurturance, and, through their illness, control over others. First discovered by a British physician in 1951, the condition was named after an eighteenth-century adventurer, Baron Karl von Münchausen, who was notorious for his outrageous stories. In 1977, a variation of this condition was identified, *Munchausen-By-Proxy Syndrome* (MBPS), in which a caregiver systematically concocts information about their child's health – even intentionally making the child sick – as a way to gain access to doctors, hospitals, and power within the health care system.

Although MBPS is more common in mothers, fathers often act as passive colluders either through physical absence or emotional distance from the family situation. To some extent, medical professionals collude as well, for instance, rarely contacting the father to gain more insight, clarify the mother's stories, or investigate his absence. Far from appearing strange, MBPS mothers may seem intelligent, articulate, and caring: the *ideal* mother. Well educated about medical conditions, they often work within the health care field. Yet, incongruently, they can lack basic social skills, display inappropriate emotions, and be simply 'too intense' to deal with.[79] For example, a MBPS mother might exhibit almost gleeful excitement when her child's situation seems most dire or not appear relieved when test results return negative. Obsessed with obtaining medical treatment, her child's fabricated 'illness' often requires extensive medical attention, invasive testing, numerous surgeries, intravenous medication, and long-term care.

Yet these 'doctor addicts' are not interested in hearing medical advice. They are only interested in getting physicians to take action. When one doctor denies them the attention they need, they obsessively seek treatment with another medical professional or different facility. Serious forms of child abuse, more than 1,200 cases of MBPS are reported annually in the United States alone. Many more cases undoubtedly exist. One recent study found that, when finally detected, up to 25 percent of the sickened child's siblings had already died under similar suspicious circumstances.[80]

Within this unfolding medical drama, the MBPS mother manufactures a starring role for herself as the 'perfect mother' in a fantasized relationship with the symbolically 'powerful' physician and the 'comforting' health care environment. This fantasy evolves to represent a second chance at a longed-for relationship with a knowledgeable and supportive father figure through the physician and nurturing family unit through the hospital. Satiating the mother's need to revenge her feelings of powerlessness, these powerful symbols are ultimately denigrated by the deceitful MBPS process, manipulated into conducting unnecessary medical procedures on the helpless, trusting child.

The critical dynamic is the MBPS mother's need to be in a relationship with physicians and medical institutions in order to feel important and in control. The child is just an object, used to gain access and maintain that power dynamic connection. Physicians get drawn into the MBPS mother's narcissistic ritual through a complicated need to be perceived as caring and concerned and their own narcissism to solve the difficult case and be seen as competent among their peers.

ORGANIZATION-IN-THE-MIND

To understand how MBPS relates to Joshua Loveday's death, we can use a social construct called the *organization-in-the-mind* to examine the interrelatedness between individuals, groups, and the wider organizational system. This model allows us to consider the actions of individuals as reflections of unconscious assumptions, images, and fantasies held about the organization instead of behavior resulting from individual psychopathologies.[81]

Everyone within an organization has a mental image of how it works. Although these diverse ideas are not often consciously negotiated, discussed, or agreed on openly, they nonetheless exist in the minds of employees, customers, and the community. As a result, a hospital like BRI exists both in the brick and mortar of its buildings as well as in the social reality constructed within people's minds.[82] In other words, we see individuals as if they were characters in a drama unfolding within an organization, taking action on behalf of the entire system.[83] Viewing the organization as "imbued with character" where individuals' emotions are at play on a larger collective scale helps us explore the way certain behaviors reflect positive or negative organizational character traits that affect team performance.[84]

For instance, Dr. Dhasmana's dedication and sense of perfectionism informed his desire to retrain his surgical team with Dr. Brawn, enhancing their teamwork and operating room techniques. Yet other organizational character traits can be more destructive and can "dominate the actions of organizational members from within an unconsciously perverse social structure."[85] It is the presence of these latter traits – and their influence in creating a toxic team environment at BRI – that we next explore.

Let us now adopt a hypothetical perspective – a paradigm of 'what if' – to examine the *organization-in-the-mind* of Bristol employees as a way to understand the breakdown in teamwork that led to Joshua's death.

'What if' Bristol's Pediatric Cardiology Unit was like a child being abused by its MBPS mother, neglected by its emotionally withdrawn father, and ignored by medical professionals colluding in the dynamic? In other words, '*what if*' anxieties and defenses within the Bristol system as a whole prompted Dr. Bolsin to take up a role similar to that of a MBPS mother, the surgeons Dr. Wisheart and Dr. Dharmana to enact the role of father, and NHS management to collude as medical professionals?

To understand MBPS, organizationally speaking, requires an exploration of the parallels between the group dynamics of MBPS and those within the PCU at Bristol. There are a number of similarities. Like a MBPS mother, Dr. Bolsin sought out one medical professional after another, more than twenty-five in total, to share his confusing and inaccurate Bolsin-Black data about the PCU, the symptoms of his 'sick' child. He lied and manipulated to suit his needs, while simultaneously depicting himself as the victim, misunderstood, isolated, and powerless. Similar to an MBPS mother, he claimed these actions were solely motivated out of concern for children's health. Yet when he was advised numerous times to clarify his research results and then use the proper channels of communication to openly discuss his concerns, he never did. In fact, several months before Joshua's death, he had another perfect opportunity.

Three BRI doctors invited Dr. Bolsin to dinner with the aim of surfacing his concerns about pediatric cardiology services and clearing the air within the unit. Yet, Dr. Bolsin did not speak up. He recalled, I would have "contributed to a debate" if someone else started it, but "I did not want to raise the issue" myself. Instead, he said, he wanted others to take action. "That was why I was going through every other route possible to press alarm bells to get somebody to come and deal with the issue."[86] Similar to the MBPS mother, Dr. Bolsin seemed to revel in the spotlight and the power he gained by manipulating others to take action based on his information. As long as the *organization-in-the-mind* stayed sick, Dr. Bolsin retained his central role of providing important information to other doctors and the outside medical community.

Like many MBPS mothers, Dr. Bolsin reported feeling isolated, uninformed, treated unfairly, rejected, and forced into a support role by his profession vis-à-vis the powerful cardiac surgeons. He believed he had more to offer and was outraged, for example, when unit surgeons and cardiologists provided information in application for 'Trust' status without consulting him, prompting his letter to Dr. Roylance. Although MBPS mothers are typically critical of the hospital's treatment of their child, they often talk with laudatory terms about the physician himself. This is an important part of the MBPS fantasy, preying on the doctor's narcissism. Similarly, Dr. Bolsin was known to describe Dr. Dhasmana as a deeply caring, hardworking doctor who could be found at all times day and night serving the needs of his patients. In fact, Dr. Bolsin called him "the best paediatric cardiac surgeon in the South West region."[87] He also noted that Dr. Wisheart was pleasant, easy to work with, "had a lot of experience within the Health Service," and "was a very good manager."[88]

It is difficult to reconcile these competing images and the purpose they served organizationally, but the MBPS model as an example of the *organization-in-the-mind* once again proves helpful. Like Dr. Bolsin, MBPS mothers often work within the health care field, identifying with doctors as an idealized parent, which allows them to deny their own intense dependency needs. Yet they find themselves in a perplexing bind: While they need doctors to project their unresolved ego needs upon, they simultaneously devalue the very people they seek nurturance from. Therefore, although MBPS mothers crave attention, they are unable to accept the care they do receive as genuine, leaving them trapped in a hopelessly escalating cycle of frustration.[89]

Similarly, Dr. Bolsin seemed to need to both idealize Dr. Dhasmana as 'the best surgeon' and Dr. Wisheart as 'the best manager' to satisfy his dependency needs while also demonizing them for their role in children "dying unnecessarily." He simultaneously craved attention from the outside medical community, yet he could not accept that people were interested and listening. As Dr. Prys-Roberts noted, this perplexing double-bind led Dr. Bolsin to act out, becoming overly emotional and highly frustrated at times. Although numerous colleagues urged him to calm down, think before he acts, use appropriate communications channels, and talk with the surgeons directly, he could not because he did not want to risk facts intruding into his fragile fantasy. If the surgeons could remain 'all bad' in his organization-in-the-mind, then Dr. Bolsin could remain 'all good' in his intentions and actions.

COMPULSION TO REENACT

After so many years of turmoil at BRI, one might expect that Dr. Bolsin might finally 'relax' and use the established channels for research and communication his colleagues had hoped. This would not be the case because another commonality between MBPS mothers and Dr. Bolsin is the compulsive need to reenact the drama as a way to brazenly defy the moral order and draw more people into their charade, feeding their insatiable desire to be needed and admired. As a result, the perverse culture bred more perversion.

In October 1994, just three months before Joshua's death, Dr. Bolsin provided evidence of this behavior when he produced yet another disturbing piece of poorly researched data, antagonizing the surgeons even more. In a one-page memo, he reported that "one surgeon" at BRI "was statistically worse than the other" and recommended that "serious attention must now be paid to the surgical activity" of Dr. Wisheart. Like his other data, this report did not gain much credence.

The political suicide implicit in this gesture becomes increasingly puzzling when one considers that Dr. Wisheart, now BRI's medical director, had stopped performing the challenging pediatric operations months prior, deferring them to the younger surgeon, Dr. Dhasmana. Around this same time, the Trust finally committed to a new pediatric facility, unifying open-heart surgeries at BRI with the other services at the children's hospital up the hill, and hiring a full-time pediatric cardiac surgeon – all important developments for BRI. Yet, strangely, just as things started to look brightest for the future of the PCU, Dr. Bolsin intensified his organizational disturbances.

OMBPS FATHERS

With obvious trepidation on the part of some unit doctors – secret telephone calls to the Department of Health and side meetings between the surgeon, cardiologist, and medical director the day before surgery – we are still left wondering why Joshua's operation went forward.

To understand this, we must now examine how the pediatric cardiology surgeons, Dr.'s Wisheart and Dhasmana, enacted roles as the absent and neglectful fathers in the MBPS organizational drama. They were either too busy or emotionally distant to get fully involved in the 'mother's' activities or the health of their 'sick child', the PCU. Although it is clear that Dr. Bolsin never directly shared his data or his concerns with the surgeons, it is difficult to understand why they remained so aloof. Apparently, like the MBPS family dynamic in which it is nearly incomprehensible that fathers do not suspect something unusual is occurring, it is hard to reconcile the surgeons' inaction.

Yet we know of Dr. Dhasmana's eagerness to perfect his surgical skills and make his mark, bringing Bristol into the forefront as a leading pediatric cardiac surgery center. It is possible that these personal goals motivated him not to ask questions and to pursue his individual agenda at the expense of the general good, particularly the babies; for example, not fully disclosing the risks of Joshua's operation to his parents. The narcissism and denial required by the surgeons to turn a 'blind eye' to this organizational undercurrent seems a conscious attempt to disguise a paradoxical reality all too evident – that no length of learning curve would have allowed Dr. Dhasmana to perfect the challenging 'switch' operation. The operation would always be risky, and babies with this rare birth defect will die. Joshua's statistical chance of survival without an operation was only about 11 percent. This was what remained unspeakable.

Although Dr.'s Dhasmana and Wisheart were certainly aware of the mortality rates, the system – through parents, managers, other health care professionals, and the community – worked to deny the risk and instead placed increasing pressure on the surgeons, whose narcissism caused them to collude in the fantasy of their omnipotence. The purpose of this dysfunction was to develop a diversion to serve as an organizational defense, avoiding the pain that facing reality would cause. For instance, the pain of accepting that many babies died during the risky pediatric cardiology procedures to facilitate a 'learning curve' and that doctors cannot cure everybody.

This is a difficult emotional process. As Dr. Bolsin's mentor, Dr. Prys-Roberts, noted, Dr. Bolsin had great difficulty accepting his role in a baby's death. Ironically, although he claimed to be seeking an "open review" of the unit's performance, through his actions he was instrumental in keeping key information hidden so it would not have to be dealt with openly. If Dr. Bolsin had heeded the advice of numerous colleagues to come forward with his data, discuss it with his surgical colleagues, and use the established communication channels, he might have helped break the complex chain of events that led to Joshua's death.

Yet, perhaps we have been asking the wrong question. Perhaps the question is not 'why did Joshua die', but why was Joshua's death – among all the other babies' deaths at Bristol over this seven-year period – the proverbial 'straw that broke the camel's back'? It has become clear that anxieties associated with the risky pediatric cardiac surgeries activated certain defenses within BRI and the PCU. Although the surgeons seemed to reconcile the statistical odds of babies dying by using their 'learning curve' metaphor, others, like Dr. Bolsin, were agitated by the reality that many of these sick babies would die without surgery and might very well die with it. Unable to accept this uncomfortable reality, the organization activated Dr. Bolsin, among others, to create a complicated organizational undertow that slowly built up over the years until it was nearly impossible for the surgical team to perform effectively. Preying on the surgeons' sense of omnipotence, these organizational dynamics led the doctors to increasingly ignore the escalating impact of outside stressors and press forward with the surgeries in an effort to 'save the day' one more time.

This coexisting organizational dynamic – in which the fantasy that doctors could save all babies and the reality that many babies might nonetheless die – might have continued for several more years except for one fact: The PCU's dilemma would soon be cured. The hospital hired a new experienced pediatric cardiac surgeon, and the split-site hospital facilities that had previously fragmented surgeons' energies were now to be united under one roof. Although this might seem to be what Dr. Bolsin wanted all along, like an MBPS mother, once these changes took effect he would no longer enjoy his previous power as unit whistle-blower and might instead be left feeling unneeded and unwanted as the repercussions of his actions took full effect.

Finally, and perhaps most disturbing, Dr. Bolsin seems oblivious to the social impact of his actions on others and the detrimental result for team performance. Even after Joshua's death, Dr. Bolsin's supervisor recalled, Dr. Bolsin had "no objection to working with any of the cardiac surgeons," ignoring the impact of his actions and "the fact that the relationship between" surgeon and anesthetist in the operating room "at critical times is of paramount importance. If there is tension and difficulty, then there is a risk of increasing mortality." "The fact that" Dr. Bolsin "was happy shows no insight into the feelings of the surgeons"[90] or awareness of his impact on unit teamwork and surgical outcomes. But it does show Dr. Bolsin's desperate need to remain connected to the surgeons. Joshua's death became 'the last straw' because on one level Dr. Bolsin knew the upcoming organizational changes would cure the PCU's 'illness', steal his spotlight, and sever his special relationship with the wider medical community.

Although we have discussed these dynamics as 'individual' behaviors, it is important once again to emphasize how these complex dynamics were interrelated, woven within the dysfunctional hospital culture over a long period of time, and insulated from change by the boundaries between professional disciplines. Perhaps most alarming is Lord Taylor's inquiry summation that "even today it is still not possible to say, categorically, that events similar to those which happened in Bristol could not happen again in the UK; indeed, are not happening at this moment."[91]

6

US Airways Flight 1549 – Thinking through Crisis

"Even in those early seconds, I knew this was an emergency that
called for thinking beyond what's usually considered appropriate".[1]
Captain Chesley 'Sully' Sullenberger III, US Airways
Flight 1549, after landing his airliner on the Hudson River
Copyright © 2009 by Chesley B. Sullenberger III.
Reprinted by permission of HarperCollins Publishers.

On January 15, 2009, US Airways Flight 1549 departed New York City
at 3:25 P.M. en route to Charlotte, North Carolina. The flight was proceeding uneventfully as the Airbus A320 lifted off LaGuardia Airport's
Runway 4, gently climbing over the snowy city.

"What a view of the Hudson today!" the captain, Chesley 'Sully'
Sullenberger III, exclaimed as the crew completed their after-takeoff
checklist.[2]

"Yeah!" his copilot, First Officer Jeffrey Skiles, agreed while flying
the jet.

Suddenly, just ninety seconds after takeoff, the airliner struck a
large flock of Canada geese ahead and to the right in a V formation.

"Birds!" the captain yelled. With no time to react or avoid, the aircraft ingested several twelve-pound water fowl into both engines.

"Whoa! Oh, shit!" the copilot exclaimed.[3]

Geese hit the windshield, nose, and wings in rapid succession like
pelting hail. "It sounded like it was 'raining birds'" the captain recalled.[4]
They filled the windscreen, "large dark birds" like a "black and white
photograph."[5]

The New York metropolitan area had experienced an increase in nonmigratory giant Canada geese settling around its airports, causing nearly eighty bird strikes in the preceding decade. Yet, most bird strikes ended with little consequence because FAA certification requires aircraft engines to continue producing thrust as birds disintegrate passing through. Similarly, of the almost 100,000 wildlife strikes reported nationwide since 2000 – most likely just a fraction of the number of deer (763), coyotes (252), rabbits (182), rodents (120), turtles (74), opossums (59), armadillos (16), alligators (14), and birds actually hit – only about 4 percent resulted in substantial aircraft damage.[6] Yet, US Airways Flight 1549 ended differently.

Just 200 knots and 2,900 feet above the ground, the captain took over the flight controls. "My aircraft," he called.

"Your aircraft," Skiles confirmed.

Later, Sullenberger recalled this moment. "I knew immediately it was very bad. I could feel the [climb] momentum stopping and the airplane slowing."[7] He felt vibrations, could smell "cooked bird," and felt "a dramatic loss of thrust." It had to be a complete loss of power in both engines. "I heard the noise of the engines chewing themselves up inside," he added,[8] and "was surprised at how symmetrical the loss of thrust was"; there was no yaw or sideward motion.[9] "It was shocking," "startling," and "eerily quiet."[10] "I knew very quickly that this was an unparalleled crisis."[11] "It was the worst sickening pit-of-your-stomach, falling-through-the-floor feeling I've ever felt in my life."[12]

The situation was dire. Back in the cabin, Flight Attendants Donna Dent and Sheila Dail recalled it was "quiet as a library." The only sound was the engines freewheeling in "a kind of rhythmic rumbling and rattling, like a stick being held against moving bicycle spokes."[13]

Up front, the captain radioed for assistance. "Cactus 1539 [sic] hit birds. We lost thrust in both engines. We're turning back towards LaGuardia."[14]

Air Traffic Controller (ATC) Patrick Harten received the captain's call and knew he had to act quickly and decisively. He immediately stopped all departures and responded. With a reputation for being careful and diligent, the 34-year-old had worked thousands of flights, and several emergencies, over his decade on the job. During those challenges, he had remained calm and acted intelligently.[15] He was the right man to be on duty that day.

"Do you want to try to land runway one three?" he inquired, the shortest turn for the Airbus-turned-glider.

"We're unable," the captain replied. "We may end up in the Hudson."

"Okay, what do you need to land?"

"I'm not sure we can make any runway. What's over to our right anything in New Jersey? Maybe Teterboro."

"Off to your right is Teterboro Airport," Harten offered. "Do you want to try and go to Teterboro?"

"Yes."

As Captain Sullenberger flew, First Officer Skiles attempted the dual-engine failure checklist designed for a high-altitude emergency where there would be ample time to complete the lengthy procedures. Although stressed, the captain nonetheless had the presence of mind to reach up and start the *auxiliary power unit*, not part of the checklist, but critical later in providing additional electrical power to the floundering jet.

Ninety seconds before touchdown, the airliner passed over the George Washington Bridge at 1,260 feet – with less than 700 feet of clearance – and Sullenberger made his cabin announcement.

"This is the captain. Brace for impact!" he instructed. And the flight attendants immediately reverted to their training, calling out, "Brace, brace brace! Heads down! Stay down! Brace, brace brace!" almost in unison.[16]

Both engines dead and attempts to restart futile, the jet floated earthward, shoreline bluffs of New Jersey to the right and New York City skyscrapers to the left. An illusion, First Officer Skiles recalled, that "felt as if we were sinking into a bathtub."[17]

Meanwhile, with no time to waste, Harten used his radar scope's touch screen feature to contact his colleagues in the Teterboro Control Tower, notifying them an emergency flight was inbound. Less than one minute had passed since he had been alerted about the emergency. "Cactus 1529 [sic] turn right two-eight-zero. You can land runway one at Teterboro," he radioed.

Descending through 1,000 feet and falling fast, the captain recalled "I knew intuitively" that landing on the Hudson River might be our only option. "I could see the area around Teterboro moving up in the windscreen, a sure sign that our flight path would not extend that far."[18] And he knew they were running out of time. "Put simply, we were too low, too slow, too far away, and pointed in the wrong direction" to make any airport.[19]

"We can't do it," Captain Sullenberger radioed.

"Ok, which runway would you like at Teterboro?"

"We're gonna be in the Hudson."

"I'm sorry, say again, Cactus?" Although Harten heard, his mind could not comprehend that the river might offer the struggling aircraft the safest landing option. So he continued to provide information, desperately trying to get the airliner back to solid ground.

"Cactus 1549 [sic], radar contact lost. You also got Newark airport off your two o'clock in about seven miles," Harten said, not giving up. "Cactus 1529 [sic], you still on?"

Just twenty seconds from impact, Captain Sullenberger heard these calls but did not respond. He had made his decision and was focusing on the task at hand. With the icy water fast approaching and the ground proximity warning system automatically barking out alerts – "Too low, gear," "Too low, terrain," "Caution, terrain," "Terrain, terrain. Pull up, pull up" – Captain Sullenberger asked his copilot a final question:

"Got any ideas?"
"Actually not."

Moments later, the Airbus skidded across the surface of the Hudson River, sending up huge plumes of water until it came to rest just north

FIGURE 6.1. US Airways Flight 1549 floating on the Hudson River.[20]

of New York City's 39th Street ferry dock. Less than six minutes had elapsed since takeoff.

The aircraft hit the water in a wings-level, nose-up attitude, going 125 knots with the landing gear up and flaps partially extended – a near-perfect water landing configuration. To many passengers and crew in the front of the aircraft, the landing felt "like a log ride at Six Flags" amusement park, "it was that smooth."[21] Even Captain Sullenberger recalled turning to his copilot observing, "Well, that wasn't as bad as I thought."[22] Others were not as amused.

The sink rate of approximately thirteen feet per second – not uncommon if this was a normal approach to a runway landing – was three times faster than the Airbus belly was engineered to withstand. Water immediately began to stream in through the cargo holds.[23] As a result, passengers and crew in the back of the aircraft reported quite "a different story."[24] Their landing experience was much more harrowing as the icy water quickly poured in, submerging the rear exits and blocking their egress. Flight Attendant Doreen Welsh recalled, "The back of the plane hit first," and "it was violent. Horrible." Cargo doors on the underside of the aircraft sprung open, filling the fuselage with water. "Garbage cans" and "coffee pots were floating" by "and things

FIGURE 6.2. Emergency responders arrive alongside the sinking US Airways Flight 1549.[25]

were flying. It was crazy back there," Ms Welsh recalled. "There was no doubt in my mind it was over." She knew she wasn't going to get out alive. "I just went crazy and started yelling [at] people and pushing people and getting people to go over the seats." Then, "as I was getting up, I thought I might actually live," and felt the range of emotions from "accepting death" to "seeing life. It was unbelievable."[26]

Within four minutes of the crash, an ad hoc flotilla of waterway ferries, Coast Guard vessels, and police-, fire-, and tug-boats converged on the scene. The frigid temperatures and icy waters were a concern as helicopters dropped police divers into the water to help passengers egress while the wreckage slowly sank, tail low, drifting south with the current.[27]

Yet, the rescue really began inside the aircraft. Because the aft doors were submerged below the waterline, the emergency slides, which double as life rafts, were unusable. That meant a majority of the passengers needed to evacuate using the over-wing exits, not recommended in a

FIGURE 6.3. US Airways Flight 1549 escaping passengers await rescue.[28]

water landing as it could leave them vulnerable, standing in water on the airplane's slippery wing. Because both forward doors were above the water, they were opened but only the right slide automatically inflated. The left slide had to be manually deployed.

One flight attendant recalled, "I could see that the water was below me, so I opened my door and my emergency escape chute automatically inflated." Then the passengers "started coming" but "there was no pushing and shoving"; it was quite orderly.[29]

Passengers and crew worked together in "controlled panic"[30] to get everyone out safely. And after just three-and-a-half minutes, 95 men, 52 women, 2 little girls, and a baby boy, plus the 5 crew members – a total of 155 people had successfully egressed. Only five people were seriously injured, seventy-eight received medical treatment, and twenty-six were transported to local hospitals. The rest were treated for hypothermia and sent home.[31]

US Airways Flight 1549 is included in this study as a positive example of teamwork, not only because the accident ended without fatalities. What remains unique about this illustration compared with the previous examples discussed is the extraordinary manner in which dozens of highly trained specialists from a myriad of high-risk professions made sense of a rapidly evolving crisis, spontaneously working together with civilians under intense time pressure to address an unprecedented emergency situation. Pilots, air traffic controllers, flight attendants, maritime operators, military members, medical personnel, law enforcement, and emergency responders, as well as the passengers themselves, analyzed a quickly evolving predicament and took action to avert disaster. Without these acts of self-authorization in which individuals instinctively stepped up, exercising leadership, containing their anxiety, and working together to get the job done, this scenario might have unfolded differently – more akin to the teamwork breakdown that followed the Hillsborough football crush. In fact, there are several infamous aviation examples of passengers surviving a plane crash, only to die during the evacuation.

In 1985, for example, a British Airtours 737 was destroyed when an engine malfunction on the ground created a fire before takeoff in Manchester, England. Only 80 of the 137 occupants safely escaped in what should have been a fairly routine egress, prompting calls for research into the impact of cabin configurations and passenger behavior on flow rates during evacuation.

In 1991, a similarly confusing emergency evacuation occurred at Los Angeles International Airport, resulting in thirty-four deaths, when USAir Flight 1493, a Boeing 737, landed on top of SkyWest Flight 5569, a small turboprop, holding for takeoff on the same runway. Autopsies of bodies trapped in the 737 wreckage revealed that nearly all died from asphyxia, inhaling smoke and other toxins, not from injury incurred during the crash. In fact, the NTSB found ten dead bodies piled in the aisle waiting to egress, less than eight feet from the over-wing exits and safety. Survivor interviews revealed that evacuation was slowed because first, the nearest passenger "froze," unable to open the over-wing exit. And second, a passenger altercation erupted, blocking egress.[32]

Other examples of crowd panic resulting in stampede, trampling, or crush abound, making the fatality-free emergency evacuation of Cactus 1549 – let alone the glider-like water landing – an anomaly in itself. Yet, this does not infer that the US Airway scenario was error-free. Mistakes were made. For instance, flight attendants were unclear until they began their evacuation that the aircraft had landed on water. The captain might have reduced this confusion if he had announced, "Brace for *water* impact" before touchdown, rather than the standard "Brace for impact." Many passengers disembarked without life vests, some dragged luggage outside with them, and a few even jumped into the frigid water attempting to swim to safety. Given the short time available and lengthy restart and ditching procedures, pilots did not complete all checklists or select the 'ditching' switch, which may have helped improve water-tight integrity. Some ferries pulled too close to survivors, raising fears that the life rafts might be swamped or punctured. Police helicopters' strong downdrafts kicked up cold surface spray, further exacerbating survivors' hypothermia. And it took several hours before an accurate passenger manifest could be assessed to determine if everyone had indeed evacuated safely.

Nonetheless, good teamwork by trained professionals and passengers alike – along with a fair amount of luck – ultimately prevented this crisis situation from escalating to catastrophe. This is an uplifting ending to a potentially harrowing story. What can we learn from this scenario that will help us think through crisis if we are confronted by an unexpected emergency in the future – whether as professionals in our work or as passenger-bystanders?

SYSTEMIC INFLUENCES

In each of the previous chapters, we examined how systemic influences aligned with individual behaviors and group dynamics in a 'window of accident opportunity' as a way to understand the complex inter-relatedness of factors contributing to team breakdown and disaster. We considered, for instance, how military budget cuts led to routine public relations cruises distracting crews and diminishing safety vigilance; how hooliganism and piecemeal stadium renovations led to flow control problems and overcrowding; how U.S. government airline deregulation led to rapid aviation industry expansion, skilled employee shortages, and regulatory challenges; and how restructuring socialized medicine in the UK led to short-term goal setting and organizational overreach. These factors impacted military, police, aviation, and surgical teams' operations in challenging new ways.

In each case, we found systemic changes and technological developments were rarely evaluated beforehand for their potential to influence team performance. Markedly absent, for instance, were proactive efforts to consider the influence of Hillsborough stadium modifications on policing and spectator flow, airline deregulation on the resultant hiring of inexperienced pilots, A300 flight control system modifications on pilot training, or 'spaghetti noodles' on submarine sonar screens for collision avoidance. Yet, fortunately, some high-risk fields have begun to recognize the need for socio-technical analyses examining the interrelatedness of technological developments and team performance.

For instance, a study in nuclear power, an industry "in which performance depends on the coordinated activity of multi-person teams," recently observed, "There has been growing recognition that design of technology needs to consider not only individual performance but also teams."[33] Like a police control room, airplane cockpit, or submarine bridge, "the design of the [nuclear plant] control room can facilitate or hinder teamwork and the communication and crew coordination that is vital to its success."[34] In other words, just as social scientists found decades ago when researching job performance in coal mines, textile mills, and hospitals, balancing both social and technical priorities remains imperative to a team's success.

Applying a similar socio-technical framework to the analysis of Cactus 1549, we discover that, like many 'normal accidents' in high-risk fields, this team of professionals had little experience working together; no previous training for this unprecedented emergency; and sparse time to prepare, coordinate, or communicate as events unfolded. Captain Sullenberger even doubted flight simulators could mimic a dual-engine failure to a water landing. Yet, as the situation grew dire, the team spontaneously learned in the moment, making sense of the developing challenges, and assessing which actions were required to ensure success.

So how did this team confound the odds? In the following section, we will evaluate a number of seemingly chance occurrences, many the result of good timing, the cooperation of 'Mother Nature', and a fair amount of luck. Other influences were the product of years of experience and a professional climate that brought out the best in all involved, enabling them to overcome adversity that fateful day.

LUCKY BREAKS

Perhaps the greatest stroke of luck in assisting in Cactus 1549's safe water landing and casualty-free egress was the environment. With touchdown at 3:30 P.M., and sunset at 4:53 P.M., more than an hour of daylight remained for passenger rescue before dark. A nighttime evacuation would have reduced visibility, slowed operations, and increased equipment requirements while extending passenger exposure to the elements and, as temperatures dipped, exacerbating hypothermic conditions.

Given the 36 degree water temperature and 11 degree wind chill factor that wintery January day, the expeditious rescue of crash survivors was paramount. Particularly critical was the fact that the human body loses heat twenty-five times faster in cold water than air. Therefore, people had less than thirty minutes before their body core temperature would drop and hypothermia would set in. Depending on the individual's health, physical fitness, body mass index, clothing, physical activity, and posture in the water, it could take significantly less time. However, many individuals who die from cold water immersion do not die from hypothermia. They suffer a heart attack either before becoming hypothermic or hours later, after rescue. Therefore, the quality and timing of medical treatment was also vitally important to survivability.

Another environmental factor instrumental in the successful rescue of all 155 people on board was the location of the landing and state of the Hudson itself. The surface of the river was calm and boat traffic light, just before the evening rush when many New York City commuters head back home to New Jersey via high-speed catamaran ferry. Local ferry captains, most of whom had grown up working on the river, were experienced at water rescue – albeit not typically from a floating airliner – and quickly arrived on the scene from the nearby piers ready for action. Coast Guard and New York City Fire and Police Department vehicles also arrived within minutes, mobilizing their major emergency response teams.[35]

The first ferry on station, *Thomas Jefferson*, pulled up less than four minutes after touchdown, ultimately rescuing fifty-six people. Captain Vincent Lombardi radioed the Coast Guard for support, then helped deckhands, ticket agents, and bus drivers hoist survivors on to his vessel. Next the *Moira Smith* arrived, pulling passengers off the wing, and then the *Yogi Berra*, which saved twenty-four people. The fourth vessel on scene was the *Governor Thomas H. Kean*, rescuing twenty-six passengers from the sinking wing. The ferry's 19-year-old Captain Brittany Catanzaro recalled, "You train so much, you don't have to think about it. I didn't have to give any orders to the crew." They simply made sense of what was happening and knew what to do. Deckhand Cosmo Mezzina agreed, focusing on the task was the priority. "You don't look right or left. You just look right in front of you, just to save, to rescue those people."[36]

This unprecedented river rescue required a high level of innovation and ship-handling finesse, as crews navigated their powerful ferries in the strong river current, trying not to collide with one another, swamp life boats, or knock passengers off the slippery wing with their wake into the frigid water. It was an amazing orchestration of events, Captain Sullenberger recalled: "It just seemed like we were all on the same page." Even "in the stress of the moment, there was an efficient kind of order that I found absolutely impressive" as professionals stepped up, using all their skills and resources to do an effective job. And "dozens of bystanders" also joined in acting with "great compassion and bravery – and a sense of duty." Once clear of the water, the captain recalled, "there was a release of emotions" for many passengers who hugged their rescuers on board the ferries, and "deckhands" responded, removing "shirts, coats, and sweatshirts they were wearing to help warm passengers." I saw "examples of humanity and goodwill everywhere I looked," he recalled. I felt "so moved." Even the disembarkation was well thought out as ferries dropped passengers on both sides of the river, distributing survivors to several local hospitals, rather than overwhelming one medical facility. "It felt like all of New York and New Jersey was reaching out to warm us," Captain Sullenberger recalled.[37]

Two factors that helped this team work together so effectively on January 15, 2009, were professionalism and standardization. Unlike Captain Waddle, whose goals, task prioritization, and decision-making process on board the USS *Greeneville* often seemed unclear to his team, Captain Sullenberger's behavior and that of his team was consistent, predictable, and professional throughout, beginning right from their brief.

The five flight crewmembers met for the first time three days before the accident at the US Airways hub in Charlotte, North Carolina, each commuting in from their home. They began with a crew briefing, during which, Captain Sullenberger recalled, "we aligned our goals, we talked about a few specifics, set the tone, and opened our channels of communication." Important to note is how through this briefing the team proactively prepared for the possibility of irregularity before there was even a hint of any problem. The captain established a professional climate with his tone and actions, conveying to the crew what they could expect if there was a problem – that their captain would respond professionally and by the book – and they should as well.

Research shows it is essential to high-risk team success to prepare in this manner. For instance, Harvard Business School Professor Amy Edmondson's studies of surgical teams in action found that rather than educational background, medical experience, physician seniority, or institutional prestige, one of the key determinants of team performance is its ability to adapt to new ways of working. In particular, Edmondson notes, leaders must create an environment conducive to team learning in which teammates can speak up, ask questions, and take action without fear of reprisal. Team success in challenging situations "came down to the way teams were put together and how they drew on their experiences" to work together.[38]

Another important contributor to team success that day was that each individual stayed in role, completing their assigned duties. Unlike the Hillsborough police team, which fragmented under pressure, in this scenario role management was clear, strengthening the cohesiveness of the team. For instance, although Captain Sullenberger reported his "physiological reaction" to the emergency was "strong" and he had to force himself to stay "calm" and "use my training," he nonetheless contained his anxiety, setting a professional tone that others emulated. The captain reflected on how he was able to accomplish this:

> For 42 years, I had made small, regular deposits of education, training, and experience, and the experience balance was sufficient that on January 15th, I could make a sudden, large withdrawal.... Everything I had done in my career had in some way been a preparation for that moment.[39]

Similarly, Captain Sullenberger described the "amazingly good" crew coordination he experienced with First Officer Skiles on the flight deck, especially "considering how suddenly the event occurred, how severe it was, and the little time" they had to prepare. Providing an excellent example of Edmondson's 'team learning,' Sullenberger described how they adapted to their challenge: Although they "did not have time to exchange words," through "observation" and "hearing," the captain "knew" that First Officer Stiles "knew what he had to do," that they "were on the same page," and this comforted him. First Officer Stiles made similar comments. Each knew their "specific roles," what the other "was doing, and they interacted when they needed to."[40]

The interaction between flight deck and cabin was also critical. Ninety seconds before water impact, Captain Sullenberger made his announcement to the flight attendants and passengers directing them to "Brace for impact!" – the signal to prepare for an emergency landing. He recalled, "I heard the flight attendants begin shouting their commands," saying, "'Heads down. Stay down.' I could hear them clearly. They were chanting it in unison over and over again.... I felt very comforted by that. I knew immediately that they were on the same page. That if I could land the airplane, that they could get them out safely."[41]

As Sullenberger alludes, this clear role management strengthened team unity, allowing individuals to focus more effectively on their own assigned tasks. These psychologically stabilizing forces – for instance, observing his copilot completing checklists and hearing flight attendants complying with established procedures – built confidence in the team, assuring teammates that roles were clear and tasks were being accomplished. The team was thinking through crisis. This confidence helped other teammates concentrate on their tasks, such as Captain Sullenberger's challenge of landing on water. If he had been distracted by teammates not completing their duties, the situation may have ended differently.

Captain Sullenberger credits *Crew Resource Management* (CRM) training for giving the crew "the skills and tools that they needed to build a team quickly and open lines of communication, share goals, and work together."[42] Since the airline industry has become "ultrasafe," he argues, "where it's possible to go several calendar years without a single fatality," it is "easy to forget what's really at stake" flying airplanes and what it takes to succeed. "We make it look too easy," he adds. The challenge is "to remain alert and vigilant and prepared, never knowing when or even if one might face the ultimate challenge."[43]

Communication outside the aircraft was also a key factor in the team's success. Excellent selfless communication displayed by Patrick Harten and his fellow ATCs prevented the emergency situation from deteriorating further. A marathon runner and ATC veteran whose father had also been a controller, 34-year-old Harten "liked it best when the pressure was on."[44] During those fateful six minutes, he communicated with fourteen different people, diverting other airplanes while assisting the US Airways crew with their final landing decision. Unlike previous accidents in which ATC distracted pilots from completing critical tasks, such as Southern Airways Flight 242 discussed in Chapter 1, Harten allowed the aircrew to set the pace. When required, he asked specific pertinent questions to make sure the entire team was on the same page. When asked a question, he replied with a short specific answer. Working collaboratively with the crew, he helped them identify the resources available and set a tone of calm professional support, all under incredible stress and narrowing time constraints.[45]

It is relatively easy to point out the heroic efforts that were made by so many individuals to avert disaster that fateful day. Pilots, flight attendants, air traffic controllers, ferry crews, and emergency responders all quickly made sense of what was occurring and took action in a decentralized manner, authorizing themselves to do what they believed needed to be done, rather than waiting for outside direction from a higher authority. This 'shared mental model' of what was at stake caused people to remain calm and focused, selflessly offering any resources they had at their disposal – even the clothes off their back – not panicking, as people did during the previous evacuations discussed. Had the USS *Greeneville* crew behaved in this manner, sharing resources and information, or police officers at Hillsborough, self-authorizing to begin the rescue efforts sooner, these disasters might have ended differently. As Captain Sullenberger emphasizes, "paying attention matters...having awareness constantly matters. Continuing to build that mental model" is essential to team success.[46]

This demonstration of teamwork seems so seamless, it is hard to recognize how many pitfalls actually were avoided. Team breakdowns such as poor communication, nonstandard behavior, ambiguous task assignment, fragmented teamwork, and weak situational awareness are often identified as factors leading to disaster. Understanding how this team successfully navigated around the difficulties many other crews stumbled on is of vital importance and makes the successful landing, egress, and rescue of all on board even more impressive. In other words, understanding what the team *did not do wrong* is just as helpful as understanding what they did do right.

In order to showcase how effective this confluence of events was in supporting teamwork, it is important to take note of areas research has identified as ripe for failure. For instance, twenty years before this accident, a U.S. government *Presidential Task Force on Aircraft Crew Complement* investigated whether flight deck teams could be safely downsized from three crewmembers to two, replacing the flight engineer with aircraft automated systems. Largely untested at the time, this reconfiguration was approved based on assumptions about the advantages of advanced technology, paving the way for highly automated airliners like the A320.[47]

Yet, relatively little was known about what this downsizing would entail, the implications for teamwork, and the complexity of automating, creating a new human-machine interface. Pilots and labor unions, in particular, protested, questioning safety and the ability of two-pilot crews to effectively manage the extra workload of increasingly complex aircraft, especially in emergency situations.[48] Cactus 1549 showed that with the proper training and experience, some two-member cockpit crews can think through crisis and handle extreme emergencies, even short-fused unprecedented challenges with no established procedures or checklists. However, we need to know more about the A320's history and design, in particular, in order to fully comprehend what happened that day.

By all accounts, the A320 is a different sort of airliner with a complicated history. Built by the European consortium Airbus, this manufacturer aligned Airbus France, Airbus Deutschland, Airbus UK, and Airbus España into one company in 1970 in order to challenge American dominance in airliner manufacturing. Four years later, Airbus introduced the A300 – the quirky airplane crashed by American Airlines Flight 587 – intending to fill a gap in the mid-sized commercial jet market. Although the A300 represented a collaborative milestone in European aviation history, sales were weak for many years, with most orders placed by airlines obligated to support domestic production such as Air France and Lufthansa. Perhaps, in part, a result of the handling problems experienced by American Airlines pilots, among others, Airbus ceased manufacturing the A300 in 2006.[49]

Determined to try again, Airbus went back to the drawing board in the 1980s, committed to designing an entirely new jet. Given the growing safety concerns worldwide about pilot proficiency and the number of human factor accidents during this period (discussed in Chapter 4), Airbus engineered their new system based on the novel premise that computers can fly better than pilots and in some emergency situations should even override human inputs entirely.[50] The result was the A320: a mid-sized, fuel-efficient, two-engine composite jet with state-of-the-art *glass cockpit* technology and digital *fly-by-wire* flight control system. Launched in 1987, there are now more than 3,800 A320s in operation, making it one of the best-selling commercial jets of all time, which helped Airbus achieve its goal as a world class competitor.[51]

One of the most unique aspects of the A320 is its digital fly-by-wire system, replacing flight control rods and cables, which previously provided a mechanical link between pilot inputs and airplane movement, with electronic signals and flight control computers. Monitoring environmental characteristics, flight parameters, and pilot inputs, computers ensure the airliner is operated within established flight envelopes before positioning flight control surfaces; even overriding pilot inputs if deemed unsafe. If First Officer Molin had been piloting an A320 instead of an A300, for instance, the crash of American Airlines Flight 587 could never have occurred because computerized systems would have inhibited his aggressive flight control inputs.

Although the A320 was the first commercial airliner to adopt a fly-by-wire flight control system, NASA was actually the first to experiment with designs back in 1972, modifying an F-8C Crusader to test the possibilities. Today, many aircraft including the Airbus A380, Boeing 777, new 787 *Dreamliner*, and NASA Space Shuttle incorporate fly-by-wire systems. The weight savings over conventional systems improves fuel efficiency, and redundant digital circuitry provides system reliability, improving safety. However, not all fly-by-wire designs are the same. Boeing believes humans should retain control, designing soft protection limits that can be overridden. "The pilot in control of the aircraft should have the ultimate authority," says Boeing spokesperson, John Cashman, director of flight crew operations.[52] Airbus disagrees, incorporating hard protection limits, or 'laws', that pilots cannot bypass into its fly-by-wire system. Which design is better remains unclear.

Yet, as cockpit automation increased, unexpected problems surfaced, particularly relating to Airbus' hard limits. This was due, in part, to a paradigm shift requiring pilots to adjust from a model of humans 'operating' machines to pilots 'communicating' with technology in its own language, as if it was a virtual crewmember.[53] Several studies found that as automation expanded, giving aircraft systems more autonomy and authority, like the A320, unanticipated burdens were placed on pilots who struggled to stay abreast of the state of the technology. These changes increased cockpit workloads in new ways, not diminishing them as previously assumed. As a result, increased automation required the development of a sophisticated knowledge of the programming, intentions, and operating parameters of the technology and an ever-vigilant awareness of the system's status. These new demands changed the airline pilot role from active operator to passive resource manager.

Research revealed that one of the major problems with high levels of cockpit automation, like the A320, is 'automation surprises' when systems do not behave as pilots anticipate.[54] Add to this the findings of a recent NTSB study that reported that in more than 80 percent of major accidents, the captain is the pilot flying. We find Cactus 1549's emergency landing a scenario ripe for failure with a highly automated system and the captain at the controls.[55] The NTSB results were unequivocal: Captains lose situational awareness "earlier, quicker, and more often when they are at the controls" in an emergency than when their copilots are flying.[56] The additional burden of flying the aircraft increases the captain's workload while narrowing cognitive functioning and impacting sense-making capacities and the ability to maintain the 'big picture'. This individual failure has implications for teamwork as well because copilots only correct captain's mistakes 20 percent of the time, making lack of assertiveness a major contributor in many accidents as well. Some possible explanations for this reluctance to speak up are inexperience, poor situational awareness, fear of reprisal like Hillsborough, or – as in the case of the USS *Greeneville* – the sincere belief that the captain knows what he or she is doing.[57]

In sum, we find that the Cactus 1549 team confounded the research odds when the captain took over the flight controls from his copilot, successfully working with the Airbus automation as a 'technology team player', unfazed by the distractions and automation surprises that research predicts might occur in these unusually stressful situations without losing situational awareness. This is particularly impressive given the unusual aircraft configuration of the water landing – landing gear up with only partial flaps – and the fact no runway information could be programmed into the computerized navigation system to assist in the approach.

One reason this team may have successfully avoided the hazards that research predicts could have undermined their performance was their extensive professional experience. We have already highlighted the ferry crew's knowledge of the river and Air Traffic Controller Patrick Harten's decade on the job, including handling several emergencies. Add to this the five-member US Airways flight crew's combined total of nearly 150 years in aviation, and we find experience to be a common denominator.

Captain Sullenberger, 57 years old, joined the airlines after a successful Air Force career, logging almost 20,000 mishap-free flight hours, nearly 10,000 as captain and 5,000 in the A320. Similarly, 49-year-old First Officer Skiles, hired in 1986, had almost 20,000 flight hours and previously served as captain until aviation industry cuts forced him back into the copilot seat. Although Skiles had just completed A320 training, transitioning from the Boeing 737 only about a week before the accident, Captain Sullenberger noted that this recent training provided a confidence and familiarity with emergency procedures that enabled the team to access checklists in an expeditious manner. Flight attendants Doreen Walsh, Sheila Dail, and Donna Dent were also airline veterans. Fifty-eight-year-old Doreen had thirty-eight years aloft, and Sheila, 57, and Donna, 51, each had more than twenty-six years flying.

But how much experience is enough? In his book *Outliers*, best selling author Malcolm Gladwell provides some guidance about the time it takes to become successful in one's profession. Studying a wide range of experts in a variety of fields, Gladwell observes that "ten thousand hours of practice is required to achieve the level of mastery associated with being a world class expert – in anything." Citing study after study of composers, basketball players, fiction writers, ice skaters, concert pianists, chess players, master criminals, and computer entrepreneurs, Gladwell claims 10,000 hours of 'practice' is a general requirement for true expertise.[58]

This number easily applies to nearly all of the professionals involved in the water landing and rescue that day, particularly the flight crew.

However, once again, it is important to note the confluence of systemic influences that culminated in this level of aviation acumen being a resource available to the team for use that day.[59] Prior to 9/11, the odds of finding pilots and flight attendants with this level of experience and seniority flying together were very low. As a result of the massive industry downsizing that ensued, it became more typical. The best example of this industry readjustment is First Officer Skiles, who had thousands of hours of experience as captain but was nonetheless serving as copilot on Flight 1549, an important resource for the team.

Although this crew's extensive experience proved pivotal to averting disaster on January 15th, the aviation industry will most likely not continue to support this level of experience in the future. A 2009 white paper by the Air Line Pilots Association (ALPA), the largest airline pilot's union in the world, notes how the fallout from 9/11 significantly altered the business models of major air carriers, encouraging them to cut costs by parking larger airplanes and furloughing their more experienced and therefore more expensive airline pilots, shifting flying to commuter affiliates and their regional jets (RJ) to save money.[60] Since their introduction, RJs have grown in size and performance capability from about 40 seats in 1991 to upward of 110 with a range of 2,000 nautical miles today. At this size and distance, RJs now blur the boundaries between the narrow-body jets nearly all major airlines once flew, like DC-9s with about 100 seats and 1,000-mile range, and early 737 models with about 100 seats and 1,800-mile range.[61]

For years, strong unions like ALPA controlled this outsourcing through labor groups and contract negotiations at the major air carriers. But after 9/11, with most contracts voided by bankruptcy judges, airline management was free to negotiate anew, and regional airlines now jumped at the chance to expand service. Delta Air Lines, for instance, now has nine commuter airline affiliates – Atlantic Southeast Airlines, Chautauqua, Comair, Compass Airlines, Freedom Airlines, Mesaba, Pinnacle, Shuttle America, and SkyWest – flying a variety of RJs under the Delta Connection name.[62]

This strategy has proven to be especially profitable over the past few years, increasing major airlines' virtual network while reducing overhead costs. A Delta 737–300, for instance, requires eighty-one passengers to break even but their commuter partner Comair only requires twenty-one flying a regional jet on a similar route.[63] Moreover, an average Delta pilot earns about $120,000 per year whereas a Comair pilot averages $36,000.[64] One recent industry study estimated that RJs can accommodate "80%–85% of passenger demand in the top U.S. domestic markets," making it the airplane of choice well into the future.[65]

Passengers have also demonstrated a clear preference for jets rather than the noisy vibrating turboprops the regional airlines previously flew. And the *European Aviation Safety Agency* (EASA) found good cause. Their study of global aviation accidents between 1997 and 2006 determined: "On average, the fatal accident rate for turboprops was three times that for jets, based on flights flown, and nearly seven times greater when using hours flown as the rate measure."[66] *The Wall Street Journal* reported that one commuter carrier developed a passenger "turboprop avoidance factor," calculating ticket sales would increase by as much as 20 percent just by switching from turboprops to RJs on some routes.[67]

So why should it be of concern that major airlines are shifting much of their domestic flying to their commuter partners who are now flying large, complex regional jets; and, most importantly, how does this relate to Cactus 1549? Similar to Captain Sullenberger's observations about the importance of pilot judgment, skill, and initiative in managing crisis, ALPA emphasizes that "the best and most important safety feature on any airplane is a well-trained, highly motivated and professional pilot."[68] Although both applaud the technological advances that have been made in aircraft design, they nonetheless emphasize when systems malfunction, severe weather threatens, or unplanned events occur, flight crews must quickly and accurately assess the situation and take appropriate action.

Whereas the combination of this experienced team proved invaluable for Cactus Flight 1549, the furloughing of experienced airline pilots by major airlines and outsourcing of flying to their regional partners who employ cheaper, "low-experience pilots" raises safety concerns. ALPA argues that because of the high cost of initial pilot training (about $50,000), low starting pay of commercial pilots (about $20,000), uncertain career prospects, and diminishing chance of ever flying one of the dwindling numbers of large jets at a major carrier, it is difficult to attract top notch applicants. In particular military pilots, formerly the backbone of commercial aviation, are increasingly staying in the service, attracted by signing bonuses and new generations of sophisticated aircraft. Because there are fewer experienced military pilots to hire, ALPA emphasizes, regional airlines lower their minimum employment criteria even further, often hiring "low-experience pilots" whose "previous flight time has been accumulated in small, slow, single-engine aircraft" with "limited minimal operational knowledge, skills, professionalism, and/or proficiency" – just like First Officer Molin.[69]

This means that a pilot with no college degree, little ground training, and as little as 250 flight hours accumulated via flight instruction, sightseeing tours, or banner tows, could be at the controls of your next commercial flight flying a complex regional jet. As discussed in Chapter 4, low-experience pilots not only represent a safety risk but place an inordinate amount of pressure on the captain to instruct and mentor while performing his or her own duties.

Ironically, this is all perfectly legal by current FAA standards. ALPA notes with concern, "today's archaic regulations allow airlines to hire low-experience pilots into the right seat of high-speed, complex, swept-wing jet aircraft in what amounts to on-the-job training with paying passengers on board."[70] Unless significant changes are made in the regulations, "this trend of hiring pilots with less and less experience is expected to continue well into the future."[71] As a result, ALPA concludes, "a complete overhaul of pilot selection and training methods is needed."[72]

Perhaps more than any other airline, US Airway's company history exemplifies the gritty, do-what-it-takes struggle to survive displayed on the Hudson River that fateful day. Since its founding in 1939, US Airways changed its name four times – from All American Airways to Allegheny Airlines in 1952, to USAir in 1979, and finally US Airways in 1996 – adopted several smaller airlines – such as Piedmont, Trump Shuttle, Lake Central, Mohawk, Empire, and Pacific Southwest Airlines (PSA) – and weathered Chapter 11 bankruptcy a record three times.

In 2005, US Airways emerged yet again from bankruptcy protection, partnering with Phoenix-based America West Airlines, creating the largest low-cost airline in America and adopting the 'Cactus' call sign. In many ways, the resumes of the Cactus 1549 crews embody these organizational struggles. Doreen Welsh started her career in 1970 with Allegheny Airlines, which morphed into USAir and then US Airways as the company expanded its network to compete during the post-deregulation period. Sullenberger, first hired by PSA in 1980, changed to a USAir uniform in 1988 when PSA was bought out.[73]

Airline mergers are often unsettling for employees who routinely lose money, benefits, control over their schedules – and sometimes even their jobs – with little time to prepare or adjust. And, because pilot seniority establishes the order for promotion, aircraft assignment, work schedules, and pay, disputes over the integration of seniority lists can be particularly contentious. US Airways and America West pilot unions, for example, have yet to agree on integration terms requiring the companies – which merged five years ago – to still run largely separate flight operations as unions battle it out in court.

Tensions like these make it particularly difficult for employees to concentrate at work. Take for example the Northwest Airline pilots who, out of radio contact for an hour, overflew their Minneapolis destination by 150 miles in October 2009 with 147 passengers on board. After investigating the incident, the NTSB reported, "The crew stated they were in a heated discussion over airline policy, and they lost situational awareness."[74] That same week, a Delta Air Lines crew also lost situational awareness when they landed their 767 with 194 passengers on a taxiway at their hub airport, Atlanta-Hartsfield International, instead of their assigned runway.[75] Just months before these two incidents, Delta had acquired Northwest through merger, creating what one airline analyst called the "tsunami of airline consolidations."[76] The deal nearly fell through when a standoff emerged between the two pilot unions, each wanting greater seniority for their labor group.

In another post-9/11 labor-related incident, United Airlines was forced to cancel a flight when the captain announced to passengers that "he was too upset to fly" after a dispute with another employee about wearing his hat. The pilots' union had urged pilots to remove their hats in protest of a managerial decision setting aside $130 million in stock in an executive incentive plan while cutting routes and laying off employees. It was a sign "to show management that" pilots were "serious about regaining what was stripped" from employees "during bankruptcy."[77]

The Cactus 1549 crew was neither immune to this industry turmoil nor the organizational pressures of their company's merger with America West. In fact, they even discussed it while on the ground at LaGuardia the day of the accident. Noticing a Northwest jet taxiing behind them during engine start, First Officer Skiles commented, "wonder how the Northwest and Delta pilots are getting on."

"I wonder about that too," Captain Sullenberger responded. "I have no idea ... hopefully better than we and [America] West do."

"Be hard to do worse," Skiles quipped.

"Yeah ... Well I hadn't heard much about it lately, but I can't imagine it'd be any better," Sullenberger replied.[78]

Although technically a violation of the FAA's sterile cockpit rules, these types of conversations are common on the flight deck of nearly every airline today as pilots struggle to cope with the drastic changes that have befallen their profession. In fact, the chaotic state of the post-9/11 aviation industry generated such widespread concern in the U.S. Congress, the Government Accounting Office (GAO) was tasked to investigate the implications of airline bankruptcies, mergers, loss of pension plans, high fuel prices, and even re-regulating the struggling industry. In response, the GAO published eight separate reports between 2002 and 2009 examining the aviation industry in detail.[79]

One study claimed that "the airline bankruptcy process is well developed and understood," even discussing the liquidation of employee pension plans and offering examples of the significant loss of benefits senior airline employees like Captain Sullenberger will experience when they retire. Yet they nonetheless claim there is "no evidence" that bankruptcy "harms the industry."[80] Another report noted: "The historically high number of airline bankruptcies and liquidations is a reflection of the industry's inherent instability," yet it did not investigate the implications of this instability for employees.[81] In fact, not one of the government's reports discussed the impact of this tumultuous climate of outsourcing, mergers, downsizing, furloughs, and changing work rules on teamwork, safety, or employee job performance.

In addition to the eight government reports, two books were released just months after Cactus 1549's Hudson River landing that prove helpful in our socio-technical analysis of the post-9/11 airline industry. The first, by William Langewiesche titled *Fly By Wire*, posits that it was not extraordinary teamwork or exceptional piloting skills that saved US Airways Flight 1549 from disaster. It was instead the A320's advanced technology – in particular, the fly-by-wire hard protection limits – that averted disaster on the Hudson that afternoon. A feat of engineering "genius," Langewiesche leads the reader to deduce that this "semi-robotic airplane" practically landed itself on the surface of the frigid river. Not only is the A320 "easy to fly," he argues, but "it is nearly pilot proof" and "in the extreme will intervene to keep people alive" just like it did on January 15, 2009.[82]

The second book, written by Captain Sullenberger himself is titled *Highest Duty*. Countering the 'pilot-proof' technology claims, Captain Sullenberger attributes the successful outcome of this near disastrous event to socio-factors such as effective teamwork, Crew Resource Management training, and the extensive experience of his crew. In particular, he argues, that the integration of advanced technology like the A320's fly-by-wire system and one-size-fits-all checklist and procedures cannot trump pilot judgment, good sense making, and initiative in dealing with unexpected emergencies. "I've come across a number of people over the years who think that modern airplanes, with all their technology and automation, can almost fly themselves," Captain Sullenberger says. "That's simply not true."[83]

It is fascinating to be offered such diverging interpretations of events occurring on that wintery day in New York. Were we witness to a feat of engineering genius as the world's first semi-robotic airliner saved 155 lives by landing itself safely on the Hudson River; or is technology a workload management tool to assist pilots but "no substitute for experience, skill, and judgment" by the crew on the flight deck during an emergency, as Sullenberg argues?[84] And, given these divergent viewpoints, how should we address the safety concerns that have been raised – by further expanding the power of technology to override humans or through better management of the piloting profession?

Aviation industry leaders have been grappling with these concerns for decades as divergent mindsets emerged divided, in part, about where to best place loyalty, trust, and power within the aviation infrastructure. After all, pilots were responsible for the extensive number of *Controlled Flight into Terrain* (CFIT) and *Loss of Control in Flight* accidents, like those described in Chapter 4. Pilots were also the ones who crashed American Airlines Flights 11 and 77 and United Airlines Flights 93 and 175 into the World Trade Center Towers and Pentagon on September 11, 2001. And human factors remain steadfastly central in nearly all aviation accidents.

In many ways, these conflicting perspectives represent an epilogue to rethinking 'normal accidents' (discussed in Chapter 1) and the post-deregulation quandary (introduced in Chapter 4), and a prologue to the socio-technical challenges that await many high-risk fields. Perhaps Langewiesche is right: The Airbus design with its hard envelope protections that override pilot inputs is best.

Yet before we commit to this perspective, let us consider the nine A320 crashes that have occurred worldwide, resulting in nearly five hundred fatalities since the aircraft was introduced in 1989. Although nine crashes in more than two decades of service is not an unusually high number when compared to other commercial airliners, what is of concern is that nearly every accident can be categorized into three areas related to the A320's fly-by-wire system. Faulty component design, system malfunction, or operator confusion about use of the advanced technology underlie each of the nine accidents.[85] Once again, understanding how these failures occurred illuminates other pitfalls that were successfully avoided on January 15, 2009.

For instance, in 1992 Air Inter Flight 148 crashed into the side of a mountain when the flawed design of the autopilot mode selector switch allowed pilots to select a 3,300 foot per minute descent rate rather than the desired 3.3 degree flight path angle while on final approach to landing.

In 1993, Lufthansa Flight 2904 skidded off the runway after touchdown when thrust reversers and brakes failed, inhibited by onboard flight computers that determined the sink rate was so low the jet could not be landing. Similarly, Gulf Air Flight 071 experienced a flight control failure on takeoff due to a faulty microchip in the aircraft's fly-by-wire computer system, resulting in runway overrun and nose gear collapse when pilots attempted to abort. And a Philippine Airlines A320 overran the runway on landing in 1998 when thrust reversers and ground spoilers failed to deploy because yet another flight computer malfunction prevented engine power reduction to idle, setting off a chain reaction. In 2000, another fly-by-wire system malfunction caused Gulf Air Flight 072 to crash on go-around after a visual approach to Bahrain International Airport. At approximately 1,000 feet the jet entered a rapid descent, increasing speed to 280 knots in a severe nose down attitude and crashed into the sea about a mile north of the airport.

Finally in 1990, Indian Airlines Flight 605 entered a steep descent and crashed half a mile short of the Bangalore-Hindustan runway, catching fire and killing ninety-seven people. The crash was attributed to pilots' confusion about the fly-by-wire auto-flight system, in particular, 'idle/open descent mode,' which kept the power at minimum on short final approach. This crash caused Indian aviation authorities to ground the fourteen A320s operating in their country at the time, reigniting debate in France over whether the highly computerized A320 was too complicated to fly.

The French Airline Pilots Union (FAPU), never a supporter of the A320s fly-by-wire design or the two-pilot configuration, urged that the jet be grounded in France as well. "It's a supercomplicated aircraft," Jean-Claude Bidot of FAPU observed, and "is sometimes put into operation by people who aren't qualified."[86] Yet officials at Airbus countered that there was no evidence that the aircraft was at fault in the crash. "The Indian authorities took the decision to ground the fleet of A320s," an Airbus spokesperson stated, but "appear to have done that without any justification."[87]

The last of the nine accidents involves yet another example of pilot confusion about the fly-by-wire technology and 'idle/open descent mode.' In an eerie case of foreshadowing, this crash occurred in 1988 – two years before the Indian Airlines accident – yet few people heeded the early warning flags the incident should have raised about the fly-by-wire system. The accident flight, Air France Flight 296, was the fifth A320 off the Airbus assembly line and third purchased by Air France, entering service just three days before the crash. On board, an experienced Air France flight crew was demonstrating the flight characteristics of the A320 at an air show in eastern France. The captain was an excellent pilot, highly skilled, and recently charged with establishing Air France's new A320 program. He briefed his crew on the details of his flyby with care: First, they would overfly the airport in the landing configuration at low speed and low altitude. Then they would go around for a second pass at high speed, demonstrating the various protection envelopes of the fly-by-wire system. Having completed these maneuvers many times at altitude during training, the captain felt certain he understood the complicated technology and could predict when the protection envelopes would kick in. Unfortunately, this proved inaccurate.

Available to watch on www.youtube.com,[88] the approach initially seems normal as the jet slowly overflies the runway in front of fifteen thousand spectators, nose high, landing gear and flaps extended, as pre-briefed. Unbeknownst to the crew, their troubles begin as the airliner passes through one hundred feet, and flight computers assume the pilot intends to land. When the captain slams the throttles forward expecting an abrupt power surge, the engines struggle, taking several seconds to power-up from idle. Meanwhile, the jet continues to slowly drift down the runway, eventually crashing into trees at the far end. Of the 136 people on board, 34 required hospitalization and 3 died. Why did this crash occur – was it simply pilot error?

One could argue that this crash, just three months after the A320 was first introduced, was the first warning sign of a flawed technical design that went unrecognized – a *latent* error, lurking within the system. An alarming fifty-two *Operational Engineering Bulletins* (OEB) were issued in the first year of A320 operations. Akin to a product recall, OEBs notify operators about aircraft system anomalies and provide direction about ways to proceed. This unusually high number of manufacturer warnings gives an indication of the challenges experienced as the airplane went into service, a discrepancy that required about twenty of the A320s fifty main computers to undergo modifications.[89]

Given these technical problems, perhaps Captain Sullenberger was right and the aviation industry needs to refocus its priorities – less on technical developments and short-term financial bottom lines – and more on the social, attracting "the best and brightest" to "the airline piloting profession" as it has in generations past.[90]

CONCLUSION

Today, the aviation industry is at a cross roads not unlike many other high-risk fields, facing challenges instigated by cost-saving measures, industry downsizing, and the increasing availability of technology. The dilemma centers on whether pilot/operators should continue to be entirely in control and paid salaries commensurate with this high level of responsibility, or should management/executives, system designers, and manufacturers claim the reigns, increasing automation and placing human operators in a more passive role. Yet, just like GAO reports investigating the post-9/11 aviation industry, alarmingly absent from many of these economic and technological conversations is consideration of the socio-technical impact on employee job performance and the teamwork of frontline operators.

Captain Sullenberger observes, "It's important as we transition from one generation of pilots to the other that we pass on some of the institutional knowledge. No matter how much technology is available, an airplane is still ultimately an airplane" and "basic skills may ultimately be required when either automation fails or it's no longer appropriate to use it." In addition, "nothing happens in isolation," he notes. "Culture is important in every organization," particularly one that "values safety in a way that's congruent, that our words and our actions match."[91]

On June 11, 2009, the NTSB concluded three days of public hearings in Washington DC investigating the Hudson River landing.

Juxtaposed with the solemn news about the disappearance of Air France Flight 447 over the Atlantic Ocean, an Airbus A330 with 228 people on board, and the fifty fatalities in the Colgan Air Flight 3407 crash near Buffalo, the US Airways near-miss success story provided the peculiar comfort of a modern miracle. Yet, our fascination with miracles may prevent us from getting a more important message: It takes a team to think through a crisis. After enduring near-record job losses, foreclosures, ponzi schemes, government bailouts, and a seemingly endless parade of greedy executives who just don't seem to get it, Americans have been desperate for an old-fashioned, stand-up guy to save the day. Enter 'Captain Sully,' the 'hero pilot' as he is now known to millions.

Yet, at the NTSB hearings, our 'hero pilot' testified about an unsung hero, celebrating the "importance of Crew Resource Management" and "a dedicated, well-experienced, highly trained crew that can overcome substantial odds, work together as a team." It wasn't just "one thing" that proved essential that day, Captain Sullenberger emphasized, it was "many things that in aggregate added up." Yet, because most reports explain disaster as the result of a single flawed decision made by an operator (e.g., 'pilot error'), it seems reasonable to assume that in avoiding disaster Captain Sullenberger became the 'hero'. However, this assumption is dangerous, as Captain Sullenberger himself attests.

Teamwork was the hero averting disaster that day. The "successful outcome" of events on January 15, 2009, "was achieved by the actions of many," Captain Sullenberger notes.

> Lives were saved due to the combination of a very experienced, well-trained crew: First Officer Jeff Skiles and Flight Attendants Donna Dent, Doreen Welsh, and Sheila Dail, all of whom acted in a remarkable display of teamwork, along with expert air traffic controllers, the orderly cooperation of our cool-headed passengers, and the quick and determined actions of the professional and volunteer first responders in New York City.[92]

Thinking through crisis in order to make sense of an unprecedented challenge, this diverse group of professionals authorized themselves to take action, each doing their part to contribute to the safe landing and rescue.

What the 'miracle on the Hudson' has shown us is that we don't need another singular hero, not even a technical one. A lone individual cannot manage the plethora of data that technologically advanced systems produce. We need teams who can think through crisis, sustaining a vigilant curiosity about their operating environment, a proactive concern for safety, and attentiveness to the possibility for failure, even when events seem to be proceeding normally. In sum, what averted this disaster was not only the excellent landing on the Hudson River but the spontaneous support and professional teamwork of pilots, passengers, air traffic controllers, flight attendants, medical personnel, ferry drivers, police, coast guard, firefighters, and other emergency responders. In addition, the location, time of day, and calm sea state all allowed for an expeditious rescue of all on board within minutes of their landing. If any of these links in the accident chain had been broken, this situation would have ended differently.

7

Team Resource Management

One thing that becomes apparent when considering the previous chapters' case studies is that teamwork is an elusive thing. Through the analysis of the USS *Greeneville* disaster, for instance, we learned that the wider organizational system can sometimes demand skills from leaders to serve external purposes that then undermine the high-risk team's operational performance. The Hillsborough football stadium disaster showed us the dangers of a centralized leadership hierarchy when an inexperienced commander is working with an experienced team facing an unpredictable challenge. In the case of American Airlines Flight 587, we saw how a lack of organizational collaboration between designers and operators of complex systems can align with individual and team failures to end in disaster. And finally, through the example of the Bristol Royal Infirmary, we learned about the high price of organizational overreach and its detrimental impact on team performance in high-risk situations.

Just as Charles Perrow predicted, these unconventional failures challenged *Greeneville* sailors, Hillsborough police, American Airlines pilots, and Bristol medical professionals in unanticipated ways as one unexpected failure stressed different parts of the system in unusual ways, causing increasingly unanticipated results. Trained to respond 'by the book', it was difficult for each of these teams to think through their crises, managing anxieties and evolving their mental model of the unfolding disaster as new data emerged. The result was that *Greeneville* sailors increasingly deferred to their charismatic captain's expertise, the Hillsborough police force fragmented, airline operators and aerospace manufacturers deadlocked, and Bristol doctors retreated to the safety of their professional groups.

Crisis, or impending disaster, changes team dynamics. As the human mind attempts to resolve dissonance, stressed teams are prone to taking the path of least resistance as a way to manage anxiety, either falling back on familiar patterns or seizing upon the first action-oriented solution that surfaces, especially if introduced by an authority figure.[1] Reflecting on the emerging team dynamics and how they are impacting performance – which could have averted disaster for the *Greeneville* crew, Hillsborough police, American pilots, or Bristol doctors – is rarely considered, although there may be ample time for it.

These teamwork failures make clear that what professionals working in today's complex high-risk operating environments often need is not more technical training, as previously assumed, but rather an increased capacity to tolerate uncertainty and think through crisis, processing in the moment as information becomes revealed. To accomplish this, teams must work effectively together to manage anxieties and resist the tendency to jump to conclusions and prematurely take action. The example of US Airways Flight 1549 is an excellent illustration of how alert individuals from a variety of professions – pilots, air traffic controllers, flight attendants, Coast Guard, police, firefighters, ferry operators, and medical personnel – teamed up quickly, learning to collaborate in a high-stress environment in order to avert catastrophe.

This analysis reveals that in order to break the accident chain of events and avoid 'normal accidents,' employees in high-risk fields need more than technical competence, charisma, and take-charge decisiveness. Today's leaders need: cultural awareness; an understanding of authority issues and how both overt and covert group processes can impede team performance, often in fatal ways; comprehension of the impact of technology on the pace and complexity of team operations; and sophisticated sense-making skills in order to manage team learning, evolve operations and incorporate new information as it emerges. To support these developments, even technical and professional fields once strictly guided by licensing, qualifications, and regulations, such as aviation, firefighters, law enforcement, maritime, medicine, military, nuclear power, off-shore oil rigs, and railroads, must become more flexible and collaborative than ever before. And the leadership and teambuilding training programs for groups operating in these high-risk environments must follow suit, developing the creative problem solvers our complex, evolving systems require.

This approach can be applied to a number of businesses. The high stakes associated with today's globalized businesses demand that diverse groups of individuals be able to form 'swift-starting action teams,' collaborating to solve complex problems on short-fused tasking in dynamically changing environments, just like flightdeck crews or operating room teams.[2] Shorter product life cycles, especially in high-tech industries, ratchet up the pace, requiring employees with differing areas of highly specific technical expertise to come together quickly and collaborate to get new products to market in a timely fashion or risk putting the organization's future on the line. Just like in high-risk fields, these business experts need sophisticated teambuilding skills because the differing viewpoints that promote creativity, innovation, and sound decision making can also lead to interpersonal conflicts that waste time, erode trust, and fragment the team.[3] In contrast, businesses designed to learn from experience, continuously improving their processes, can keep pace with advancing technologies and the ever-changing demands of the marketplace, making them more likely to survive and thrive under pressure, just like high-risk teams.[4]

As Wendy Kopp, founder and CEO of *Teach for America*, succinctly notes, "The world seems to be moving faster and faster, so you have to figure out how to drive things proactively instead of just becoming reactive."[5] Even the U.S. military is adapting as counterinsurgency strategies in Iraq and Afghanistan demanded new ways of thinking.

New doctrines now support that successful operations require an understanding of how local people view the situation, who they trust, and what is important to them.[6] A recently published point paper by U.S. Army Special Forces Major Jim Gant, titled *One Tribe at a Time*, exemplifies this need.[7]

Working directly with Afghanistan's centuries-old tribal systems, Gant proposes the Army develop small groups of specially trained soldiers with "cultural awareness," "street smarts," and intuitive decision-making skills who can "comprehend the extensive networks, influences, and idiosyncrasies of the mission" and the "constantly changing" environment in Afghanistan. Under this plan, six member *Tribal Engagement Teams* (TET) would "essentially go native," moving off U.S. bases to live in local villages with weapons, ammunition, and money, empowering tribal leaders to improve security and fight insurgents. The military would have to grant teams an unusual amount of authority to make fast decisions without using the typical chain of command and autonomy to mix with locals and modify uniform regulations like growing beards. Yet, Gant feels this innovative team strategy – essentially empowering the team to think through crisis – is the only way to win the war.[8]

BRIEF HISTORY TEAMWORK

Although teamwork in today's technologically advanced high-risk fields is evolving in new ways due to the challenges of our increasingly complex operating systems, people have worked in groups for thousands of years developing tools to assist them. Hunter-gatherer societies employed a form of teamwork to hunt animals and forage for edible plants for more than two million years. At the end of the Mesolithic period, most societies transitioned to agricultural methods, collaborating to farm the land and develop tools to support their work. Perhaps one of the biggest impetuses to change Western thinking about teams, technology, and the workplace was the *Industrial Revolution*, which began as the result of technological and social developments in the late eighteenth century. For example, steam engines powered by fossil fuels, furnaces used to make metals, and weaving looms that manufactured cloth at a rapid pace fundamentally changed the workplace, influencing the way work was organized. Technology has always had an impact on team performance.

In 1914, Henry Ford shocked the world when he paid automobile assembly-line workers $5 per day ($104 in 2008 dollars),[9] more than doubling previous worker pay rates to produce his classic Model T – only available in black because black paint dried faster. Ford's strategy proved extremely profitable because the pay attracted skilled employees and increased assembly-line productivity by reducing turnover and training costs. Yet, these technological developments took their toll as an early automobile workers union president noted: "Skilled mechanics may be in the factories, but they get little or no chance to use their skill," frustrating workers as psychological stress and repetitive motion injuries combined to make the assembly line a hazardous work environment. As one Ford worker observed, "If I keep putting on Nut No. 86 for about 86 more days, I will be Nut No. 86 in the Pontiac bughouse."[10]

Around this same time period *scientific management* or *Taylorism* was developed by Frederick Winslow Taylor,[11] expanding Ford's mass production efficiency methods by applying *task optimization* to other forms of manufacturing. Yet, similar to Ford, by ignoring the interrelatedness of technology, teamwork, and the social aspects of work, Taylorism squelched innovation and dehumanized the workplace. It created organizations that were steeply hierarchical and overly bureaucratic and industrial work that was repetitive, tedious, and demoralizing for employees. In contrast Mary Parker Follett, one of the first to observe the advantages of a more collaborative work environment in her 1925 essay *The Giving of Orders*,[12] argued for a less hierarchical worker-management interface, suggesting instead that workers and foremen study a situation together and develop a mutually beneficial solution to which they were both committed: a revolutionary approach at the time.[13]

Between 1927 and 1932, Elton Mayo conducted his famous study of women telephone relay assembly-line workers at the Hawthorne Works of the Western Electric Company in Chicago, exploring the relationship between employees and their work environment. Mayo's '*Hawthorne experiments*' were perhaps the first to show that worker performance and satisfaction was influenced by numerous interrelated environmental variables and that a more decentralized structure, in which workers had more control over their own tasks, can improve performance and productivity. In short, Mayo realized that organizations are complex interactive systems and that the social aspects of the workplace fulfill essential human needs not previously identified – important concepts when considering teamwork in high-risk fields.[14]

Ironically, the World Wars became a human laboratory of sorts, deepening our understanding of the psychology of teamwork. For example, military leaders' identification of *shell shock*, today's version of post-traumatic stress syndrome, alerted us to the powerful impact the work environment has on people's psychological stability. The loss of a unit's leader or key personnel could easily lead to rampant shell shock as the fabric of the team unraveled under stress. Similarly, other innovations, such as officer selection using *leaderless groups* and therapeutic communities at Northfield Hospital, advanced the field's understanding of the interrelated nature of environment, productivity, and health within high-risk fields.[15]

After World War II, the Tavistock Institute of Human Relations was founded in London in 1947 to apply lessons learned during war to peacetime organizations. Research based on a *socio-technical* approach conducted by Elliott Jaques at Glacier Metal Company,[16] Eric Trist in British coal mines,[17] A. K. Rice with weavers at Calico Mills in India,[18] and Isabel Menzies Lyth with hospital nurses in the UK[19] proved hugely influential. For instance, these researchers found that although new coal mining equipment was available, "productivity failed to increase in step with increases in mechanization."[20] In other words, as industries became more technologically advanced, output actually decreased as social factors such as employee turnover, absenteeism, and labor disputes increased, taking a toll on productivity.

As evidenced by Ford's assembly-line workers' complaints, Mayo's Hawthorne study, leadership research during the World Wars, and Tavistock scientists' socio-technical theory, it becomes clear that teams have social as well as technical needs, and the work environment must attend to both for optimal performance. Study after study found that although new, faster technologies were adopted in coal mines, assembly lines, metal foundries, and fabric mills, productivity did not increase until social aspects and human needs were considered as well. In contrast to Ford and Taylor's image of isolated workers acting as interchangeable cogs accomplishing individual tasks, these studies highlighted factors impacting team performance, providing a lens to view both human elements and technological imperatives within organizations without subverting either.[21]

Between 1950 and 1970, the Japanese economy metamorphosed from a war-torn country into one of the richest nations on earth influenced, in part, by American statistician and 'father of the modern quality movement' W. Edwards Deming.[22] Relatively unknown in the United States at the time, Deming introduced Japanese businesses to *Statistical Process Control* and *Total Quality Management*, instilling a dedication to quality and productivity, principles that led to the global success of Toyota and then later Proctor and Gamble, Ritz Carlton, and Harley-Davidson, among others.[23] Like Ford and Taylor, Deming emphasized efficiency, what he called *kaizen* or continuous process improvement. Yet like socio-technical researchers, Deming strongly believed in the competence and motivation of the average worker to do his or her job with pride if management created a productive work environment.[24]

HISTORY OF CRM

About this same time period, jet aircraft emerged as the mainstay of commercial air travel, drastically reducing both mechanical problems and the number of aviation accidents. As mechanical reliability increased, it became clear that human errors played a part in 70 percent to 80 percent of aircraft mishaps, shocking aviation industry leaders and alerting government regulators. Convinced they desperately needed a new team training model that would address aviation's entrenched ethos and the complex authority dynamics of teams operating in stressful environments, NASA held the first workshop in 1979 called *Resource Management on the Flight Deck*. At this meeting, the term *Cockpit Resource Management* emerged as the process of training crews to reduce pilot error by making better use of the human resources available on the flight deck. This later changed to *Crew Resource Management* (CRM) when dispatchers, flight attendants, and mechanics joined pilots in the training. Eventually CRM was integrated with flight simulator training and became an integral part of all aviation programs, leading to the creation of a wider organizational 'safety culture.'[25]

United Airlines initially took the lead, developing the first comprehensive CRM program in 1981. But it was a rocky beginning. Heavily influenced by the thinking of management consultants Robert Blake, an early *National Training Laboratories* (NTL) enthusiast, and his cofounder of Scientific Methods Inc., Jane Mouton, United's training was based on management efficiency programs popular at the time called "personal growth programs" or "sensitivity training."[26] This highly personal approach did not sit well with pilots who felt it had little to do with leadership, management, or aviation. Typically linear thinkers, many pilots were ill-equipped emotionally and psychologically to deal with what felt like an onslaught of judgmental, personal criticism masked as 'feedback' from peers and, most troubling, subordinates. These NTL-based feedback exercises and role-playing scenarios became notorious among pilots. Unfortunately, many participants were forever alienated by this approach, creating staunch critics of the value of team training programs. Some even questioned whether leadership and teamwork are innate skills, impossible to teach.[27]

Yet, several researchers have countered that claim. For instance, in his best selling book, Daniel Goleman observes that *emotional intelligence* "can be as powerful, and at times more powerful, than IQ" as a determinant of successful performance.[28] Similarly, other research has shown that almost 90 percent of the competencies necessary for success in leadership positions are social and emotional in nature, not technical skills as previously assumed.[29] These emotional intelligence skills, such as the ability to manage anxiety and frustrations, stay motivated, control impulses, be resilient, and keep fear and distress from swamping the ability to think, are critical to decision making under conditions of stress.[30] Moreover, most relevant to the development of new team training, Goleman notes these crucial emotional competencies can be learned.[31] Yet, emotional intelligence largely has been overlooked in leadership and team training, especially in high-risk fields. New brain research demonstrating that the emotional and cognitive centers of the brain are far more integrated than previously thought has given credence to the concept of emotional intelligence, an idea once considered an oxymoron because emotions convey the idea of irrationality and unreasonableness.[32]

Similarly, Malcolm Gladwell explores in his best seller, *Blink: The Power of Thinking without Thinking*, how humans have two different decision-making processes. The first process is a "conscious strategy." Slow and deliberate, we attempt to recall things we have previously learned to puzzle out an answer through logic. The second strategy is "fast and frugal," operating "entirely below the surface of consciousness" using "weirdly indirect channels" like a sweaty palm or fluttery stomach to send messages.[33] In the military, we would call this a 'gut-check'. Gladwell calls it "thin-slicing" – the "ability of our unconscious to find patterns in situations and behaviors based on very narrow slices of experience," which can be exploited in the decision-making process.[34]

Extraordinary performers in many fields have this sixth sense, an uncanny ability to read into a situation using very narrow slivers of experience. When making decisions quickly or under duress, we naturally use the second, more intuitive strategy. Most importantly, like Goleman, Gladwell concludes it is possible to shape and manage these unconscious reactions through team training. These snap judgments and first impressions can be "educated and controlled."[35] As a result, even leaders in highly specialized and technical fields can – and should – develop skills of observation, analysis, and reflection in order to improve their job performance.

Today, CRM-influenced programs have spread from aviation to a variety of high-risk, team-oriented fields around the world such as the armed forces, emergency planning, firefighting, law enforcement, medicine, merchant navy, military, nuclear power, off-shore oil industry, and railroad.[36] As a result, one can now find CRM-related research published in a variety of nonaviation journals such as the *Association of Operating Room Nurses Journal*,[37] *British Medical Journal*,[38] *Cognition, Technology & Work*,[39] *Disaster Prevention and Management*,[40] *Human Relations*,[41] *International Journal of Quality in Health Care*,[42] *Journal of American College of Surgeons*,[43] *Journal of International European Industrial Training*,[44] *Journal of Nursing Administration*,[45] *Journal of Perinatal & Neonatal Nursing*,[46] *Journal of Risk Research*,[47] *Management Communication Quarterly*,[48] *Team Performance Management*,[49] *The American Surgeon*,[50] and even *The New Yorker* magazine,[51] to name a few. These studies typically provide evidence that poor leadership and teamwork combine with communication failures and authority issues and role conflicts to become common human factors' precursors to accidents in high-hazard, high-reliability industries. Yet, few methods are offered to provide professionals in these high-risk fields with the requisite *team* skills the research suggests is required and their jobs demand.

Instead, the culture in most high-risk organizations supports the view that as individuals gain operational or field experience, rising through the organizational ranks, they will naturally acquire the leadership, communication, teambuilding, and sense-making skills on the job. In this environment, people often believe that what new employees need is technical training tied to strict individual measures of observable competencies – passing a written examination, firing a weapon accurately, flying a checkflight, successfully conducting an operation, or completing a rescue maneuver within prescribed time limits – based on technical job requirements and established industry standards.

Although we know teams operating in high-risk environments need teamwork as well as technical skills, the unspoken assumption is that new employees will acquire these less valued 'soft' skills over time. More and more we find this does not occur, or does not occur effectively under given time constraints. It is not until professionals are thrust into leadership roles in response to operational necessity, like Captain Waddle on board the *Greeneville*, Chief Duckenfield at Hillsborough, or First Officer Molin at American Airlines, among others, that the gaps in their skills and training become evident. As it was in these cases, it is unfortunately often in hindsight as the result of an accident.

QUALITY MANAGEMENT

In the 1980s, *Lean Six Sigma* and other quality improvement strategies began to emerge, focusing on data assessment, not behavioral analysis, as a way to improve workplace productivity.[52] Now in use by the U.S. military and most major manufacturers, Lean Six Sigma is a combination of two business improvement techniques: *Lean*, focusing on eliminating waste and shortening the product production cycle time; and *Six Sigma*, focusing on improving quality and reducing product variability. You might notice neither emphasize the social aspects of work that were found to be so important to team performance in previous social science research.

Rapidly gaining in popularity, this more quantitative approach influenced CRM research as well. More recently, some studies attempted to find a "universal rationale" or "error management approach" that can be "used to measure team performance to include data on error types and error management."[53] Yet, even Lean Six Sigma experts concede the best data cannot help an organization succeed if they do not have effective teams: "Time and again, at company after company, experience shows that being able to deal effectively with the human element of improvement is a more critical determinant of team success than the rational, analytical processes and tools."[54] Once again, the field offers few specific ways to organize, train, and lead these important work teams to succeed in carrying out their process improvements. As a result, we need a new paradigm of teamwork and team training.

Swedish human factors Professor Sydney W. A. Dekker provides some guidance, noting it is time for human factors, CRM, and system safety management to emerge as a stand-alone discipline providing the innovation, vocabulary, models, and ideas that the field needs to progress. In contrast to data-driven strategies aimed at developing a universal error management approach to predict and evaluate errors, Dekker argues the real challenge is to understand how apparently safe systems can '*drift into failure*' as part of the normal work done by normal people in seemingly normal organizations.[55] As the name implies, "drift into failure is about a slow, incremental movement of systems operations toward the edge of their safety envelope" during "the banality" of everyday organizational life.[56] No system is immune.[57]

Not so much the result of technical errors or mechanical malfunctions, this 'drift' is about how efficiently, or inefficiently, organizations adapt to change within their environments. Proactively examining routine, day-to-day operations for latent errors before an accident occurs, not waiting until disaster strikes, is critical to improving team performance. For instance, are routine workplace challenges used as data to support wider organizational change efforts and team performance improvement measures, or are employees encouraged to solve problems on their own?

One interesting hospital study found that nurses' sense of independence and feelings of competence were often derived from coping with the obstacles within their workplace. Although this behavior may have solved problems in the short-term, it reduced the organization's ability to detect underlying causes of reoccurring problems and undermined organizational change efforts aimed at improving the health care system.[58] Other research, supporting the USS *Greeneville*'s three tenets, noted that back-up behavior – knowing how and when to back up teammates – is what "makes a team a team."[59] Especially critical under periods of high workloads and stress, successful teams monitor one another's performance, ask for assistance, provide feedback and coaching, and offload tasks to ensure errors are mitigated and team goals are achieved. This capability to shift one's role and responsibilities to assist others and reduce stress requires observation, flexibility, and adaptability, ultimately developing a shared cognition within the team.[60]

Although researchers have found that ongoing, informal input from frontline employees, especially when provided to formal authority figures with the power to take action, is vital to an organization's ability to learn, innovate, and adapt[61]; we still know very little about the intrapersonal dynamics of speaking up.[62] Why is it, for example, individuals like Petty Officer Seacrest, Lieutenant Junior Grade Coen, and the *Greeneville* crew did not offer their input, backing one another up as was their submarine's tenet?

Once again, Dr. Amy Edmondson at Harvard Business School proves helpful, suggesting that it is "*how* leaders promote speaking up both within and outside of their teams" that influences results. By acknowledging their own fallibility, appreciating differences, being open to new ideas, and emphasizing teamwork, leaders can create a climate of psychological safety that can effectively offset the power imbalance within the team, encouraging team members to speak up.[63] In her study of the integration of a new cardiac surgery technique at two different hospitals, Edmondson and her research team found that in order to speed up team learning, leaders must: remain accessible, not aloof; specifically ask for input, not assume people will speak up; and admit their mistakes, asking for help when needed.[64] But, how can people learn these skills?

A NEED FOR TRAINING

While technological developments have driven high-risk systems to become increasingly complex, expanding the potential for *latent* errors, the leadership, teambuilding, and creative problem-solving skills required to compensate for this fact have not emerged as rapidly. Human resistance to change, organizational culture, and technically focused training programs often diminish, not enhance, the creative problem-solving skills required to compensate. A new, more *present* leadership model would support leaders who can communicate across many different boundaries, manage themselves in multiple roles, and hone reflective capacities using emotional intelligence to enhance thinking and inform actions when under pressure. Such leaders would understand how authority dynamics affect formal and informal leadership roles and be better able to manage resistance to change.

Driven in large part by advancing developments in technology, the use of teams in all sorts of workplaces has expanded drastically over the past decade. As systems become more technologically complex, demanding more input while creating and displaying more data than any one person could possibly utilize effectively, a new form of team must emerge to accomplish cognitively based tasks in contrast to the assembly-line work of previous decades. This team development imposes new requirements for increased communication, performance coordination, and shared mental modeling. Yet as Bowers, Salas, and Jentsch note in *Creating High-Tech Teams*, despite advances in our understanding of the nature of effective teamwork brought about by collaborations across industries, "there is still very substantial gaps in our knowledge."[65] To this I would add especially in high-risk fields where systemic pressures such as time urgency, peer pressure, exposure to personal risk, professional competitiveness, interpersonal conflicts, reputation management, and living with the weighty repercussions of one's decisions often combine to make team decision making a particularly stressful activity. It is time for us to catch up. Yet, Bowers observes that even as we conduct this team research the extensive "level of technology being acquired and deployed in the workplace is changing the nature of teamwork at least as fast as it is being researched."[66]

To counter this fast-paced change, the next evolution of team improvement strategies must focus on helping teams to think, learn, create, and innovate in order to meet the needs of our complex, dynamic operating environments. Developing the ability to think through crisis will allow teamwork to evolve and adapt as quickly as the changing nature of the workplace itself, preparing teams to handle the unprecedented challenges we know 'normal accidents' may impart.

A WORKING MODEL

Identifying and understanding covert dynamics, like the lack of assertiveness, speaking up, and other authority issues we found in several previous accidents, is important for successful high-risk team performance, yet most team training only obliquely engages with this topic. In existing CRM training models, this phenomenon might be called principles of good judgment, effective decision making, or awareness of hazardous attitudes. The essence of these concepts focuses on the individual's 'perception' of what is going on and the ability to distinguish between correct and incorrect technical solutions.[67] Rarely

does training address that there might be multiple, correct perceptions of reality occurring, thereby revealing the challenge for high-risk
teams to learn to negotiate through conflict. Surfacing conflicts – not
avoiding them – is an important way to improve team performance
in high-risk fields. In other words, once one accepts that group life
is complex, not linear, and influenced by a number of powerful yet
unseen variables, it becomes clear that high-risk teams need a complex
'toolbox' of skills in order to be effective.

LEADERSHIP

To operate effectively, teams need to establish a professional climate
in which they can surface and discuss conflicts and errors in a timely
manner, maintaining a shared sense of situational awareness while
effectively managing resources. The way a leader solicits input is as
important as the act itself. If a leader takes an authoritarian approach
or responds defensively, the team is likely to feel that speaking up is
unsafe. In contrast, if a leader is democratic, supportive, and open to
questions and challenges, team members are likely to feel greater psychological safety for speaking up. In other words, both invitation and
appreciation are needed to convey the inclusiveness that helps teams
feel that their input is valued.[68]

Depending on the team's task, the well functioning team does not
become overly preoccupied with the leadership hierarchy but allows
the most qualified individual to emerge and lead as required by operational scenarios. If a team has a number of tasks to manage, as most
high-risk teams do, each member may exercise leadership at different
times to accomplish the team's goals. Unless there is an operational
necessity to react quickly, it is often best for a team to operate in a decentralized manner, allowing all resources to be utilized most efficiently.
As was evident in the Hillsborough disaster, needlessly implementing
a rigid centralized hierarchy can stifle team communication, inhibit
innovation, and quash creative thinking during a crisis.

Although decentralized, clear *formal authority roles* still remain: A police chief, military officer, or airline captain does not relinquish his or her *authority role* or its corresponding responsibility. Yet, depending on the nature of a team's task, the person occupying the formal authority role may not be the most suitable leader at all times and can relinquish leadership to a better suited teammate. If Chief Duckenfield had considered a more decentralized leadership structure, he might have been able to take better advantage of the extensive experience his team had policing football at Hillsborough.

COMMUNICATION

Communication is sometimes called the glue that holds the team process together, yet its complexity is often a misunderstood and undervalued skill in high-risk professions. For instance, we often think of communication in an all-or-nothing way – we are understood or misunderstood, persuaded or unmoved, agreed or disagreed with – ignoring the fact that there is much ambiguity and innuendo in the communication process. In fact, words are only a small part of the communication process. A large part of communication is conveyed via body language and other nonverbal means. For example, identity characteristics such as race, gender, sexual orientation, religion, age, height, weight, attractiveness, professional experience, hobbies, family connections, friendships, and a list of other factors, all become influential as recipients decide how much *authority* to award the sender and his or her message. Recipients are constantly judging whether the sender seems credible or trustworthy and whether the message is believable.

Recipients of communication are not the only ones judging; the sender must also assess the intelligence, language skills, expectations, and personality characteristics of the intended audience. For instance, when collaborating with professionals from different organizations, the effective communicator must be wary of alienating others through the use of jargon not easily understood outside professional circles.

He or she should also consider the audience's potential reaction to the message when choosing words. Is this a message that was expected and generally agreed with, or is it difficult news for the recipients to hear?

Many high-risk team models of communication still reflect a centralized, command-and-control paradigm, emphasizing communication as the exchange of "information" and "instructions" from one leader to recipients in a manner that they can clearly and correctly understand.[69] Yet, if effective high-risk teams can operate in a more decentralized fashion, sharing the leadership role depending on the task, then communication becomes a complex *act of authorizing*. Consider whose words get heard and recalled during stressful conditions. Often it is people who have been awarded *authority*, whether formally or informally, by the team.

There are at least five ways that effective communication is essential to high-risk teams' effective performance in the operational environment, and they often occur simultaneously: (1) open information exchange; (2) establishing work-oriented interpersonal relationships; (3) establishing predictable behavior patterns; (4) maintaining attention to task; and (5) establishing leadership.[70]

First, it is a team's collective responsibility to establish and maintain a professional climate, a climate of curiosity, and open communication to ensure the successful exchange of information. The professionalism of a team can be improved by engaging honestly and respectfully, soliciting feedback, appreciating people's efforts, and avoiding inappropriate jokes or slang. By keeping the climate professional, teammates stay open to learning from experience, creating an environment that is conducive to innovation, growth, and creativity. We saw the detrimental impact of the poor information exchange between the crew on board the USS *Greeneville*, police at Hillsborough, Airbus manufacturers and American Airlines operators, and Bristol doctors on their respective teams' performance.

Second, by collectively creating and maintaining a professional climate, the high-risk team can establish work-oriented interpersonal relationships. Conversely, in an unprofessional climate, people often feel uncomfortable and grow mistrustful, interested more in self-preservation than creating a healthy team environment. Rather than committing to the team's vision, recognizing there is a collective, inter-dependence to their relationship, organizing in a systemic way, and sharing leadership roles, individuals begin to act more like a crowd – interested in only satisfying their own needs and desires. This team failure became particularly acute at Bristol hospital when the doctors split along professional boundaries and at Hillsborough when the police force individualized.

Third, although high-risk teams establish predictable behavior patterns through the use of manuals, checklists, standard operat-ing procedures, and training, it is also important to have a common language that can flag areas of concern as they emerge. For example, 'C.U.S.' words – the words *concern, uncomfortable*, and *safety* – can be used as communication red flags to signal that things are not going well. Through the use of this common phraseology, all crew members understand that an important safety concern is being expressed that needs to be addressed as soon as possible. The use of C.U.S. words would have been particularly helpful for Lieutenant Junior Grade Coen and Petty Officer Seacrest as a way to flag their growing concern about safety on board the *Greeneville*.

Fourth, in addition to 'C.U.S.' words, *The Big Three – inquiry, advocacy*, and *assertiveness* – can be used as a communication strategy to maintain team members' attention to task. When a team member feels *concerned* or *uncomfortable* about an unfolding event, the first step is to clearly state what is being experienced and inquire if other team members are experiencing the same thing. This communication strategy keeps all team members focused on the safe completion of the team's task. For instance, rather than Flight 587's Captain States simply saying, "You all right?" when First Officer Molin hit the turbulence, he might have *inquired* more specifically: "Why are you responding so aggressively on the flight controls?" If an adequate response is not received, the next step is to advocate a plan of action in a clear and articulate manner. Avoiding fuzzy phrases, slang, and metaphors, a teammate should be polite, but assertive, stating his or her position. Captain States could have *advocated*, "I'm *uncomfortable* with your flight control inputs," and then *asserted*, "I have the controls."

In another example, one strategy that could have been used on board the USS *Greeneville* would have been for Lieutenant Commander Pfeiffer, Lieutenant Sloan, Lieutenant Junior Grade Coen, or Petty Officer Seacrest to *inquire* directly to Captain Waddle whether he intended to complete all four training maneuvers and be late returning to port, or cut the maneuvers short in order to arrive on time. They could have *advocated* a reduction to the training schedule, and when pushed by the captain, they could have *assertively* told him they needed more time. They could have *inquired* whether the captain really expected Coen to prepare the submarine for periscope depth in five minutes and *advocated* a more reasonable plan that would have complied with standard operating procedures. Yet, this did not happen.

Fifth, communication should be used to establish leadership roles and surface conflicts in order to avoid a *groupthink* environment. In this more open environment, leaders do not shy away from conflict but actively work to explore the issues as a learning opportunity. In addition, the leader strives to support a climate in which uncertainties and complexities of group process can be examined. Being aware of a group's tendency to scapegoat, the successful leader is willing to take action when warranted to redirect group antagonism. Finally, a leader understands his or her 'role' and manages personal and professional boundaries in a manner that builds trust within the team. By using her or his emotional intelligence and instincts, a leader can uncover many of the covert activities that debilitate team performance. If Dr. Bolsin had more of this skill at Bristol hospital, he might have understood how his behavior was undermining the operating room team's performance.

SENSE MAKING

Sense making is the process of constructing a mental model of current events by comparing and evaluating one's perception of reality 'outside' with what one is experiencing 'inside' one's head. Although this may seem simple, sense making in organizational life is often a puzzling experience. As previously discussed, groups often create multiple, conflicting interpretations of reality, all of which are plausible and occurring simultaneously at a rapid pace.[71] For instance, one could argue First Officer Molin was flying Flight 587 out of the turbulence, as Captain States assumed, or he was breaking the airplane; Lieutenant Junior Grade Coen was dangerously slow and methodical to a fault, or carefully diligent in his duties; and Captain Waddle was a charismatic role model and mentor for his crew, or an overcontrolling bully. Given the multitude of conflicting interpretations and the time urgency of most decision-making scenarios in technical, high-risk fields, how can we become more efficient sense makers?

First, we must *identify the correct problem*, remaining vigilantly *curious* about others, ourselves, and our environment and *gathering information* to help keep our perceptions as closely aligned to reality as possible. Making assumptions is risky business. As we *analyze* this information we naturally attempt to create order – to make sense – within our mind. For example, many crew members on board the *Greeneville* assumed that some of the training events would be cancelled. It seemed logical. Therefore, it was easy to jump to a conclusion and therefore stop processing the situation. Similarly, Chief Duckenfield seemed to assume that if police could manage the crowd control situation until kickoff, all would be well.

Once we believe we understand a situation, we think we can forget about it or, better yet, use this piece of meaning to make sense out of something else, building a house of *false reality* cards. We can avoid the house of false reality cards trap by routinely *cross-checking* what is inside our heads and bodies with the outside world. The longer we

FIGURE 7.1. Team Resource Management (TRM) sense-making cycle.[72]

can *tolerate ambiguity*, and sit with the uncertainty of a situation, the longer we can remain curious, gathering important information and thinking through crisis in order to make a reality-based assessment.

Once we have used a genuine curiosity to gather information, resisting our urge to jump to conclusions by tolerating the ambiguity of this experience, and cross-checked information to ensure it's accurate, it is time to *develop a plan* to provide a temporary guide for action. I say temporary because one should continue the sense-making cycle of gathering and cross-checking, *modifying the plan as required* as new realities emerge. Obviously, given the time constraints of some challenges in high-risk teams, the sense-making cycle may be quite quick.

In this case, the time critical nature of the situation requires a more centralized leadership approach, clear direction from a central source. But in most cases, there is more time than one initially believes to make sense of a situation.

For instance, even when pilots are confronted by an engine fire in flight, clearly one of the most hazardous emergencies, they are still trained to refer to a checklist and confirm the presence and exact location of the fire with fellow aircrew. Before securing the burning engine, they confirm that they have their hand on the correct selector before moving any switches or levers. Although this may take a minute or two, history has shown more than a few pilots have shut down the good engine in flight in a confused state of sense making. It is often the inability to tolerate ambiguity as important facts become clear that forces us to make mistakes.

The *Greeneville* team's failure to make proper sense of the impending collision can be traced back to a number of contributing factors using the sense-making cycle. To begin, Captain Waddle and his crew failed to identify the correct problem: their submarine's operation in waters where imminent collision was possible. If they had even remotely considered that there were potential obstacles to their surfacing, they would have been curious why they had so little information about vessels in their area and begun processing more data. If members of the control team had cross-checked data, their sense of the 'big picture', and analyzed the information available to them, they would have realized that no one had a clear sense of situational awareness. Instead, Coen and Seacrest tolerated ambiguity too effectively, trusting that Captain Waddle was all-knowing. Although Coen observed that the captain "did not follow standards" during ascent to periscope depth nor "perform his visual search in the manner that [he] was trained," he nonetheless emphasized "the CO is the most experienced submarine officer on board a submarine. He is highly trained and highly experienced." Therefore, "I had no reason to believe that he would perform a less-than-safe search of the area."[73]

TEAMWORK

Good *teamwork* can be thought of as the successful integration of the other elements. By creating a more decentralized team environment, if situations permit, in which people can share the leadership role, assigning duties based on skill not job title, teams can think through crisis and innovate to meet the needs of often unprecedented challenges. By communicating openly and professionally, without inappropriate jokes or confusing jargon, using common communication strategies such as 'C.U.S.' words and The Big Three, teams can successfully exchange information, establish predictable behavior patterns, and balance the workload by maintaining good situational awareness and attention to the task.

One way to assess the effectiveness of teamwork is to examine three areas of high-risk team performance: decision making, workload management, and error management.

First, observe how information is shared and decisions are made within the team. Is input solicited from a variety of areas or are decisions made by one person, behind closed doors with little feedback from outside?

Second, assess the manner in which the workload is managed. Are tasks solely the responsibility of certain individuals or is everyone *authorized* to pitch in and help when required? Conversely, are individuals allowed to become saturated by the extent of their workload while others sit idly by?

Finally, how are the inevitable human errors managed within the team or organization? Is it assumed that some errors will naturally occur or is there pressure to achieve an unattainable level of perfection? When errors are made, how is it handled? Are individuals scapegoated?

An excellent example of teamwork within a high-risk organization is Southwest Airlines. Southwest's management fosters a corporate culture in which employees can have fun and be themselves. This decentralized culture encourages *leadership* by delegating responsibility, empowering employees to make decisions as experts in their work area. When a Southwest 737 pulls into the gate, employees *communicate* and coordinate activates in order to get the airplane 'turned around' and out on time – usually within twenty minutes. That means pilots may unload baggage, flight attendants may load cases of soda and peanuts, and gate agents may clean newspapers and trash off the passengers seats. No one needs to be told to help out; as a team they *make sense* of the situation and develop a plan after evaluating the tasks that need to be accomplished. As a result, the team balances the workload to achieve their goal: the twenty-minute turnaround.

CONCLUDING THOUGHTS

Dozens of books have been written about teams over the past decade; for example, '*Team-Building, Instant Team-Building, Team Players and Teamwork, Team Cognition, Cross-Functional Teams, X-Teams, Leading Teams, The 17 Indisputable Laws of Teamwork, Intellectual Teamwork, The Wisdom Of Teams, The 17 Essential Qualities of a Team Player, The Discipline Of Teams, Remaking Teams, Why Teams Don't Work,*' and '*Overcoming The Five Dysfunctions Of A Team*'.[74] Although this list is a positive indication of the growing interest in improving ways of working effectively together, few authors agree on which factors are essential. Even the regulators of high-risk professions, such as medical licensing boards or the FAA, agree teamwork is essential and the repercussions of team failures often catastrophic. Yet, they nonetheless provide little in the way of specific guidance.

The FAA, for example, has endorsed human factors training and teambuilding in aviation for years, now requiring Crew Resource Management at all commercial airlines. However, they remain reluctant to dictate specific criteria for these training programs or provide evaluation guidance.[75]

One challenge is that it is difficult to bridge the gap between theory and application. Although Charles Perrow advised in *Normal Accidents* that "we should give risky systems more quality control and training than we do,"[76] he does not elaborate on details. Even James Reason conceded "that the bulk" of his book *Human Error*, a mainstay in the field, "has favoured theory rather than practice."[77] This leaves the daunting challenge to practitioners to make the important 'theoretical' lessons learned relevant for teams in operation.

Some solutions have been offered. For example, personality measurements developed after World War II such as Blake and Mouton's *Managerial Grid* or *Myers-Briggs* Type Indicator remain popular because they provide simple, formulaic solutions to the complex problem of teambuilding. Still in use today in employee screening by 89 of the Fortune 100 companies, *Myers-Briggs* is administered to 2.5 million Americans per year.[78] At a cost of about $150 per test,[79] this makes predicting teamwork a lucrative business. A similarly simplistic explanation of the complexity of group dynamics can be found in another popular theoretical model, Tuckman and Jensen's from the 1970s: *forming, storming, norming, performing*, and *adjourning*.[80] Once again, this model remains in vogue in leadership and teambuilding programs because it satiates people's craving for simple explanations to difficult teambuilding problems.

Even many aviation researchers have given up on the challenge of developing methods to improve teamwork and have instead focused on reducing mistakes through *Threat Error Management* (TEM) programs. Akin to "defensive driving" strategies for motorists,[81] TEM assumes mistakes are inevitable. Therefore, programs help crews manage external threats, pilot errors, and undesired aircraft states through observable and measurable behavioral markers. Although TEM programs have been adopted at many airlines, they do relatively little to help crews innovate, improve situational awareness in unprecedented emergencies, develop shared mental models, or enhance teamwork in ways research has shown is needed.

In contrast, what we have learned over the course of this book is that teams operate in unpredictably cyclic, not linear, ways and team chemistry, more than technical prowess, is often a powerful determinant of team success. Four of the five major case studies, here – *Greeneville*, Hillsborough, American Airlines and Bristol hospital – involved highly trained and technically proficient individuals. Yet, in each case, teamwork broke down.

We also found that a team's ability to think through crisis, tolerate ambiguity, and learn to make sense as unprecedented challenges unfold was key to averting disaster in United Airlines Flight 232 and US Airways Flight 1549. This suggests that personality measures, linear phases, or easy steps cannot ensure team success. Rather, what teams need are team learning tools; analytic strategies that heighten the group's awareness of preexisting situational givens, such as individual psychology, group dynamics, and systemic factors; and controllable operational variables, such as leadership, communication, teamwork, and sense making so that teams can learn to operate more effectively in a wide range of dynamically evolving environments.

In order to "deal effectively with the human element," creating a *kaizen* environment of continuous process improvement, high-risk fields must embrace what Follett, Mayo, Deming, and socio-technical researchers, among others, argued for more than fifty years ago. A socio-technical approach to training and workplace design is one in which social requirements and technical factors are in balance so that their teams can excel. In short, leaders and managers in high-risk fields must consider the optimization of both human factors and technological imperatives equally within organizations and training programs. How might this be accomplished?

By understanding the dynamics of leadership and authority and its impact on team performance more holistically, training protocols can be developed that will enable people to think critically in unprecedented situations. This offers colleges and universities a new role: to incorporate safety awareness and teamwork in educational programs.

In aviation, this may also help address concerns voiced by the NTSB[82] and Captain Sullenberger,[83] when he testified to Congress about the 'loss of seasoning' in future generations of commercial pilots. In addition, serious consideration needs to be made into the "overhaul of pilot selection and training," which ALPA called for in their 2009 white paper. Additionally, investigations into the impact of the current tumultuous aviation industry climate of outsourcing, mergers, downsizing, furloughs, and changing work rules on teamwork, safety, or employee job performance are needed before it is too late.

In conclusion, effective leaders need to be able to simultaneously manage both the tasks and the processes by which their teams operate. Successful teams need people who can identify, confront, and vent their anxieties, rather than becoming debilitated by them and either thoughtlessly jumping to action or seeking to scapegoat. Organizations need to develop an inclusive culture that accepts complexity, tolerates ambiguity, surfaces conflict, and supports a learning process at all levels.[84]

Therefore, the training challenge is complicated. First, training must help develop high-risk team's ability to think through crisis in order to puzzle out solutions to unfamiliar, ill-defined, complex problems while also managing the communication processes required to keep the team intact.[85] To begin with, training can familiarize people with previous accidents by examining case studies in an academic setting, exploring the flawed decision-making chain that often leads to team breakdown and disaster such as those covered here. Using a structured analysis model, individuals can develop the cognitive skills required to analyze how a series of errors in judgment ultimately culminate in disaster, building critical thinking skills.

Yet, this training format does little to address the second challenge – managing the leadership and communication processes required to keep the team from fragmenting under pressure like Chief Duckenfield's police force at Hillsborough stadium. To accomplish this development, training must also include strategies that actively engage the team in mental exercises, communication activities, and sense making through experiential learning opportunities that do not alienate the learner. Mixing instructional designs based on different learning theories allows training to build on the strengths of each, enhancing knowledge transfer and maintaining relevance when transitioning from the 'schoolhouse' to the 'frontline'. Just as methods for analysis of organizational disaster have matured to include performance breakdown and team learning, it is now time to embrace a more holistic approach to high-risk team performance analysis and training. As United Airlines Flight 232 and US Airways Flight 1549 have shown, it is possible to successfully think through crisis.

NOTES

INTRODUCTION

1. Fraher, A. L. 2005a. *Group Dynamics in High-Risk Teams: A "Team Resource Management" Primer.* New York: iUniverse Publications.
2. Flin, R. 1996. *Sitting in the Hot Seat: Leaders and Teams for Critical Incident Management.* New York: John Wiley & Sons.
3. Klein, G., Orasanu, J., Calderwood, R., and Zsambok, C. (eds.) 1993. *Decision making in Action.* New York: Ablex.
4. See for instance: Serfaty, D. and Michel, R. 1990. *Toward a Theory of Tactical Decision Making Expertise.* In Proceedings of the Symposium on Command and Control Research. Monterey CA: 257–69. Klein et al., 1993; Flin, 1996. Zsambok, C. and Klein, G. 1996. *Naturalistic Decision Making.* Hillsdale, NJ: Lawrence Erlbaum.
5. Flin, 1996: 172. Serfaty and Michel, 1990: 257–69.
6. Langewiesche, W. 2009a. *Fly By Wire: The Geese, the Glide, the Miracle on the Hudson.* New York: Farrar, Straus and Giroux: 21–2.
7. Levinson, N. G. 2009. "The Need for New Paradigms in Safety Engineering." In C. Dale and T. Anderson (eds.), *Safety-Critical Systems: Problems, Process and Practice*: 3–22. London: Springer-Verlag.
8. Fraher, A. L. 2004a. Systems Psychodynamics: The Formative Years of an Interdisciplinary Field at the Tavistock Institute. *History of Psychology,* 7(1): 65–84.
9. Neumann, J. E. 1999. Systems Psychodynamics in the Service of Political Organizational Change. In R. French & R. Vince (Eds.), *Group Relations, Management, and Organization*: 54–69. Oxford, England: Oxford University Press.
10. Ho, C. B., Oh, K. B., Pech, R. J., Durden, G., and Slade, B. 2009. *Crisis Decision Making.* New York: Nova Science Publishers Inc.

CHAPTER 1

1. Perrow, C. 1984. *Normal Accidents: Living with High-Risk Technologies.* New York: Basic Books: 5.
2. National Transportation Safety Board (NTSB). 1978. Southern Airways Flight 242 (Report number: NTSB/AAR-78/03): 33–4. Accessed online on 22 April 2010: http://libraryonline.erau.edu/online-full-text/ntsb/aircraft-accident-reports/AAR78–03.pdf
3. NTSB, 1978.
4. NTSB, 1978: 83.
5. "Precip" refers to precipitation.
6. NTSB, 1978: 72.
7. NTSB, 1978: 73.
8. NTSB, 1990: 4.
9. National Transportation Safety Board (NTSB). 1990. United Airlines Flight 232 (Report number: NTSB/AAR-90/06). Accessed online on 22 April 2010: http://libraryonline.erau.edu/online-full-text/ntsb/aircraft-accident-reports/AAR90–06.pdf
10. Reason, J. 1990. *Human Error.* Cambridge: Cambridge University Press: 173.
11. Reason, 1990: 202.
12. Stein, M. 2004. "The Critical Period of Disasters: Insights from Sense-Making and Psychoanalytic Theory." *Human Relations,* 57(10): 1243–61.
13. Kayes, D. C. 2004. "The 1996 Mount Everest Climbing Disaster: The Breakdown of Learning in Teams." *Human Relations,* 57(10): 1263–84.
14. Edmondson, A. C. 2003. "Speaking up in the Operating Room: How Team Leaders Promote Learning in Interdisciplinary Action Teams." *Journal of Management Studies,* 40(6): 1419–52.
15. Schwartz, H. S. 1987. "On the Psychodynamics of Organizational Disaster: The Case of the Space Shuttle Challenger." *Columbia Journal of World Business.* Schwartz, H. S. 1989. "Organizational Disaster and Organizational Decay: The Case of the National Aeronautics and Space Administration." *Industrial Crisis Quarterly,* 3: 319–34. Stein, 2004.
16. Weick, K. E. 1993. "The Collapse of Sensemaking in Organizations: The Mann Gulch Disaster." *Administrative Science Quarterly,* 38: 628–52. Weick, K. E. 1995. *Sensemaking in Organizations.* Thousand Oaks: Sage.
17. Flin, R. H. 1995. "Crew Resource Management for Teams in the Offshore Oil Industry." *Journal of European Industrial Training,* 19(9): 23–7.
18. Fraher, A. L. 2004b. "Flying the Friendly Skies: Why U.S. Commercial Airline Pilots Want To Carry Guns." *Human Relations,* 57(5): 573–95.
19. Emphasis added. Schwartz, 1989: 319.
20. Edmondson, 2003. Fraher, A. L. 2005a. "Team Resource Management (TRM): A Tavistock Approach to Leadership in High-Risk Environments." *Organisational and Social Dynamics,* 5(2): 163–82. Kayes, 2004. Stein, 2004.
21. Kayes, 2004: 1264.

22. Weick, K. E. and Sutcliffe, K. M. 2001, *Managing the Unexpected.* San Francisco: Jossey-Bass. Frankel, A. S., Leonard, M. W., and Denham, C. R. 2006. "Fair and Just Culture, Team Behavior, and Leadership Engagement." *Health Research and Educational Trust*, 41(4): 1690–709.

CHAPTER 2

1. Interview of LT. Michael J. Coen USN, 27–28 September 2001. National Transportation Safety Board (NTSB). 2001. Collision between the U.S. Navy Submarine USS *Greeneville* and Japanese Motor Vessel *Ehime Maru* near Oahu, Hawaii (Report number: NTSB/DCA-01-MM-022): 150.
2. NTSB, 2001; United States Navy Court of Inquiry (COI). 2001. Record of proceedings of a Court of Inquiry convened at Trial Service Office Pacific by order of Commander In Chief United States Pacific Fleet to inquire into a collision between *USS Greeneville* (SSN 772) and Japanese M/V *Ehime Maru* that occurred off the coast of Oahu, Hawaii, on 9 February 2001. Naval Station Pearl Harbor, Hawaii. Accessed online on 22 April 2010: http://www.cpf.navy.mil/news_images/special_projects/cpfnews/coidownloadtran-scripts.html

    Waddle, S. 2002. *The Right Thing*. Nashville, TN: Integrity Publishing.
3. COI, 2001: 8.
4. Admiral T. Fargo, personal communication, April 23, 2001.
5. U.S. Navy photo; NTSB, 2001: 4.
6. Emphasis added; COI, 2001: 145.
7. COI, 2001: 13.
8. *Ehime* Prefecture photo; NTSB, 2001: 2.
9. COI, 2001: 18.
10. NTSB, 2001: 17.
11. COI, 2001: 18.
12. NTSB, 2001: Sloan interview: 25–6.
13. NTSB, 2001: Coen interview: 5–6.
14. COI, 2001: 19.
15. NTSB, 2001: 13.
16. NTSB, 2001: Coen interview: 62–6.
17. NTSB, 2001: 13.
18. NTSB, 2001: 12.
19. NTSB, 2001: 15.
20. COI, 2001: 31.
21. NTSB, 2001: Sloan interview: 57.
22. NTSB, 2001: Sloan interview: 45.
23. COI, 2001: 33.
24. COI, 2001: 33.
25. COI, 2001: 112.
26. COI, 2001: 125.

27. COI, 2001: 34. NTSB, 2001: 16.
28. COI, 2001: 38.
29. NTSB, 2001: Coen interview: 27–8.
30. Waddle, 2002: 127.
31. COI, 2001: 57.
32. COI, 2001: 58. NTSB, 2001: 24.
33. COI, 2001: 305.
34. Waddle, 2002: 36.
35. Waddle, 2002: 24.
36. Waddle, 2002: 29–30.
37. Waddle, 2002: 64.
38. Waddle, 2002: 76.
39. NTSB, 2001: Waddle interview: 37.
40. Waddle, 2002: 84–5.
41. Sciolino, E. 4 March 2001. "Greeneville's Skipper Known for Devotion to His Job and Crew." *New York Times.*
42. Waddle, 2002: 85–7.
43. NTSB, 2001: 40.
44. NTSB, 2001: Pfeiffer interview: 210.
45. NTSB, 2001: Waddle interview: 34.
46. NTSB, 2001: Waddle interview: 34.
47. NTSB, 2001: 42.
48. NTSB, 2001: Coen interview: 10.
49. NTSB, 2001: Coen interview: 10.
50. COI, 2001: 32.
51. Waddle, 2002: 107.
52. Waddle, 2002: 108.
53. NTSB, 2001: Waddle interview: 2–3.
54. Bing, D. 2007. *Crowding Out the Space: The Weakness of a Strong Leader.* Philadelphia: Center for Applied Research. Accessed online on 28 May 2009: http://www.ispso.org/Bing2007BridgerPaper.pdf
55. NTSB, 2001: Coen interview: 27–8.
56. NTSB, 2001: Pfeiffer interview: 73–4.
57. NTSB, 2001: Waddle interview: 30–1.
58. NTSB, 2001: Pfeiffer interview: 139.
59. NTSB, 2001: Pfeiffer interview: 16–17.
60. NTSB, 2001: Sloan interview: 45–6.
61. NTSB, 2001: Pfeiffer interview: 86. COI, 2001: 739.
62. Reason, 1990: 202.

CHAPTER 3

1. Police Constable S. Smith's statement found in the Parliamentary Archives, Houses of Parliament, Westminster London, among over 1,000 police and witness statements made after the Hillsborough disaster.

2. Gary Burns, personal communication, undated, Accessed online on 23 May 2008: http://www.contrast.org/hillsborough/history/gary.shtm

3. Taylor, R., Ward, A. and Newburn, T. (eds). 1995. *The Day of the Hillsborough Disaster: A Narrative Account.* Liverpool: Liverpool University Press: 2.

4. Taylor, The Right Honorable Lord Justice. 1989. *The Hillsborough Stadium Disaster: Interim Report.* Presented to Parliament by the Secretary of State for the Home Department by Command of Her Majesty: 7 [paragraph 47].

5. Taylor, 1989: 7 [paragraph 48].

6. Taylor, 1989: appendix 1.

7. Taylor, 1989: 9 [paragraph 57].

8. Taylor et al., 1995: 25.

9. Taylor et al., 1995: 28.

10. Phillips, J. D. August 1990. *The Hillsborough Stadium Disaster Inquiry and Report.* Deputy Chief Constable Report, Devon and Cornwall Constabulary held at Parliamentary Archives, House of Parliament, London: 82 [paragraph 7.24]; 85 [paragraph 7.30].

11. Taylor et al., 1995: 32.

12. Taylor et al., 1995: 59.

13. Taylor 1989: 9 [paragraph 59].

14. Taylor 1989: 9 [paragraph 58].

15. Scraton, P. 1999. *Hillsborough: The Truth.* Edinburgh: Mainstream Publishing Projects Ltd: 48.

16. Taylor, 1989: Duckenfield interview: 4.

17. Superintendent Bernard Murray personal communication, 3 May 1989: 8.

18. Taylor et al., 1995: 31.

19. Scraton, 1999: 50.

20. CCTV video footage, Parliamentary Archives, House of Parliament, London.

21. Phillips, 1990: 108 [paragraph 8.14].

22. Taylor, 1989: 34 [paragraph 197].

23. Scraton, 1999: 52.

24. Police Sergeant Robert Burns, personal communication, undated: 2–3.

25. Superintendent Bernard Murray, personal communication, 3 May 1989: 9.

26. Inspector Paul Hand-Davis, personal communication, 27 April 1989: 3.

27. Taylor, 1989: 11 [paragraph 65].

28. Police Constable Michael Buxton, personal communication, 12 May 1989: 2.

29. Police Constable Michael Buxton, personal communication, 12 May 1989: 2.

30. Emphasis added. Police Constable Michael Buxton, personal communication, 12 May 1989: 2.

31. Police Constable Michael Buxton, personal communication, 12 May 1989: 2.

32. Superintendent Roger Marshall, personal communication, 3 May 1989: 15–16.

33. PC Trevor Bichard, personal communication, 5 May 1989: 7.

34. Taylor, 1989: 12 [paragraph 67].

35. Gary Burns, personal communication, undated. Accessed online on 1 June 2008: http://www.contrast.org/hillsborough/history/gary.shtm

36. Taylor et al., 1995: 33, 55–6.
37. Taylor et al., 1995: 48.
38. Taylor et al., 1995: 50–51.
39. Taylor et al., 1995: 33, 55–6.
40. Gary Burns, personal communication, undated. Accessed online on 1 June 2008: http://www.contrast.org/hillsborough/history/gary.shtm
41. Gary Burns, personal communication, undated. Accessed online on 1 June 2008: http://www.contrast.org/hillsborough/history/gary.shtm
42. Taylor et al., 1995: 47.
43. Taylor et al., 1995: 48.
44. Taylor, 1989: 18 [paragraph 109].
45. Taylor, 1989: 13 [paragraph 77].
46. Taylor, 1989: 14 [paragraph 80].
47. Scranton, 1999: 74.
48. Inspector Trevor Harvey, personal communication, undated: 5.
49. Scranton, 1999: 69.
50. Scranton, 1999: 64.
51. Taylor, 1989: 15 [paragraph 82–3].
52. Inspector Trevor Harvey, personal communication, undated: 5–6.
53. Inspector Trevor Harvey, personal communication, undated: 5–6.
54. Inspector Trevor Harvey, personal communication, undated: 5–6.
55. Scranton, 1999: 65–6.
56. Taylor, 1989: 40 [paragraph 231].
57. Taylor, 1989: 49 [paragraph 278].
58. Taylor, 1989: 44 [paragraph 251].
59. Taylor, 1989: 50 [paragraph 284].
60. Taylor, 1989: 50 [paragraph 283].
61. Taylor, 1989: 40 [paragraph 231].
62. Cited in Fishwick, N. 1989. *English Football and Society, 1910–1950*. Manchester: Manchester University Press: vi.
63. Frosdick, S. and Marsh, P. 2005. *Football Hooliganism*. Devon, UK: Willan Publishing: 10.
64. Frosdick and Marsh, 2005: 10–11.
65. Finn, G. 1994. "Football Violence – A Societal Psychological Perspective." In R. Giulianotti et al. (eds) *Football, Violence and Social Identity*: 90–127. London: Routledge: 95.
66. Frosdick and Marsh, 2005: 13.
67. The term *hooligan* originated from an immigrant gang, the Houlihans, which terrorized London in the nineteenth century.
68. Brimson, D. 2007. *March of the Hooligans: Soccer's Bloody Fraternity*. New York: Virgin Books: 81. Walvin, J. 1986. *Football and the Decline of Britain*. London: Macmillan: 66.
69. Walvin, 1986: 122.
70. Murphy, P., Williams, J., and Dunning, E. 1990. *Football on Trial: Spectator Violence and Development in the Football World*. London: Routledge: 71.

71. Frosdick and Marsh, 2005: 156.
72. http://www.urbandictionary.com/define.php?term=blag accessed on 9 August 2008.
73. Buford, B. 1991. *Among the Thugs*. London: W. W. Norton & Company: 103.
74. Between 1889 and 1910, fifty-nine of the current league football clubs moved into grounds they now occupy (Taylor, 1989: 5 [paragraph 27]).
75. Taylor, 1990: 5 [paragraph 27].
76. Taylor, 1990: 5 [paragraph 30].
77. Robson, G. 2000. *"No One Likes Us, We Don't Care": The Myth and Reality of Millwall Fandom*. Oxford: Berg: 4.
78. Sir Norman Chester Centre for Football Research. 2002. *Football Stadia after Taylor: Fact Sheet Number 2*. University of Leicester: 12.
79. Murphy et al., 1990: 39.
80. Taylor, 1990: 6 [paragraph 33].
81. Walvin, 1986.
82. Frosdick and Marsh, 2005: 93.
83. Taylor, I. 1987. "British Soccer after Bradford." *Sociology of Sport Journal* 4 (1): 171–91.
84. Buford, 1991: 114.
85. Buford, 1991: 217.
86. Frosdick and Marsh, 2005: 89.
87. Frosdick and Marsh, 2005: 89.
88. Sir Norman Chester Centre for Football Research. 2001. *Football Stadia after Taylor: Fact Sheet Number 1*. University of Leicester: 5.
89. Taylor, 1989: 5–6 [paragraph 36–9].
90. Taylor et al., 1995: 35.
91. Taylor 1989: 13 [paragraph 71].
92. Police Constable Trevor Bichard, personal communication, 5 May 1989: 8.
93. Interviews and CCTV footage reveal that this "club official" is most likely a plain-clothes Inspector sent down to the field by Chief Duckenfield to take control of the situation.
94. Woman Police Constable Fiona Richardson, personal communication, 30 April 1989: 2.
95. Taylor, 1989: 13 [paragraph 72].
96. Scranton, 1999: 62.
97. Taylor et al., 1995: 51.
98. Police Constable David Frost, personal communication, undated; Detective Constable Dennis Anthony Cerrone personal communication, undated.
99. Police Constable S. Smith, personal communication, 17 May 1989: 6.
100. Detective Constable Dennis Anthony Cerrone, personal communication, undated.
101. Police Constable David Frost, personal communication, undated.
102. Police Constable Roy Green, personal communication, 15 May 1989: 1.
103. Police Constable Roy Green, personal communication, 15 May 1989: 8.
104. Police Constable Roy Green, personal communication, 15 May 1989: 9.

105. Police Constable Paul Branston, personal communication, undated.
106. Police Constable Iain Alastair Paterson, personal communication, 3 May 1989: 5.
107. Taylor, 1989: 40 [paragraph 231].
108. Taylor, 1989: 50 [paragraph 284].

CHAPTER 4

1. Air Safety Week. October 25, 2004a. *American Airlines Tries to Pin Blame on Design Defect.* Accessed online June 25, 2010: http://findarticles.com/p/articles/mi_m0UBT/is_41_18/ai_n6284079/
2. National Transportation Safety Board (NTSB). 2004. American Airlines Flight 587. (Report number: NTSB/AAR-04/04). Accessed online on 25 March 2010: http://libraryonline.erau.edu/online-full-text/ntsb/aircraft-accident-reports/AAR04-04.pdf
3. NTSB, 2004, appendix B.
4. NTSB, 2004: 8.
5. NTSB, 2004: 50.
6. NTSB, 2004: 51.
7. Air Traffic Control spacing requirements: Federal Aviation Administration (FAA). 1998. *Air Traffic Control Handbook* (FAA Order 7110.65) states that the minimum separation for heavy airplane behind another heavy airplane is 2 minutes or 4 nautical miles (paragraphs 3–9–6; 5–5–4). NTSB (2004) reports JAL Flight 47 and American Airlines Flight 587 were separated at all times by at least 4.3 nm horizontally and 3,800 feet vertically (3, Footnote 11).
8. NTSB, 2004: 27–9.
9. For more information about use of composite materials in aerospace engineering see: http://composite.about.com/od/referencematerials/l/blpreface.htm and http://www.centennialofflight.gov/essay/Evolution_of_Technology/composites/Tech40.htm
10. NTSB, 2004: 68–70.
11. NTSB, 2004: 160.
12. Chart compiled by author using *Research and Innovative Technology Administration* (RITA) data, U.S. Bureau of Transportation Statistics. Accessed online on 25 April 2010: http://www.bts.gov/programs/airline_information/
13. *New York Times.* November 22, 1987. "F.A.A Begins Review of Standards for Pilots." *New York Times.*
14. Lavin, C. H. January 11, 1989. "Pilots Scarce, Airlines See 30-year-olds as Captains." *New York Times.*
15. First Officer Sten Molin's commuter airline employers: First Holiday Airlines, then Catskill Airlines, and later Business Express where he flew mid-sized twin-engine propeller planes such as the DeHavill and Twin Otter, Beech-99, and Shorts 360 as a first officer (NTSB, 2004).

16. *New York Times*, 1987.
17. National Transportation Safety Board (NTSB). 1987. Continental Airlines Flight 1713 (Report number: NTSB/AAR-88/09). Accessed online on March 25, 2010: http://libraryonline.erau.edu/online-full-text/ntsb/aircraft-accident-reports/AAR88–09.pdf
18. NTSB, 1987: 10.
19. NTSB, 1987: 11.
20. NTSB, 1987: 38.
21. NTSB, 1987: 38.
22. National Transportation Safety Board (NTSB). 1993a. GP Express Airlines Flight 861. (Report number: NTSB/AAR-93/03). Accessed online on March 25, 2010: http://libraryonline.erau.edu/online-full-text/ntsb/aircraft-accident-reports/AAR93–03.pdf
23. NTSB, 1993a: 31.
24. National Transportation Safety Board (NTSB). 1993b. Scenic Air Tours Flight 22. (Report number: NTSB/AAR-93/01). Accessed online on March 25, 2010: http://libraryonline.erau.edu/online-full-text/ntsb/aircraft-accident-reports/AAR93–01.pdf
25. NTSB, 1993b: 51.
26. National Transportation Safety Board (NTSB). 1994a. GP Express Airlines N115GP. (Report number: NTSB/AAR-94/01). Accessed online on March 25, 2010: http://libraryonline.erau.edu/online-full-text/ntsb/aircraft-accident-summaries/AAR94–01S.pdf
27. NTSB, 1994a: 12.
28. NTSB, 2004: Rockliff interview: 239.
29. NTSB, 1987: 37.
30. NTSB, 2004: 134.
31. NTSB, 2004: 134.
32. Federal Aviation Administration (FAA). 1996. *Challenge 2000*. Recommendations for Future Aviation Safety Regulation. Accessed online on 23 November 2008: http://www.nexacap.com/press_releases/C2000_final.pdf
33. Hall, J. 25 June 1996. Chairman National Transportation Safety Board testimony before the Committee on Transportation and Infrastructure, Subcommittee on Aviation, House of Representatives. Accessed online on 30 November 2008 http://www.ntsb.gov/Speeches/former/hall/jh960625.htm
34. Gore, A. 1996. White House Commission on Aviation Safety and Security: Final Report to President Clinton. Accessed online on 23 November 2008: http://www.fas.org/irp/threat/212fin~1.html
35. NTSB, 2004: 23–4.
36. NTSB, 2004: 24.
37. *Air Safety Week*, 2004a. NTSB, 2004.
38. NTSB, 2004: 50
39. NTSB, 2004: Lavelle interview: 37–9.
40. Cessna Aircraft Company. 1978. *Cessna-152 Information Manual*: 4–19.

41. Federal Aviation Administration. 1999. *Flight Instructor Handbook*. Accessed online on 23 January 2009: http://www.faa.gov/library/manuals/aviation/media/FAA-H-8083-9.pdf
42. National Transportation Safety Board (NTSB). 2002. Cessna 310 crash in San Dimas CA. (Report number: NTSB/ LAX02FA214). Accessed online on 25 April 2010: http://www.ntsb.gov/ntsb/GenPDF.asp?id=LAX02FA214&rpt=fa
43. NTSB, 2004: Attachment H; Exhibit 2-S.
44. Wald, M. L. 1 October 2007. "Fatal Airplane Crashes drop 65%." *New York Times*.
45. Wald M. L. and Maynard, M. 13 April 2008. "Behind Air Chaos, an FAA Pendulum Swing." *New York Times*.
46. Wald and Maynard, 2008.
47. COMPANY NEWS. 2 June 2004. "F.A.A. Fines American and Boeing $3.3 Million." *New York Times*.
48. Bailey, J. 9 April 2008. "American Canceling More Flights for Inspection." *New York Times*.
49. Wald, M. L. 7 March 2008. "F.A.A. Fines Southwest Air in Inspections." *New York Times*.
50. Wald and Maynard, 2008.
51. Wald, 2007.
52. Douglas, J. A. August 2006. "Editorial Page: Not Good Enough." *Aviation Safety World*: 5. Accessed online on 20 January 2009: http://www.flight-safety.org/asw/aug06/asw_aug06.pdf
53. Darby, R. August 2006. "Commercial Jet Hull Losses, Fatalities Rose Sharply in 2005." *Aviation Safety Week*: 51–2. Accessed online on 20 January 2009: http://www.flightsafety.org/asw/aug06/asw_aug06.pdf
    See also *Boeing Statistical Summary Commercial Jet Airplanes Accidents Worldwide*. Accessed online on 20 January 2009: http://www.boeing.com/news/techissues/pdf/statsum.pdf
54. Union of Concerned Scientists. 11 February 2008. "No Space for Aviation Safety at NASA." Accessed online on 20 January 2009: http://www.ucsusa.org/scientific_integrity/abuses_of_science/nasa-pilot-survey.html
55. CNN. 31 December 2007. "Report Containing Thousands of Pilot Complaints is Released." Accessed online on 20 January 2009: http://www.cnn.com/2007/TECH/space/12/31/nasa.airsafety/index.html
56. Union of Concerned Scientists, 2008.

CHAPTER 5

1. Kennedy, I. July 2001. *The Report of the Public Inquiry into Children's Heart Surgery at Bristol Royal Infirmary 1984–1995*. Presented to Parliament by the Secretary of State for Health by Command of Her Majesty. Dhasmana interview: 41–2.

2. Congenital heart abnormalities occur in about 6 of every 1,000 live births each year, approximately 3,500 babies in the UK alone. Fifty percent of these babies will not survive into adulthood without surgery.

3. Liebman J, Cullum L, and Belloc N. 1969. "Natural History of Transposition of the Great Arteries: Anatomy and Birth and Death Characteristics." *Circulation*, 40: 237–62.

4. Martins, P. and Castela, E. 2008. "Transposition of the Great Arteries." *Orphanet Journal of Rare Diseases*, 3: 27. Accessed online on 27 March 2009: http://www.pubmedcentral.nih.gov/articlerender.fcgi?artid=2577629#B50

5. http://www.chdinfo.com/aa/aa120797.htm;
   http://www.driscollchildrens.org/DCHweb/AboutDriscoll/content/cardio_arterial_switch_procedure.asp
   http://yourtotalhealth.ivillage.com/Arterial+Switch+Operation.html?pageNum=1

6. BBC News. 8 June 1998. "Our Rights Were Ignored." Accessed online on 1 July 2009: http://news.bbc.co.uk/2/hi/special_report/1998/05/98/the_bristol_heart_babies/105918.stm

7. Kennedy, 2001: 4.

8. Margaret Thatcher Foundation. 23 September 1987. "Interview for Woman's Own ('no such thing as society') with journalist Douglas Keay." Accessed on 27 March 2008: http://www.margaretthatcher.org/speeches/display-document.asp?docid=106689

9. Paton, C. 21 November 2008. "Griffiths Report could have Freed NHS from Politics." *Health Service Journal*. Accessed online on 21 March 2009: http://www.hsj.co.uk/opinion/2008/11/griffiths_report.html

10. Jones, K. 2006. *The Making of Social Policy in Britain: From the Poor Law to New Labour*. London: Continuum International Publishing Group: 181–4.

11. Kennedy, 2001: 68.

12. Kennedy, 2001: 68.

13. For example, the Association of Paediatric Anaesthetists in 1973, the Paediatric Intensive Care Society in 1987, and the British Cardiology Association in 1991.

14. Kennedy, 2001: 59–60.

15. Kennedy, 2001: 46.

16. Helmreich, R. L. and Musson, D. M. 2000. "Surgery as Team Endeavour." *Canadian Journal of Anesthesia*, 47: 391–2.

17. See for example, Bogner, M. S. 1994. *Human Error in Medicine*. Hillside NJ: Lawrence Erlbaum and Associates. Helmreich and Musson, 2000. Makary, M. A., Sexton, J. B., Freischlag, J. A., Holzmueller, C. G., Millman, E. A., Rowen, L. and Pronovost, P. J. 2006. "Operating Room Teamwork among Physicians and Nurses: Teamwork in the Eye of the Beholder." *American College of Surgeons*, 202(5): 746–52.

18. Kennedy, 2001: Bolsin interview: 132.

19. Kennedy, 2001: Dhasmana interview: 16.

20. Kennedy, 2001: Dhasmana interview: 16–7.

21. Kennedy, 2001: Dhasmana interview: 16–7.
22. Kennedy, 2001: Dhasmana interview: 67.
23. Kennedy, 2001: Dhasmana interview: 45.
24. Kennedy, 2001: Dhasmana interview: 47.
25. Kennedy, 2001: Dhasmana interview: 47.
26. Belli, E., Lacour-Gayet, F., Serraf, A., Alkhulaifi, A. M., Touchot, A., Bruniaux, J. and Planche, C. 1999. "Surgical Management Of Transposition Of Great Arteries Associated With Multiple Ventricular Septal Defects." *European Journal of Cardio-Thoracic Surgery*, 16(1): 14–20. Accessed online on 27 March 2009: http://cat.inist.fr/?aModele=afficheN&cpsidt=1895532
27. Kennedy, 2001: Dhasmana interview: 71.
28. Kennedy, 2001: Dhasmana interview: 46–7.
29. Kennedy, 2001: Dhasmana interview: 50.
30. Kennedy, 2001: Dhasmana interview: 59.
31. Kennedy, 2001: Dhasmana interview: 42–3.
32. Kennedy, 2001: Dhasmana interview: 47.
33. Kennedy, 2001: Dhasmana interview: 50.
34. Kennedy, 2001: Dhasmana interview: 11.
35. Kennedy, 2001: Dhasmana interview: 53.
36. This figure represents evidence presented during the inquiry and was gleaned from UK Cardiac Surgical Registry Data 1990–1992.
37. Kennedy, 2001: Prys-Robert interview: 4–5.
38. Kennedy, 2001: Prys-Robert interview: 5.
39. Kennedy, 2001: Prys-Robert interview: 5.
40. Dr. Stephen Bolsin, personal communication, 7 August 1990.
41. Kennedy, 2001: Bolsin interview: 111.
42. Kennedy, 2001: Bolsin interview: 56.
43. Kennedy, 2001: Bolsin interview: 108.
44. Kennedy, 2001: Roylance interview: 67–8.
45. Kennedy, 2001: Bolsin interview: 57.
46. Avenues available were to: approach the surgeons directly; speak to the Chairman of the Medical Committee; request a special topic meeting with his colleagues; ask to add his topic to the agenda of one of their regularly scheduled audit meetings; or ask the cardiac surgery audit coordinator to present his concerns at the more informal evening meetings held monthly in people's homes.
47. Kennedy, 2001: Bolsin interview: 113–14.
48. Kennedy, 2001: 139.
49. Kennedy, 2001: Bolsin interview: 53.
50. Kennedy, 2001: Prys-Roberts interview: 45–6.
51. Dr. Alison Hayes, personal communication, 1999: 1.
52. Kennedy, 2001: 144.
53. Kennedy, 2001: Pryn interview: 129–30.
54. Dr. Jane Ashwell, personal communication, 13 December 1993.

55. Dr. Stephen Bolsin, personal communication, 10 February 1994.
56. Kennedy, 2001: Bolsin interview: 98.
57. Examples include:
    Professor Gianni Angelini, professor of cardiac surgery, University of Bristol;
    Dr. Jane Ashwell, senior medical officer, Department of Health;
    Dr. Andrew Black, senior lecturer in anesthesia, Bristol University;
    Dr. William Brawn, consultant pediatric cardiac surgeon, Diana Princess of Wales Hospital, Birmingham;
    Dr. Alan Clement, consultant in anesthesia, BRI;
    Dr. Ian Davies, consultant in anesthesia, BRI;
    Professor Paul Dieppe, dean, faculty of medicine, University of Bristol;
    Dr. Peter Doyle, general surgeon, Department of Health;
    Professor John Farndon, professor and head of surgery, University of Bristol;
    Dr. Phil Hammond, columnist with *Private Eye Magazine*;
    Dr. Alison Hayes, consultant pediatric cardiologist, BRI;
    Mrs. Janet Maher, UBH/T general manager, directorate of surgery;
    Dr. Sally Masey, consultant anesthesiologist, BRI;
    Dr. Chris Monk, clinical director of anaesthesia, BRI;
    Professor John Norman, Department of Anaesthesia, University of Southampton;
    Mrs. Kathleen Orchard, general manager, directorate of surgery UBHT;
    Dr. Stephen Pryn, consultant in anesthesia and intensive care, BRI;
    Professor Cedric Prys-Roberts, professor of anesthesia, University of Bristol;
    Dr. John Roylance, chief executive, UBHT;
    Dr. Susan Underwood, consultant anesthesiologist, BRI;
    Professor John Vann-Jones, clinical director of cardiac services, BRI;
    Dr. Sheila Willatts, consultant anesthesiologist, BRI; member, Council of Royal College of Anesthetists;
    Dr. N. Brian Williams, consultant anesthesiologist, BRI;
    Dr. John Zorab, director of anaesthesia and medical director, Frenchay Hospital, Bristol.
58. Dr. Peter Martin, personal communication, 11 January 1995: 1.
59. Dr. Chris Monk, personal communication, 11 January 1995: 2.
60. Kennedy, 2001: Dhasmana interview: 30.
61. Kennedy, 2001: Dhasmana interview: 39.
62. Kennedy, 2001: Dhasmana interview: 57–8.
63. Dr. Chris Monk, personal communication, 11 January 1995: 2.
64. Kennedy, 2001: Dhasmana interview: 78.
65. Sexton, J. B., Thomas, E. J., and Helmreich, R. L. 2000. "Error, Stress, and Teamwork in Medicine and Aviation." *British Medical Journal*, 320: 748.
66. Groopman, J. 2 May 2005. "A Model Patient." *The New Yorker*: 52.
67. Makary et al., 2006.

68. Sexton et al., 2000: 748.
69. Makary et al., 2006: 746–52.
70. Kennedy, 2001: 1.
71. Kennedy, 2001: 7.
72. Kennedy, 2001: 4–5.
73. Kennedy, 2001: 2.
74. Kennedy, 2001: 3.
75. Kennedy, 2001: 15.
76. Weicke, 1995: 338.
77. Long, S. 2008. *The Perverse Organisation and its Deadly Sins.* London: Karnac Books: 1–3.
78. Long, 2008: 15.
79. Schreier, H. A. and Libow, J. A. 1993. *Hurting for Love: Munchausen by Proxy Syndrome.* London: Guildford Press: 87.
80. Gregory, J. 2003. *Sicken: The True Story of a Lost Childhood.* London: Century.
81. Armstrong, D. 2005. *Organization in the Mind.* London: Karnac Books.
82. Shapiro, E. R. and Carr, A. W. 1991. *Lost in Familiar Places: Creating New Connections between the Individual and Society.* New Haven, CT: Yale University Press.
83. Armstrong, 2005.
84. Long, 2008: 1–3.
85. Long, 2008: 1–3.
86. Kennedy, 2001: Bolsin interview: 180–2.
87. Kennedy, 2001: Bolsin interview: 8.
88. Kennedy, 2001: Bolsin interview: 89.
89. Schreier and Libow, 1993: 87.
90. Kennedy, 2001: Monk interview: 42.
91. Kennedy, 2001: 11.

CHAPTER 6

1. Sullenberger, C. 2009a. *Highest Duty.* New York: William Morrow Publishers: 211.
2. Sullenberger, 2009a: Appendix B (Full CVR transcript available). Full transcript also available online at: http://www.faa.gov/data_research/accident_incident/1549/media/Full%20Transcript%20L116.pdf
3. Sullenberger, 2009a: 206.
4. National Transportation Safety Board (NTSB). 2009a. *Operations/Human Performance Group Chairmen Interview Summaries – Flight Crew* (Docket No. SA-532; Exhibit No. 2-B): 11. Accessed online on 13 June 2009: http://www.ntsb.gov/Dockets/Aviation/DCA09MA026/418999.pdf
5. NTSB, 2009a: 11.
6. Sullenberger, 2009a: 208.
7. Sullenberger, 2009a: 209.

8. Sullenberger, 2009a: 208,
9. NTSB, 2009a: 12.
10. Sullenberger, 2009a: 209.
11. Sullenberger, 2009a: 209.
12. Couric, K. 2009a. Interview on *60 minutes*. "Flight 1549: A Routine Takeoff Turns Ugly." Accessed online on 30 April 2009: http://www.cbsnews.com/stories/2009/02/08/60minutes/main4783580.shtml
13. Sullenberger, 2009a: 209.
14. Sullenberger, 2009a: Appendix B.
15. Sullenberger, 2009a: 217.
16. Sullenberger, 2009a: 235.
17. Sullenberger, 2009a: 236.
18. Sullenberger, 2009a: 230.
19. Sullenberger, 2009a: 223.
20. National Transportation Safety Board (NTSB). 2009e. *US Airways Flight 1549: Attachment 4 Photographs.* (Docket No. SA-532; Exhibit No. 6E) Washington DC (Report number: DCA09MA026). Accessed online on 25 June 2010: http://www.ntsb.gov/Dockets/Aviation/DCA09MA026/420144.pdf
21. Passenger Mark Hood, personal communication, 15 January 2009. Accessed online on 2 May 2009: http://www.nytimes.com/interactive/2009/01/15/nyregion/20090115-plane-crash-970.html
22. Couric, 2009a.
23. Langewiesche, W. 2009a. *Fly By Wire: The Geese, the Glide, the Miracle on the Hudson.* New York: Farrar, Straus and Giroux: 180.
24. Couric, K. 2009b. Interview on *60 minutes*. "Flight 1549: Saving 155 Souls in Minutes." Accessed online on 30 April 2009: http://www.cbsnews.com/stories/2009/02/08/60minutes/main4783586.shtml
25. National Transportation Safety Board (NTSB). 2009d. *US Airways Flight 1549: Attachment 1 Photographs.* Washington DC (Report number: DCA09MA026). Accessed online on 25 June 2010: http://www.ntsb.gov/Dockets/Aviation/DCA09MA026/423126.pdf
26. Couric, 2009b.
27. Wilson, M. and Baker, A. 16 January 2009. "In Icy Water, Quick Rescue Kept Death Toll at Zero." *New York Times*: A1 & A25.
28. NTSB, 2009e: 3.
29. Couric, 2009b.
30. Sullenberger, 2009a: 243.
31. National Transportation Safety Board (NTSB). 2009c. US Airways Flight 1549: Preliminary Report (Report number: DCA09MA026). Accessed online 2 May 2009: http://www.ntsb.gov/ntsb/GenPDF.asp?id=DCA09MA026&rpt=p
32. National Transportation Safety Board (NTSB). 1991. USAir Flight 1493 and Skywest Flight 5569 Collision (Report number: NTSB/AAR-91/08). Accessed online on 3 January 2010: http://libraryonline.erau.edu/online-full-text/ntsb/aircraft-accident-reports/AAR91-08.pdf

33. O'Hara, J. M. and Roth, E. M. 2005. "Operational Concepts, Teamwork, and Technology in Commercial Nuclear Power Stations." In Clint Bowers, Eduardo Salas, and Florian Jentsch (eds) *Creating High-Tech Teams: Practical Guidance on Work Performance and Technology*. Washington, DC: American Psychological Association: 139–59.
34. O'Hara and Roth, 2005: 156.
35. Heightman, A. J. 15 January 2009. "Airplane Crash Showcases Emergency Readiness." *Journal of Emergency Medical Services*. Accessed online on 3 May 2009: http://www.jems.com/news_and_articles/columns/Heightman/airplane_crash_showcases_emergency_readiness.html;jsessionid=FEFF8843 6DD201F3E0A501172810D9BF
36. Dwyer, J. 17 January 2009. "Old Hands on the River Didn't have to be told what to Do." *New York Times*: A17.
37. Sullenberger, 2009a: 249–51.
38. Edmondson, A., Bohmer, R., and Pisano, G. 2004. "Speeding Up Team Learning." In *Harvard Business Review on Teams That Succeed*: 77–98. Boston: Harvard Business School Publishing: 130.
39. Air and Space Smithsonian. 18 February 2009. *Interview with Captain Sullenberger: Sully's Tale*. Accessed online 2 May 2009: http://www.airspacemag.com/flight-today/Sullys-Tale.html
40. NTSB, 2009a: 30.
41. Couric, 2009a.
42. NTSB, 2009a: 30.
43. Langewiesche, 2009a: 20–1.
44. Langewiesche, 2009a: 47.
45. Lowy, J. 24 February 2009. "Controller Thought Plane That Ditched Was Doomed." *Associated Press*. Accessed online on 2 May 2009: http://www.abcnews.go.com/Politics/wireStory?id=6944354
46. Langewiesche, 2009a: 23.
47. Last, S. and Adler, M. 1991. *British Airways Airbus A-320 Pilots' Autothrust Survey*. (SAE tech paper 912225). Warrendale, PA: Society of Automotive Engineers.
48. Last and Adler, 1991.
49. See   http://www.airbus.com/en/presscentre/pressreleases/pressreleases_items/07_03_06_A300_final_assembly.html
50. Langewiesche, 2009a: 16.
51. See http://www.airbus.com/en/aircraftfamilies/a320/a320/performance.html
52. Wallace, J. 20 March 2000. "Unlike Airbus, Boeing lets Aviator Override Fly-By-Wire Technology." *Seattle Post-Intelligencer*. Accessed online on 3 January 2010: http://www.seattlepi.com/business/boe202.shtml
53. Card, S. K., Moran, T. P., and Newell, A. 1983. *The Psychology of Human-Centered Approach*. Hillsdale, NJ: Erlbaum.
54. See for instance: Billings, C. E. 1996. *Aviation Automation: The Search for a Human-Centered Approach*. Hillsdale, NJ: Erlbaum. Norman, D. A. 1990. "The 'Problem' with Automation: Inappropriate Feedback and Interaction,

not 'Over-Automation.'" *Philosophical Transactions of the Royal Society of London, 327, 585–93.* Sarter, N. B. and Woods, D. D. 1994. "Pilot Interaction with Cockpit Automation II: An Experimental Study of Pilots' Model and Awareness of the Flight Management and Guidance System." *International Journal of Aviation Psychology*, 4: 1–28. Sarter, N. B. and Woods, D. D. 1997. "Team Play with a Powerful and Independent Agent: Operational Experiences and Automation Surprises on the Airbus A-320." *Human Factors*, 39(4): 553–69.

55. National Transportation Safety Board (NTSB). 1994b. *Safety Study: A Review of Flight-Crew Involved, Major Accidents of U.S. Air Carriers, 1978 through 1990.* Washington DC (NTSB No. PB 94–917001).

56. Jentsch, F., Barnett, J., Bowers, C. A., and Salas, E. 1999. "'Who is flying this Plane Anyway? What Mishaps tell us about Crew Member Role Assignment and Air Crew Situation Awareness." *Human Factors*, 41(1): 11–12.

57. Jentsch et al., 1999: 10.

58. Gladwell, M. 2008. *Outliers: The Story of Success.* New York: Little, Brown and Company: 40.

59. Sullenberger, 2009a: 25.

60. Air Line Pilots Association (ALPA). September 2009. *Producing a Professional Airline Pilot: Candidate Screening, Hiring, Training, and Mentoring.* Air Line Pilots Association White Paper. Accessed on 1 January 2010: http://www.alpa.org/portals/alpa/pressroom/inthecockpit/ProducingProfessionalPilot_9–2009.pdf

61. Gaal, S. T. and Husain, A. 2008. *Large Regional Jets – The Next Battleground*: 4. Accessed online 5 January 2010: http://www.skyworkscapital.com/region-aljets.pdf

62. Accessed on 5 January 2010: http://www.delta.com/planning_reservations/plan_flight/aircraft_types_layout/index.jsp

63. United States Department of Transportation (US DOT). June 1998. *Profile: Regional Jets and Their Emerging Roles in the U.S. Aviation Market.* Office of the Assistant Secretary for Aviation and International Affairs. Accessed online 5 January 2010: http://ostpxweb.dot.gov/aviation/domav/regjets.pdf

64. Accessed online on 15 May 2010: www.glassdoor.com

65. Gaal and Husain, 2008.

66. Civil Aviation Authority (CAA). 21 July 2008. *Global Fatal Accident Review 1997–2006.* United Kingdom Safety Regulation Group (CAP 776): 1. Accessed online 6 January 2010: http://www.caa.co.uk/docs/33/CAP776.pdf

67. US DOT, 1998.

68. ALPA, 2009.

69. ALPA, 2009: 1.

70. ALPA, 2009: 1.

71. ALPA, 2009: 4.

72. ALPA, 2009: 1.

73. See http://www.usairways.com/en-US/aboutus/pressroom/history/chronology.html

74. CNN. 29 October 2009. *Airliner Crew Flies 150 miles past Airport.* Accessed online on 30 January 2010: http://www.cnn.com/2009/TRAVEL/10/22/airliner.fly.by/index.html

75. CNN. 21 October 2009. *FAA Probes Plane's Landing on Atlanta Airport's Taxiway.* Accessed online on 30 January 2010: http://www.cnn.com/2009/US/10/21/georgia.taxiway.incursion/index.html

76. Associated Press. 13 December 2006. "United and Continental in Merger Talks." *New York Times.*

77. Yu, R. 23 June 2008. "United Flight Canceled when Pilot says He's too upset to Fly." *USA Today*: 3B.

78. NTSB, 2009b: 22.

79. See for example, United States Government Accountability Office (US GAO). March 2002a. *Commercial Aviation: Air Service Trends at Small Communities since October 2000.* Testimony before the Committee on Commerce, Science, and Transportation Subcommittee on Aviation, U.S. Senate (GAO-05-834T). Accessed online on 18 December 2009: http://www.gao.gov/new.items/d05834t.pdf; United States Government Accountability Office (US GAO). July 2002b. *Commercial Aviation: Structural Costs Continue to Challenge Legacy Airlines' Financial Performance.* Report to Congressional Requesters (GAO-02-432). Accessed online on 18 December 2009: http://www.gao.gov/new.items/d02432.pdf; United States Government Accountability Office (US GAO). August 2004. *Commercial Aviation: Legacy Airlines Must Further Reduce Costs to Restore Profitability.* Report to Congressional Committees (GAO-04-836). Accessed online on 18 December 2009: http://www.gao.gov/new.items/d04836.pdf; United States Government Accountability Office (US GAO). July 2005a. *Commercial Aviation: Structural Costs Continue to Challenge Legacy Airlines' Financial Performance.* Testimony Before the Committee on Commerce, Science, and Transportation, Subcommittee on Aviation, U.S. Senate (GAO-05-834T). Accessed online on 30 January 2010: www.gao.gov/new.items/d05834t.pdf; United States Government Accountability Office (US GAO). September 2005b. *Commercial Aviation: Bankruptcy and Pension Problems Are Symptoms of Underlying Structural Issue.* Report to Congressional Committees (GAO-05-945). Accessed online on 18 December 2009: http://www.gao.gov/new.items/d05945.pdf; United States Government Accountability Office (US GAO). June 2006. *Airline Deregulation: Reregulating the Airline Industry Would Likely Reverse Consumer Benefits and Not Save Airline Pensions Structural Costs Continue to Challenge Legacy Airlines' Financial Performance.* Report to Congressional Committees (GAO-06-630). Accessed online on 19 December 2009:http://www.gao.gov/new.items/d06630.pdf;United States Government Accountability Office (US GAO). July 2008. *AIRLINE INDUSTRY: Potential Mergers and Acquisitions Driven by Financial and Competitive Pressures.* Report to the Subcommittee on Aviation Operations, Safety, and Security, Committee on Commerce, Science, and Transportation, U.S. Senate (GAO-08-845). Accessed online on 13 December 2009: http://www.gao.gov/new.

items/do8849.pdf; United States Government Accountability Office (US GAO). April 2009. Commercial Aviation: Airline Industry Contraction Due to Volatile Fuel Prices and Falling Demand Affects Airports, Passengers, and Federal Government Revenues. Report to Congressional Requesters (GAO-09–393). Accessed online on 18 December 2009: http://www.gao.gov/new. items/do9393.pdf

80. US GAO, 2005b: 19 and 27.
81. US GAO, 2005a: 20.
82. Langewiesche, 2009a: 103; 108–9.
83. Sullenberger, 2009a: 188.
84. Sullenberger, 2009a: 138.
85. Accessed online on 7 December 2009: http://www.airdisaster.com/cgi-bin/ aircraft_detail.cgi?aircraft=Airbus+A320
86. Greenhouse, S. 24 February 1990. "India Crash Revives French Dispute Over Safety of Airbus Jet." *New York Times.*
87. Greenhouse, 1990.
88. Accessed online on 7 December 2009: http://www.youtube.com/watch?v= hVZdqqPOgpw
89. Bonneau, B. 1990. "Les Crises De Nerfs De L'a320." *Aeronautique*: 94–101. Accessed online on 6 January 2010: http://catless.ncl.ac.uk/Risks/10.02.html
90. Sullenberger, C. 24 February 2009b. Statement before the Subcommittee on Aviation, Committee on Transportation and Infrastructure, United States House of Representatives. Accessed online on 7 June 2009: http://transpor-tation.house.gov/Media/file/Aviation/20090224/Sullenberger.pdf
91. Langewiesche, 2009a: 22.
92. Sullenberger, 2009b.

CHAPTER 7

1. Festinger, L. and Carlsmith, J. M. 1959. "Cognitive Consequences of Forced Compliance." *Journal of Abnormal and Social Psychology*, 5: 203–10.
2. McKinney, E. H. Jr, Barker, J. R., Davis, K. J. and Smith, D. 2005. "How Swift Starting Action Teams get off the Ground." *Management Communication Quarterly*, 19(2): 198–237.
3. Edmondson, A. C. and Nembhard, I. M. 2009. "Product Development and Learning in Project Teams: The Challenges Are the Benefits." *The Journal of Product Innovation Management*, 26: 123–38.
4. Edmondson and Nembhard, 2009: 124.
5. Kopp, W. 5 July 2009. "Corner Office: Charisma? To Her, It's Overrated." *New York Times*: 2.
6. Rubin, A. J. 21 November 2009. "In Iraq, a Blunt Civilian is a Fixture by the General's Side." *New York Times*: A6.
7. Gant, J. 2009. *One Tribe at a Time: A Strategy for Winning in Afghanistan*. Los Angeles, CA: Nine Sisters Imports, Inc: 35. Accessed online on 16 February

2010: http://blog.stevenpressfield.com/2009/10/one-tribe-at-a-time-4-the-full-document-at-last/

8. Tyson, A. S. 17 January 2010. "Can this Officer Win the War?" *The Washington Post*: B1.

9. See the following for calculation http://www.austintxgensoc.org/calculate-cpi.php accessed on 19 April 2008.

10. Meyer, S. 2008. *The Degradation of Work Revisited: Workers and Technology in the American Auto Industry, 1900–2000.* Accessed online on 1 July 2009: http://www.autolife.umd.umich.edu/Labor/L_Overview/L_Overview8.htm

11. Published in Taylor's monographs *Shop Management* in 1905 and *The Principles of Scientific Management* in 1911.

12. First presented in 1925 before a Bureau of Personnel Administration conference.

13. Follett, M. P. 1996. "The Giving of Orders." In J. M. Shafritz and J. S. Ott (eds) *Classics of Organization Theory*, (4th ed). New York: Harcourt Brace College Publishers: 58.

14. Kline, T. 1999. *Remaking Teams*. San Francisco: Jossey-Bass: 4. Mayo, E. 1933. *The Human Problems of an Industrial Civilization*. New York: The Viking Press: 1.

15. Dicks, H. V. 1970. *Fifty Years of the Tavistock Clinic*. London: Routledge and Kegan Paul. Fraher, A. L. 2004a. *A History of Group Study and Psychodynamic Organizations*. London: Free Association Books. Fraher, A. L. 2004b. Systems Psychodynamics: The Formative Years of an Interdisciplinary Field at the Tavistock Institute. *History of Psychology*, 7(1): 65–84. Fraher, A. L. 2004c. "Flying the Friendly Skies: Why U.S. Commercial Airline Pilots Want To Carry Guns." *Human Relations*, 57(5): 573–95. Harrison, T. 2000. *Bion, Rickman, Foulkes and the Northfield Experiments: Advancing on a different front*. London: Jessica Kingsley Publishers. Trist, E., and Murray, H. (eds). 1993. *The Social Engagement of Social Science: A Tavistock Anthology, Volume II: The Socio-Technical Perspective*. Philadelphia: University of Pennsylvania Press.

16. Jaques, E. 1952. *The Changing Culture of a Factory*. New York: Dryden Press.

17. Trist, E. 1993. "Introduction to Volume II." In E. Trist and H. Murray (eds), *The Social Engagement Of Social Science: A Tavistock Anthology, Volume II: The Socio-Technical Perspective*: 36–60. Philadelphia: University of Pennsylvania Press.

18. Rice, A. K. 1963. *The Enterprise and its Environment*. London: Tavistock Publications.

19. Menzies, I. E. P. 1959. "The Functioning Of Social Systems as a Defense against Anxiety: A Report on a Study of the Nursing Service of a General Hospital." *Human Relations*, 13:95–121.

20. Trist, 1993: 36.

21. Fraher, 2004a, 2004b; Kline 1999: 4
22. Leonhardt, D. 16 April 2008. "Money Doesn't Buy Happiness. Well on Second Thought ..."*New York Times*: C1.
23. Accessed online on 30 March 2008: http://www.managementwisdom.com/weddechofqua.html
24. Leonhardt, 2008: C1.
25. Fraher, A. L. 2005a. "Team Resource Management (TRM): A Tavistock Approach to Leadership in High-Risk Environments." *Organisational and Social Dynamics*, 5(2): 163–182. Fraher, A. L. 2005b. *Group Dynamics in High-Risk Teams: A "Team Resource Management' Primer*. New York: iUniverse Publications. Helmreich, R. L., Merritt, A. C., and Wilhelm, J. A. 1999. "The Evolution Of Crew Resource Management Training In Commercial Aviation." *International Journal of Aviation Psychology*, 9(10): 19–32. Weiner, E. L., Kanki, B. G., and Helmreich, R. L. (eds). 1993. *Cockpit Resource Management*. San Diego: Academic Press.
26. Blake, R. R. and Mouton, J. 1964. *The Managerial Grid*. Houston: Gulf Press. Bradford, L. P., Gibb, J. R., and Benne, K. D. 1964. *T-Group Theory and Laboratory Method*. New York: John Wiley and Sons. Cook, G. N. 1995. "Cockpit Resource Management Training: Are Current Instructional Methods Likely to be Successful?" *The Journal of Aviation/Aerospace Education Research*, 7(2): 26–34.
27. Cook 1995; Fraher, 2005a, 2005b.
28. Goleman, D. 1995. *Emotional Intelligence: Why It Can Matter More Than IQ*. New York: Bantam Books: 34.
29. Cherniss, C. 2000. "Social and Emotional Competence in the Workplace." In R. Bar-On and J. D. A. Parker (eds) *The Handbook of Emotional Intelligence*: 433–58. San Francisco: Jossey-Bass: 434.
30. Goleman, 1995: 34.
31. Goleman, 1995: 34.
32. Mayer, J. D., Salovey, P., and Caruso, D. R. 2000. "Emotional Intelligence as Zeitgeist, as Personality, and as a Mental Ability." In R. Bar-On and J. D. A. Parker (eds) *The Handbook Of Emotional Intelligence*: 92–117. San Francisco: Jossey-Bass: 93.
33. Gladwell, M. 2005. *Blink: The Power of Thinking Without Thinking*. New York: Little, Brown and Company: 10.
34. Gladwell, 2005: 23.
35. Gladwell, 2005: 15.
36. Fraher, 2005b; McKinney et al., 2005.
37. Powell; S. M. and Hill, R. K. 2006. "Home Study Program: My Copilot is a Nurse-Using Crew Resource Management in the Operating Room." *Association of Operating Room Nurses Journal*, 83(1): 178–206.
38. Gaba, D. M. 18 March 2000. "Anaesthesiology as a Model for Patient Safety in Health Care." *British Medical Journal*, 320: 785–88. Helmreich, R. L. 18 March 2000. "On Error Management: Lessons from Aviation." *British*

Medical Journal, 320: 781–5. Sexton, J. B., Thomas, E. J., and Helmreich, R. L. 2000. "Error, Stress and Teamwork in Medicine and Aviation: Cross Sectional Surveys." *British Medical Journal*, 320: 745–9.

39. Guerlain, S., Turrentine, F. E., Bauer, D. T., Calland, J. F., and Adams, R. 2008. "Crew Resource Management Training for Surgeons: Feasibility and Impact." *Cognition, Technology & Work*, 10(4): 255–65.

40. Paton, D. and Flin, R. 1999. "Disaster Stress: An Emergency Management Perspective." *Disaster Prevention and Management*, 8(4): 261–67.

41. Fraher, 2004b.

42. Haller, G., Garnerin, P., Morales, M., Pfister, R., Berner, M., Irion, O., Clergue, F., and Kern, C. 2008. "Effect of Crew Resource Management Training in a Multidisciplinary Obstetrical Setting." *International Journal for Quality in Health Care*, 20(4): 254–64.

43. Makary, M. A., Sexton, J. B., Freischlag, J. A., Holzmueller, C. G., Millman, E. A., Rowen, L., and Pronovost, P. J. 2006. "Operating Room Teamwork among Physicians and Nurses: Teamwork in the Eye of the Beholder." *Journal of American College of Surgeons*, 202(5): 746–52.

44. Flin, R. H. 1995. "Crew Resource Management for Teams in the Offshore Oil Industry." *Journal of European Industrial Training*, 19(9): 23–7.

45. Oriol, M. D. 2006. "Crew Resource Management: Applications in Healthcare Organizations." *Journal of Nursing Administration*, 36(9): 402.

46. McConaughey, E. 2008. "Crew Resource Management in Healthcare: The Evolution of Teamwork Training and MedTeams®." *Journal of Perinatal & Neonatal Nursing*, 22(2): 96.

47. Mearns, K., Flin, R., and O'Connor, P. 2001. "Sharing 'Worlds of Risk'; Improving Communications with Crew Resource Management." *Journal of Risk Research*, 4(4): 377–92.

48. Ashcraft, K. L. 2005. "Resistance through Consent? Occupational Identity, Organizational Form, and the Maintenance of Masculinity Among Commercial Airline Pilots." *Management Communication Quarterly*, 19(1): 67–90. McKinney et al., 2005.

49. Flin, R. H. 1997. "Crew Resource Management for Teams in the Offshore Oil Industry." *Team Performance Management*, 3(2): 121–29. Flin, R., O'Connor, P. and Mearns, K. 2002. "Crew Resource Management: Improving Team Work in High Reliability Industries." *Team Performance Management*, 8(3): 68–78.

50. McGreevy, J., Otten, T., Poggi, M., and Robinson, C. 2006. "The Challenge of Changing Roles and Improving Surgical Care Now: Crew Resource Management Approach." *The American Surgeon*, 72(11): 1082–8.

51. Groopman, J. 2 May 2005. "A Model Patient." *The New Yorker*: 48–54.

52. George, 2002. Robbins, H. A. and Finley, M. 2000. *The New Why Teams Don't Work*. San Francisco: Berrett-Koehler Publishers, Inc.: 6.

53. Helmreich et al., 1999.

54. George, 2002: 157.

55. Dekker, S. W. A. 2005. *Ten Questions about Human Error*, London: Lawrence Erlbaum Associates Publisher: xi.
56. Dekker, 2005: 18.
57. Dekker, 2005: 24.
58. Tucker, A. L., Edmondson, A. C., and Spear, S. 2002. "When Problem Solving Prevents Organizational Learning." *Journal of Organizational Change Management*, 15(2): 122–37.
59. Wilson, K. A., Salas, E., Priest, H. A., and Andrews, D. April 2007. "Errors in the Heat of Battle: Taking a Closer Look at Shared Cognition Breakdowns through Teamwork." *Human Factors*, 49(2): 8.
60. Wilson et al., 2007.
61. Crossan, M., Lane, H., and White, R. 1999. "An Organizational learning Framework: From Intuition to Institution." *Academy of Management Review*, 24: 522–37. Edmondson, A. C. 2002. "The Local and Variegated Nature of Learning in Organizations: A Group Level Perspective." *Organization Science*, 13: 128–46.
62. Detert, J. R. and Edmondson, A. C. 2006. *Everyday Failures in Organizational Learning: Explaining the High Threshold for Speaking Up at Work*: 4. Accessed online on 3 July 2009: http://www.hbs.edu/units/tom/docs/detert-edmondson.pdf
63. Edmondson, A. C. 2003. "Speaking up in the Operating Room: How Team Leaders Promote Learning in Interdisciplinary Action Teams." *Journal of Management Studies* 40(6): 1419–52.
64. Edmondson, A., Bohmer, R., and Pisano, G. 2004. "Speeding Up Team Learning." In *Harvard Business Review on Teams That Succeed*: 77–98. Boston: Harvard Business School Publishing.
65. Bowers, C., Salas, E., and Jentsch, F. (eds). 2006. *Creating High-Tech Teams*. Washington DC: American Psychological Association: 4.
66. Bowers et al., 2006: 5.
67. Krause, 2003: 3.
68. Nembhard, I. M. and Edmondson, A. C. 2006. "Making It Safe: The Effects of Leader Inclusiveness and Professional Status on Psychological Safety and Improvement Efforts in Health Care Teams." *Journal of Organizational Behaviour*, 27: 947–8.
69. United Airlines. 2003. *Flight Operations Manual*: 36.20.7
70. Kanki, B. G. and Palmer, M. T. 1993. "Communication and Crew Resource Management." In Earl L. Weiner, Barbara G. Kanki and Robert L. Helmreich (eds) *Cockpit Resource Management*. San Diego: Academic Press: 112.
71. Weick, K. E. and Sutcliffe, K. M. 2001. *Managing the Unexpected*. San Francisco: Jossey-Bass.: 9.
72. Fraher, 2005b: 83–4.
73. National Transportation Safety Board (NTSB). 2001. Collision between the U.S. Navy Submarine USS *Greeneville* and Japanese Motor Vessel *Ehime Maru* near Oahu, Hawaii (Report number: NTSB/DCA-01-MM-022).

Coen interview: 34. Accessed online on 22 April 2010: http://www.ntsb.gov/publictn/2005/MAB0501.pdf

74. See www.amazon.com.
75. Federal Aviation Administration (FAA). 2004. *Crew Resource Management Training* (AC 120–51E): 4. Accessed online 4 May 2010: http://rgl.faa.gov/REGULATORY_AND_GUIDANCE_LIBRARY/RGADVISORYCIRCULAR.NSF/0/80038cf51aace53686256e24005cbb23/$FILE/AC120–51e.PDF
76. Perrow, C. 1984. *Normal Accidents: Living with High-Risk Technologies*. New York: Basic Books: 257.
77. Reason, J. 1990. *Human Error*. Cambridge: Cambridge University Press: 217.
78. Belkin, L. 3 April 2008. "Dilbert the Inquisitor." *New York Times*: E1.
79. Accessed online on 16 April 2008: http://www.myersbriggs.org/
80. Tuckman, B. and Jensen, M. 1977. "Stages of Small Group Development Revisited." *Group and Organizational Studies*, 2: 419–27. Levi, D. 2001. *Group Dynamics for Teams*. Thousand Oaks: Sage: 41.
81. Merritt, A. and Klinect, J. 2006. *Defensive Flying for Pilots: An Introduction to Threat and Error Management*. The University of Texas Human Factors Research Project: The LOSA Collaborative: 10. Accessed online on 16 February 2010: http://homepage.psy.utexas.edu/HomePage/Group/HelmreichLAB/Publications/pubfiles/TEM.Paper.12.6.06.pdf
82. National Transportation Safety Board (NTSB). 1987. Continental Airlines Flight 1713 (Report number: NTSB/AAR-88/09): 38. Accessed online on 25 March 2010: http://libraryonline.erau.edu/online-full-text/ntsb/aircraft-accident-reports/AAR88–09.pdf
83. Sullenberger, C. 24 February 2009b. Statement before the Subcommittee on Aviation, Committee on Transportation and Infrastructure, United States House of Representatives. Accessed online on 7 June 2009: http://transportation.house.gov/Media/file/Aviation/20090224/Sullenberger.pdf
84. Hirschhorn, L. 1988. *The Workplace Within: Psychodynamics of Organizational Life*. Cambridge, MA: The MIT Press. Gabriel, Y. 1999. *Organizations in Depth*. Thousand Oaks, CA: Sage: 225.
85. Robertson, C. H. 2004. "Teaching Pilots Judgment, Decision-Making, & Critical Thinking." *International Journal of Applied Aviation Studies*, 4(2): 206.

BIBLIOGRAPHY

Air and Space Smithsonian. 18 February 2009. *Interview with Captain Sullenberger: Sully's Tale.* Accessed online 2 May 2009: http://www.airspacemag.com/flight-today/Sullys-Tale.html

Air Line Pilots Association (ALPA). September 2009. *Producing a Professional Airline Pilot: Candidate Screening, Hiring, Training, and Mentoring.* Air Line Pilots Association White Paper. Accessed online on 1 January 2010: http://www.alpa.org/portals/alpa/pressroom/inthecockpit/ProducingProfessionalPilot_9-2009.pdf

Air Safety Week. 25 October 2004a. *American Airlines Tries to Pin Blame on Design Defect.* Accessed online 25 June 2010: http://findarticles.com/p/articles/mi_m0UBT/is_41_18/ai_n6284079/

Air Safety Week. 25 October 2004b. *Pilot Training Concerns Raised Before Flight 587 Crash.* Accessed online on 5 December 2008: http://findarticles.com/p/articles/mi_m0UBT/is_/ai_n6284080

Armstrong, D. 2005. *Organization in the Mind.* London: Karnac Books.

Armstrong, G. 1994. "False Leeds." In R. Guilianotti and J. Williams (eds) *Game Without Frontiers.* London: Avebury.

1998. *Football Hooligans: Knowing the Score.* London: Berg.

Ashcraft, K. L. 2005. "Resistance through Consent? Occupational Identity, Organizational Form, and the Maintenance of Masculinity Among Commercial Airline Pilots." *Management Communication Quarterly,* 19(1): 67–90.

Associated Press. 13 December 2006. "United and Continental in Merger Talks." *New York Times.*

Associated Press. 18 April 2008. "New Jersey Weighs Building Another Nuclear Plant, First Since 1973." *New York Times:* C14.

Bailey, J. 9 April 2008. "American Canceling More Flights for Inspection." *New York Times.*

Bayers, P. L. 2003. *Imperial Ascent: Mountaineering, Masculinity, and Empire.* Colorado: Rocky Mountain Press.

BBC News. 8 June 1998. *Our Rights Were Ignored.* Accessed online on 1 July 2009: http://news.bbc.co.uk/2/hi/special_report/1998/05/98/the_bristol_heart_babies/105918.stm

Belkin, L. 3 April 2008. "Dilbert the Inquisitor." *New York Times*: E1–2.

Belli, E., Lacour-Gayet, F., Serraf, A., Alkhulaifi, A. M., Touchot, A., Bruniaux, J., and Planche, C. 1999. "Surgical Management Of Transposition Of Great Arteries Associated With Multiple Ventricular Septal Defects." *European Journal of Cardio-Thoracic Surgery*, 16(1): 14–20. Accessed on 27 March 2009: http://cat.inist.fr/?aModele=afficheN&cpsidt=1895532

Billings, C. E. 1996. *Aviation Automation: The Search for a Human-Centered Approach.* Hillsdale, NJ: Erlbaum.

Bing, D. 2007. *Crowding Out the Space: The Weakness of a Strong Leader.* Philadelphia: Center for Applied Research. Accessed online on 28 May 2009: http://www.ispso.org/Bing2007BridgerPaper.pdf

Bion, W. 1961. *Experiences in Groups.* New York: Basic Books.

Blake, R. R. and Mouton, J. 1964. *The Managerial Grid.* Houston: Gulf Press.

Boeing . *Boeing Statistical Summary Commercial Jet Airplanes Accidents Worldwide.* Accessed on 20 January 2009: http://www.boeing.com/news/techissues/pdf/statsum.pdf

Bogner, M. S. 1994. *Human Error in Medicine.* Hillside NJ: Lawrence Erlbaum and Associates.

Bonneau, B. 1990. Les Crises De Nerfs De L'a320. *Aeronautique*: 94–101. Accessed on 6 January 2010: http://catless.ncl.ac.uk/Risks/10.02.html

Boorstin, D. J. 1987. *The Image: A Guide to Pseudo-Events in America.* New York: Atheneum.

Boukreev, A. and De Walt, G. W. 1997. *The Climb: Tragic Ambitions on Everest.* New York: St Martin's Press.

Bowers, C ., Salas, E ., and Jentsch, F . (eds). 2006. *Creating High-Tech Teams.* Washington DC: American Psychological Association.

Bradford, L. P., Gibb, J. R., and Benne, K. D. 1964. *T-Group Theory and Laboratory Method.* New York: John Wiley and Sons.

Branch, J. 15 September 2006. "Putting All the Elements Together." *New York Times*: C12.

Braun, E. and Macdonald, S. 1978. *Revolution in Miniature.* Cambridge: Cambridge University Press.

Brimson, D. 2007. *March of the Hooligans: Soccer's Bloody Fraternity.* New York: Virgin Books.

Broder, J. M. 29 July 2005. "Police Chiefs Moving to Share Terror Data." *New York Times*: A12.

Buford, B. 1991. *Among the Thugs.* London: W. W. Norton & Company.

Card, D. July 1996. "Deregulation and Labor Earnings in the Airline Industry." *NBER Working Paper 5687*.

Card, S. K., Moran, T. P., and Newell, A. 1983. *The Psychology of Human-Centered Approach*. Hillsdale, NJ: Erlbaum.

Cessna Aircraft Company. 1978. *Cessna-152 Information Manual*.

Cherniss, C. 2000. "Social and Emotional Competence in the Workplace." In R. Bar-On and J. D. A. Parker (eds) *The Handbook of Emotional Intelligence*: 433–58. San Francisco: Jossey-Bass.

Civil Aviation Authority (CAA). 21 July 2008. *Global Fatal Accident Review 1997–2006*. United Kingdom Safety Regulation Group (CAP 776). Accessed online on 6 January 2010: http://www.caa.co.uk/docs/33/CAP776.pdf

COMPANY NEWS. 2 June 2004. "F.A.A. Fines American and Boeing $3.3 Million." *New York Times*.

CNN. 31 December 2007. *Report Containing Thousands of Pilot Complaints is Released*. Accessed online on 20 January 2009: http://www.cnn.com/2007/TECH/space/12/31/nasa.airsafety/index.html

CNN. 21 October 2009. *FAA Probes Plane's Landing on Atlanta Airport's Taxiway*. Accessed online on 30 January 2010: http://www.cnn.com/2009/US/10/21/georgia.taxiway.incursion/index.html

CNN. 29 October 2009. *Airliner Crew Flies 150 miles past Airport*. Accessed online on 30 January 2010: http://www.cnn.com/2009/TRAVEL/10/22/airliner.fly.by/index.html

Cook, G. N. 1995. "Cockpit Resource Management Training: Are Current Instructional Methods Likely to be Successful?" *The Journal of Aviation/Aerospace Education Research*, 7(2): 26–34.

Couric, K. 2009a. Interview on *60 minutes*. "Flight 1549: A Routine Takeoff Turns Ugly." Accessed online on 30 April 2009: http://www.cbsnews.com/stories/2009/02/08/60minutes/main4783580.shtml

2009b. Interview on *60 minutes*. "Saving 155 Souls in Minutes the Entire US Airways Crew Recalls the Dramatic Evacuation and Aftermath." Accessed online on 30 April 2009: http://www.cbsnews.com/stories/2009/02/08/60minutes/main4783586.shtml

Crémieux P. January 1996. "The Effect of Deregulation on Employee Earnings: Pilots, Flight Attendants, and Mechanics, 1959–1992." *Industrial and Labor Relations Review*, 49(2).

Crossan, M., Lane, H., and White, R. 1999. "An Organizational learning Framework: From Intuition to Institution." *Academy of Management Review*, 24: 522–37.

Darby, R. August 2006. Commercial Jet Hull Losses, Fatalities Rose Sharply in 2005. *Aviation Safety Week*: 51–2. Accessed online on 20 January 2009: http://www.flightsafety.org/asw/aug06/asw_aug06.pdf

Dekker, S. W. A. 2005. *Ten Questions about Human Error*. London: Lawrence Erlbaum Associates Publisher.

Detert, J. R. and Edmondson, A. C. 2006. *Everyday Failures in Organizational Learning: Explaining the High Threshold for Speaking Up at Work*. Accessed online on 3 July 2009: http://www.hbs.edu/units/tom/docs/detert-edmondson.pdf

Dicks, H. V. 1970. *Fifty Years of the Tavistock Clinic*. London: Routledge and Kegan Paul.

Dismukes, R. K. 2001. *Rethinking Crew Error: Overview of Panel Session*. Research and Technology Report. Moffett Field, CA: NASA Ames Research Center.

Douglas, J. A. August 2006. "Editorial Page: Not Good Enough." *Aviation Safety World*: 5. Accessed online on 20 January 2009: http://www.flight-safety.org/asw/aug06/asw_aug06.pdf

Dubner, S. J. 6 October 2001. "Looking for Heroes – and Finding Them." *New York Times*.

Dwyer, J. 17 January 2009. "Old Hands on the River Didn't Have to Be Told What to Do." *New York Times*: A17.

Edmondson, A. C. 1996. "Learning from Mistakes Is Easier Said than Done." *Journal of Applied Behavioral Science*, 32(1): 5–28.

2002. "The Local and Variegated Nature of Learning in Organizations: A Group Level Perspective." *Organization Science*, 13: 128–46.

2003. "Speaking up in the Operating Room: How Team Leaders Promote Learning in Interdisciplinary Action Teams." *Journal of Management Studies* 40(6): 1419–52.

Edmondson, A., Bohmer, R., and Pisano, G. 2004. "Speeding Up Team Learning." In *Harvard Business Review on Teams That Succeed*: 77–98. Boston: Harvard Business School Publishing.

Edmondson, A. C. and Nembhard, I. M. 2009. "Product Development and Learning in Project Teams: The Challenges Are the Benefits." *The Journal of Product Innovation Management*, 26: 123–38.

Edwards, E. 1988. "Introductory Overview." In E. L. Weiner and D. C. Nagel (eds) *Human Factors in Aviation*: 1–24. San Diego: Academic Press.

Elmes, M. and Barry, D. 1999. "Deliverance, Denial, and the Death Zone: A Study of Narcissism and Regression in the May 1996 Everest Climbing Disaster. *Journal of Applied Behavioral Science*, 35: 163–87.

Federal Aviation Administration (FAA). 1996. *Challenge 2000*. Recommendations for Future Aviation Safety Regulation. Accessed online on 23 November 2008: http://www.nexacap.com/press_releases/C2000_final.pdf

Federal Aviation Administration (FAA), 1998. *Air Traffic Control Handbook*. Accessed online on 23 April 2010: http://avstop.com/ac/atc/index. html

Federal Aviation Administration (FAA). 1999. *Flight Instructor Handbook*. Accessed online on 23 January 2009: http://www.faa.gov/library/ manuals/aviation/media/FAA-H-8083-9.pdf

Federal Aviation Administration (FAA). 2004. *Crew Resource Management Training* (AC 120–51E): 4. Accessed online 4 May 2010: http:// rgl.faa.gov/REGULATORY_AND_GUIDANCE_LIBRARY/ RGADVISORYCIRCULAR.NSF/0/80038cf51aace53686256e24005cbb 23/$FILE/AC120–51e.PDF

Festinger, L. and Carlsmith, J. M. 1959. "Cognitive Consequences of Forced Compliance." *Journal of Abnormal and Social Psychology*, 5: 203–10.

Finn, G. 1994. "Football Violence – A Societal Psychological Perspective." In R. Giulianotti et al. (eds) *Football, Violence and Social Identity*: 90–127. London: Routledge.

Fishwick, N. 1989. *English Football and Society, 1910–1950*. Manchester: Manchester University Press.

Flin, R. H. 1995. "Crew Resource Management for Teams in the Offshore Oil Industry." *Journal of European Industrial Training*, 19(9): 23–7.

1996. *Sitting in the Hot Seat: Leaders and Teams for Critical Incident Management*. New York: John Wiley & Sons.

1997. "Crew Resource Management for Teams in the Offshore Oil Industry." *Team Performance Management*, 3(2): 121–29.

Flin, R., O'Connor, P. and Mearns, K. 2002. "Crew Resource Management: Improving Team Work in High Reliability Industries." *Team Performance Management*, 8(3): 68–78.

Follett, M. P. 1996. "The Giving of Orders." In J. M. Shafritz and J. S. Ott (eds) *Classics of Organization Theory* (4th ed). New York: Harcourt Brace College Publishers.

Fraher, A. L. 2004a. "Systems Psychodynamics: The Formative Years of an Interdisciplinary Field at the Tavistock Institute." *History of Psychology*, 7(1): 65–84.

2004b. "Flying the Friendly Skies: Why U.S. Commercial Airline Pilots Want To Carry Guns." *Human Relations*, 57(5): 573–95.

2004c. *A History of Group Study and Psychodynamic Organizations*. London: Free Association Books.

2005a. "Team Resource Management (TRM): A Tavistock Approach to Leadership in High-Risk Environments." *Organisational and Social Dynamics*, 5(2): 163–82.

2005b. *Group Dynamics in High-Risk Teams: A "Team Resource Management" Primer*. New York: iUniverse Publications.

Frankel, A. S., Leonard, M. W., and Denham, C. R. 2006. "Fair and Just Culture, Team Behavior, and Leadership Engagement." *Health Research and Educational Trust*, 41(4): 1690–709.

Frosdick, S. and Marsh, P. 2005. *Football Hooliganism*. Devon, UK: Willan Publishing.

Gaal, S. T. and Husain, A. 2008. *Large Regional Jets – The Next Battleground*. Accessed online 5 Janaury 2010: http://www.skyworkscapital.com/regionaljets.pdf

Gaba, D. M. 18 March 2000. "Anaesthesiology as a Model for Patient Safety in Health Care." *British Medical Journal*; 320: 785–88.

Gabriel, Y. 1999. *Organizations in Depth*. Thousand Oaks, CA: Sage.

Gant, J. 2009. *One Tribe at a Time: A Strategy for Winning in Afghanistan*. Los Angeles, CA: Nine Sisters Imports, Inc. Accessed online 16 February 2010: http://blog.stevenpressfield.com/2009/10/one-tribe-at-a-time-4-the-full-document-at-last/

Garvin, D. A. Edmondson, A. C., and Francesca Gino, F. 2008. "Is Yours a Learning Organization?" *Harvard Business Review*, 86(3): 109–16.

Gawande, A. 2007. *Better: A Surgeon's Notes on Performance*. New York: Picador Books.

Gemmill, G. and Oakley, J. "Leadership: An Alienating Social Myth." In K. Grint (ed) *Leadership: Classic, Contemporary, and Critical Approaches*: 272–88. Oxford: Oxford University Press.

George, M. L. 2002. *Lean Six Sigma*. New York: McGraw-Hill.

Gilpin, D. R. and Murphy, P. J. 2008. *Crisis Management in a Complex World*. Oxford: Oxford University Press.

Gladwell, M. 2005. *Blink: The Power of Thinking Without Thinking*. New York: Little, Brown and Company.

2008. *Outliers: The Story of Success*. New York: Little, Brown and Company.

Glater, J. D. 31 October 31 2007. "Training Law Students for Real-Life Careers." *New York Times*: A22.

Goleman, D. 1995. *Emotional Intelligence: Why It Can Matter More Than IQ*. New York: Bantam Books.

1998. *Working With Emotional Intelligence*. New York: Bantam Books.

Gore, A. 1996. White House Commission on Aviation Safety and Security: Final Report to President Clinton. Accessed online on 23 November 2008: http://www.fas.org/irp/threat/212fin~1.html

Greenhouse, S. 24 February 1990. "India Crash Revives French Dispute Over Safety of Airbus Jet." *New York Times*.

Gregory, J. 2003. *Sicken: The True Story of a Lost Childhood*. London: Century

Groopman, J. 2 May 2005. "A Model Patient." *The New Yorker*: 48–54.

Guerlain, S., Turrentine, F. E., Bauer, D. T., Calland, J. F., and Adams, R. 2008. "Crew Resource Management Training for Surgeons: Feasibility and Impact." *Cognition, Technology & Work*, 10(4): 255–65.

Hall, J. 25 June 1996. Chairman National Transportation Safety Board testimony before the Committee on Transportation and Infrastructure, Subcommittee on Aviation, House of Representatives. Accessed online on 30 November 2008 http://www.ntsb.gov/Speeches/former/hall/jh960625.htm

Haller, G., Garnerin, P., Morales, M., Pfister, R., Berner, M. Irion, O., Clergue, F., and Kern, C. 2008. "Effect of Crew Resource Management Training in a Multidisciplinary Obstetrical Setting." *International Journal for Quality in Health Care*, 20(4): 254–64.

Harrison, T. 2000. *Bion, Rickman, Foulkes and the Northfield Experiments: Advancing on a different front*. London: Jessica Kingsley Publishers.

Heckscher, C. 2007. *The Collaborative Enterprise: Managing Speed and Complexity in Knowledge-Based Business*. New Haven: Yale University Press.

Heightman, A. J. 15 January 2009. "Airplane Crash Showcases Emergency Readiness." *Journal of Emergency Medical Services*. Accessed online on 3 May 2009: http://www.jems.com/news_and_articles/columns/Heightman/airplane_crash_showcases_emergency_readiness.html;jsessionid=FEFF88436DD201F3E0A501172810D9BF

Helmreich, R. L. 18 March 2000. "On Error Management: Lessons from Aviation." *British Medical Journal*, 320: 781–5.

Helmreich, R. L. and Foushee, C. 1993. "Why Crew Resource Management? Empirical and Theoretical Bases of Human Factors Training in Aviation." In E. L. Wiener, B. G. Kanki, and R. L. Helmreich (eds) *Cockpit Resource Management*: 1–41. San Diego: Academic Press.

Helmreich, R. L. and Merritt, A. C. 1998. *Culture at Work in Aviation and Medicine*. Aldershot, UK: Ashgate Publishing.

Helmreich, R. L., Merritt, A. C., and Wilhelm, J. A. 1999. "The Evolution of Crew Resource Management Training in Commercial Aviation." *International Journal of Aviation Psychology*, 9(10): 19–32.

Helmreich, R. L. and Musson, D. M. 2000. "Surgery as Team Endeavour." *Canadian Journal of Anesthesia*, 47: 391–2.

Hirsch and Macpherson. January 2000. "Earnings, Rents, and Competition in the Airline Labor Market." *Journal of Labor Economics*, 18(1): 125–55.

Hirschhorn, L. 1988. *The Workplace Within: Psychodynamics of Organizational Life*. Cambridge, MA: The MIT Press.

1997. *Reworking Authority: Leading and Following in the Post-Modern Organization*. Cambridge, MA: The MIT Press.

Hirschhorn, L. and Young, D. R. 1993. "Psychodynamics of Safety." In L. Hirschhorn and C. K. Barnett (eds) *The Psychodynamics of Organizations*: 143–65. Philadelphia: Temple University Press.

Ho, C. B., Oh, K. B., Pech, R. J., Durden, G., and Slade, B. 2009. *Crisis Decision Making*. New York: Nova Science Publishers Inc.

Jaques, E. 1952. *The Changing Culture of a Factory*. New York: Dryden Press.

Jentsch, F., Barnett, J., Bowers, C. A., and Salas, E. 1999. "Who Is Flying This Plane Anyway? What Mishaps Tell Us About Crew Member Role Assignment and Air Crew Situation Awareness." *Human Factors*, 41(1): 1–14.

Jones, K. 2006. *The Making of Social Policy in Britain: From the Poor Law to New Labour*. London: Continuum International Publishing Group.

Kanki, B. G. and Palmer, M. T. 1993. "Communication and Crew Resource Management." In E. L. Weiner, B. G. Kanki, and R. L. Helmreich (eds) *Cockpit Resource Management*: 99–136. San Diego: Academic Press.

Kayes, D. C. 2002. "Dilemma at 29,000 feet: An Exercise in Ethical Decision Making Based on the 1996 Mt Everest Disaster." *Journal of Management Education*, 26: 307–21.

2004. "The 1996 Mount Everest Climbing Disaster: The Breakdown of Learning in Teams." *Human Relations*, 57(10): 1263–84.

2006. *Destructive Goal Pursuit: The Mt Everest Disaster*. Basingstoke: Palgrave Macmillan.

Kennedy, I. July 2001. *The Report of the Public Inquiry into Children's Heart Surgery at Bristol Royal Infirmary 1984–1995*. Presented to Parliament by the Secretary of State for Health by Command of Her Majesty.

Kern, T. 2001. *Controlling Pilot Error: Culture, Environment, & CRM*. New York: McGraw-Hill.

Klein, G., Orasanu, J., Calderwood, R., and Zsambok, C. (eds.) 1993. *Decision-making in Action*. New York: Ablex.

Kline, T. 1999. *Remaking Teams*. San Francisco: Jossey-Bass.

Kopp, W. 5 July 2009. "Corner Office: Charisma? To Her, It's Overrated." *New York Times*: 2.

Krause, S. S. 2003. *Aircraft Safety: Accident Investigations, Analyses and Applications* (2nd Ed.). New York: McGraw-Hill.

Langewiesche, W. 2009a. *Fly By Wire: The Geese, the Glide, the Miracle on the Hudson*. New York: Farrar, Straus and Giroux.

June 2009b. "Anatomy of a Miracle." *Vanity Fair*: 82–91.

Langley, A. 1999. "Strategies for Theorizing from Process Data." *Academy of Management Review*, 24(4): 691–710.

Last, S. and Adler, M. 1991. *British Airways Airbus A-320 Pilots' Autothrust Survey*. (SAE tech paper 912225). Warrendale, PA: Society of Automotive Engineers.

Lavin, C. H. 11 January 1989. "Pilots Scarce, Airlines See 30-year-olds as Captains." *New York Times*.

Leonhardt, D. 16 April 2008. "Money Doesn't Buy Happiness. Well on Second Thought…." *New York Times:* C1.

Levi, D. 2001. *Group Dynamics for Teams*. Thousand Oaks: Sage.

Levinson, N. G. 2009. "The Need for New Paradigms in Safety Engineering." In C. Dale and T. Anderson (eds) *Safety-Critical Systems: Problems, Process and Practice*: 3–22. London: Springer-Verlag.

Lewis, G. 2006. *Organizational Crisis Management: The Human Factor*. New York: Auerbach Publications.

Liebman J., Cullum L., and Belloc N. 1969. "Natural History of Transposition of the Great Arteries: Anatomy and Birth and Death Characteristics." *Circulation*, 40: 237–62.

Long, S. 2008. *The Perverse Organisation and Its Deadly Sins*. London: Karnac Books.

Lowy, J. 24 February 2009. "Controller Thought Plane That Ditched Was Doomed." *Associated Press*. Accessed online on 2 May 2009: http://www.abcnews.go.com/Politics/wireStory?id=6944354

Makary, M. A., Sexton, J. B., Freischlag, J. A., Holzmueller, C. G., Millman, E. A., Rowen, L., and Pronovost, P. J. 2006. "Operating Room Teamwork among Physicians and Nurses: Teamwork in the Eye of the Beholder." *Journal of American College of Surgeons*, 202(5): 746–52.

Margaret Thatcher Foundation. 23 September 1987. "Interview for Woman's Own ("no such thing as society") with journalist Douglas Keay." Accessed online on 27 March 2008: http://www.margaretthatcher.org/speeches/displaydocument.asp?docid=106689

Martins, P. and Castela, E. 2008. "Transposition of the Great Arteries." *Orphanet Journal of Rare Diseases*, 3: 27. Accessed online on 27 March 2009: http://www.pubmedcentral.nih.gov/articlerender.fcgi?artid=2577629#B50

Maurino, D. E. 1999. "Safety Prejudices, Training Practices, and CRM: A Midpoint Perspective." *The International Journal of Aviation Psychology*, 9(4): 413–22.

Mayer, J. D., Salovey, P., and Caruso, D. R. 2000. "Emotional Intelligence as Zeitgeist, as Personality, and as a Mental Ability." In R. Bar-On and J. D. A. Parker (eds) *The Handbook Of Emotional Intelligence*: 92–117. San Francisco: Jossey-Bass.

Mayo, E. 1933. *The Human Problems of an Industrial Civilization*. New York: The Viking Press.

McConaughey, E. 2008. "Crew Resource Management in Healthcare: The Evolution of Teamwork Training and MedTeams®." *Journal of Perinatal & Neonatal Nursing*, 22(2): 96.

McFadden, R. D. 16 January 2009. "All 155 Aboard Safe as Crippled Jet Crash-Lands in Hudson: For Terrified Survivors, a Miracle." *New York Times*: A24.

McGreevy, J ., Otten, T., Poggi, M., and Robinson, C. 2006. "The Challenge of Changing Roles and Improving Surgical Care Now: Crew Resource Management Approach." *The American Surgeon,* 72(11): 1082–8.

McKinney, E. H. Jr, Barker, J. R., Davis, K. J., and Smith, D. 2005. "How Swift Starting Action Teams get off the Ground." *Management Communication Quarterly*, 19(2): 198–237.

Mearns, K., Flin, R., and O'Connor, P. 2001. "Sharing 'Worlds of Risk'; Improving Communications with Crew Resource Management." *Journal of Risk Research*, 4(4): 377–92.

Meister, D. 2003. "The Editor's Comments." *Human Factors and Ergonomics Society COTG Digest* 5: 2–6.

Menzies, I. E. P. 1959. "The Functioning Of Social Systems as a Defense against Anxiety: A Report on a Study of the Nursing Service of a General Hospital." *Human Relations*, 13: 95–121.

Merritt, A. and Klinect, J. 2006. *Defensive Flying for Pilots: An Introduction to Threat and Error Management.* The University of Texas Human Factors Research Project: The LOSA Collaborative. Accessed online on 16 February 2010: http://homepage.psy.utexas.edu/HomePage/Group/ HelmreichLAB/Publications/pubfiles/TEM.Paper.12.6.06.pdf

Meyer, S. 2008. *The Degradation of Work Revisited: Workers and Technology in the American Auto Industry, 1900–2000.* Accessed online on 1 July 2009: http://www.autolife.umd.umich.edu/Labor/L_Overview/ L_Overview8.htm

Miller, E. 1993. *From Dependency to Autonomy: Studies in Organization and Change.* London: Free Association Books.

Murphy, P. Williams, J., and Dunning, E. 1990. *Football on Trial: Spectator Violence and Development in the Football World.* London: Routledge.

National Transportation Safety Board (NTSB). 1978. Southern Airways Flight 242 (Report number: NTSB/AAR-78/03). Accessed online on 22 April 2010: http://libraryonline.erau.edu/online-full-text/ntsb/aircraft-accident-reports/AAR78-03.pdf

National Transportation Safety Board (NTSB). 1987. Continental Airlines Flight 1713 (Report number: NTSB/AAR-88/09). Accessed online on 25 March 2010: http://libraryonline.erau.edu/online-full-text/ntsb/ aircraft-accident-reports/AAR88-09.pdf

National Transportation Safety Board (NTSB). 1990, United Airlines Flight 232 (Report number: NTSB/AAR-90/06). Accessed online on 22 April 2010: http://libraryonline.erau.edu/online-full-text/ntsb/aircraft-accident-reports/AAR90–06.pdf

National Transportation Safety Board (NTSB). 1991. USAir Flight 1493 and Skywest Flight 5569 collision (Report number: NTSB/AAR-91/08). Accessed online on 3 January 2010: http://libraryonline.erau.edu/online-full-text/ntsb/aircraft-accident-reports/AAR91–08.pdf

National Transportation Safety Board (NTSB). 1993a. GP Express Airlines Flight 861. (Report number: NTSB/AAR-93/03). Accessed online on 25 March 2010: http://libraryonline.erau.edu/online-full-text/ntsb/aircraft-accident-reports/AAR93–03.pdf

National Transportation Safety Board (NTSB). 1993b. Scenic Air Tours Flight 22. (Report number: NTSB/AAR-93/01). Accessed online on 25 March 2010: http://libraryonline.erau.edu/online-full-text/ntsb/aircraft-accident-reports/AAR93–01.pdf

National Transportation Safety Board (NTSB). 1994a. GP Express Airlines N115GP. (Report number: NTSB/AAR-94/01). Accessed online on 25 March 2010: http://libraryonline.erau.edu/online-full-text/ntsb/aircraft-accident-summaries/AAR94–01S.pdf

National Transportation Safety Board (NTSB). 1994b. *Safety Study: A Review of Flight-Crew Involved, Major Accidents of U.S. Air Carriers, 1978 through 1990*. Washington DC (NTSB No. PB 94–917001).

National Transportation Safety Board (NTSB). 2001. Collision between the U.S. Navy Submarine USS *Greeneville* and Japanese Motor Vessel *Ehime Maru* near Oahu, Hawaii (Report number: NTSB/DCA-01-MM-022). Accessed online on 22 April 2010: http://www.ntsb.gov/publictn/2005/MAB0501.pdf

National Transportation Safety Board (NTSB). 2002. Cessna 310 crash in San Dimas CA. (Report number: NTSB/ LAX02FA214). Accessed online on 25 April 2010: http://www.ntsb.gov/ntsb/GenPDF.asp?id=LAX02FA214&rpt=fa

National Transportation Safety Board (NTSB). 2004. American Airlines Flight 587. (Report number: NTSB/AAR-04/04). Accessed online on 25 March 2010: http://libraryonline.erau.edu/online-full-text/ntsb/aircraft-accident-reports/AAR04–04.pdf

National Transportation Safety Board (NTSB). 2009a. *Operations/Human Performance Group Chairmen Interview Summaries – Flight Crew* (Docket No. SA-532; Exhibit No. 2-B) Washington DC. Accessed online on 13 June 2009: http://www.ntsb.gov/Dockets/Aviation/DCA09MA026/418999.pdf

National Transportation Safety Board (NTSB). 2009b. *US Airways Flight 1549: Group Chairman's Factual Report of Investigation Cockpit Voice Recorder*. (Docket No. SA-532; Exhibit No. 12) Washington DC (DCA09MA026). Accessed online on 30 January 2010: http://ntsb.gov/dockets/aviation/dca09ma026/420526.pdf

National Transportation Safety Board (NTSB). 2009c. *US Airways Flight 1549: Preliminary Report* (Report number: DCA09MA026). Accessed online 2 May 2009: http://www.ntsb.gov/ntsb/GenPDF.asp?id=DCA09MA026&rpt=p

National Transportation Safety Board (NTSB). 2009d. *US Airways Flight 1549: Attachment 1 Photographs*. Washington DC (Report number: CA09MA026). Accessed online on 25 June 2010: http://www.ntsb.gov/Dockets/Aviation/DCA09MA026/423126.pdf

National Transportation Safety Board (NTSB). 2009e. *US Airways Flight 1549: Attachment 4 Photographs*. (Docket No. SA-532; Exhibit No. 6E) Washington DC (Report number: DCA09MA026). Accessed online on 25 June 2010: http://www.ntsb.gov/Dockets/Aviation/DCA09MA026/420144.pdf

Nembhard, I. M. and Edmondson, A. C. 2006. "Making It Safe: The Effects of Leader Inclusiveness and Professional Status on Psychological Safety and Improvement Efforts in Health Care Teams." *Journal of Organizational Behaviour*, 27: 941–66.

Neumann, J. E. 1999. "Systems Psychodynamics in the Service of Political Organizational Change." In R. French & R. Vince (Eds.), *Group Relations, Management, and Organization*: 54–69. Oxford: Oxford University Press.

New York Times. 22 November 1987. "F.A.A Begins Review of Standards for Pilots." *New York Times*.

New York Times. 15 February 1997. "Making Air Travel Safer." *New York Times*.

New York Times. 2 June 2004. "F.A.A. Fines American and Boeing $3.3 Million." *New York Times*.

Norman, D. A. 1990. "The 'Problem' with Automation: Inappropriate Feedback and Interaction, not 'Over-Automation.'" *Philosophical Transactions of the Royal Society of London*, 327: 585–93.

Norris, G. 8 October 2007. "An Overview of Supersonic Flight." *Aviation Week*.

O' Hara, J. M and Roth, E. M. 2006. "Operational Concepts, Teamwork, and Technology in Commercial Nuclear Power Stations." In C. Bowers, E. Salas and Florian Jentsch (eds), *Creating High-Tech Teams*: 139–59. Washington DC: American Psychological Association.

Oriol, M. D. 2006. "Crew Resource Management: Applications in Healthcare Organizations." *Journal of Nursing Administration*, 36(9): 402.

Parasuraman, R. and Mouloua, M. 1996. *Automation Technology and Human Performance: Theory and Application*. Mahwah, NJ: Erlbaum.

Paton, C. 21 November 2008. "Griffiths Report Could Have Freed NHS From Politics." *Health Service Journal*. Accessed online on 21 March 2009: http://www.hsj.co.uk/opinion/2008/11/griffiths_report.html

Paton, D. and Flin, R. 1999. "Disaster Stress: An Emergency Management Perspective." *Disaster Prevention and Management*, 8(4): 261–67.

Patsuris, P. 26 August 2002. "The Corporate Scandal Sheet." *Forbes*. Accessed online on 6 June 2009: http://www.forbes.com/2002/07/25/accounting-tracker.html

Perrow, C. 1984. *Normal Accidents: Living with High-Risk Technologies*. New York: Basic Books.

Peters, J. W. and Bunkley, N. 16 November 2006. "The Many Lives of US Airways; Bankrupt Twice in 4 Years, and Now Bidding for a Troubled Rival." *New York Times:* C1.

Pettitt, M. A., and Dunlap, J. H. 1994. "Training Pilots or Educating Captains? A Framework for Collegiate *Ab Initio* Programs." *The Journal of Aviation/Aerospace Education and Research*, 3(1): 21–7.

Phillips, J. D. August 1990. *The Hillsborough Stadium Disaster Inquiry and Report*. Deputy Chief Constable Report, Devon and Cornwall Constabulary held at Parliamentary Archives, House of Parliament, London.

Pirie, R. B. 5 March 2001. "A Full Accounting of the USS *Greeneville* Accident." *Washington Post*: A18.

Powell, S. M. and Hill, R. K. 2006. "Home Study Program: My Copilot is a Nurse-Using Crew Resource Management in the Operating Room." *Association of Operating Room Nurses Journal*, 83(1): 178–206.

Reason, J. 1990. *Human Error*. Cambridge: Cambridge University Press.

1997. *Managing the Risks of Organizational Accidents*. Aldershot, UK: Ashgate Publishing.

2008. *The Human Contribution: Unsafe Acts, Accidents and Heroic Recoveries*. Aldershot, UK: Ashgate Publishing.

Rice, A. K. 1963. *The Enterprise and Its Environment*. London: Tavistock Publications.

1965. *Learning for Leadership*. London: Tavistock Publications Limited.

Rivera, R. 17 January 2009. "In a Split Second, a Pilot Becomes a Hero Years in the Making." *New York Times:* A19.

Robbins, H. A. and Finley, M. 2000. *The New Why Teams Don't Work*. San Francisco: Berrett-Koehler Publishers, Inc.

Robertson, C. H. 2004. "Teaching Pilots Judgment, Decision-Making, & Critical Thinking." *International Journal of Applied Aviation Studies*, 4(2): 203–20.

Robson, G. 2000. *'No One Likes Us, We Don't Care': The Myth and Reality of Millwall Fandom*. Oxford: Berg.

Rubin, A. J. 21 November 2009. "In Iraq, a Blunt Civilian is a Fixture by the General's Side." *New York Times*: A6.

Salas, E ., Bowers, C. A ., and Edens, E . (eds). 2001. *Improving Teamwork in Organizations: Applications of Resource Management*. London: Lawrence Erlbaum Associates, Publishers.

Sarter, N. B. and Woods, D. D. 1994. "Pilot Interaction with Cockpit Automation II: An Experimental Study of Pilots' Model and Awareness of the Flight Management and Guidance System." *International Journal of Aviation Psychology*, 4: 1–28.

1997. "Team Play with a Powerful and Independent Agent: Operational Experiences and Automation Surprises on the Airbus A-320." *Human Factors*, 39(4): 553–69.

2000. "Team Play with a Powerful and Independent Agent: A Full-Mission Simulation Study." *Human Factors*, 42(3): 390–402.

Schaefer, H. G., Helmreich, R. L., and Scheideggar, D. 1994. "Human Factors and Safety in Emergency Medicine." *Resuscitation*, 28: 221–25.

Schreier, H. A. and Libow, J. A. 1993. *Hurting for Love: Munchausen by Proxy Syndrome*. London: Guildford Press.

Schroeder, C. and Harms, D. 2007. "MPL Represents A State-Of-The-Art Ab Initio Airline Pilot Training Programme." *ICAO Journal* (3). Accessed online on 6 January 2010: http://www.casa.gov.au/wcmswr/_assets/main/fcl/multicrew/icaoarticle.pdf

Schwartz, H. S. 1987. "On The Psychodynamics of Organizational Disaster: The Case of the Space Shuttle Challenger." *Columbia Journal of World Business*.

1989. "Organizational Disaster and Organizational Decay: The Case of the National Aeronautics and Space Administration." *Industrial Crisis Quarterly*, 3: 319–34.

Sciolino, E. 4 March 2001. "Greeneville's Skipper Known for Devotion to His Job and Crew." *New York Times*.

Scraton, P. 1999. *Hillsborough: The Truth*. Edinburgh: Mainstream Publishing Projects Ltd.

Seamster, T. L. and Kaempf, G. L. 2001. "Identifying Resource Management Skills For Airline Pilots." In E. Salas, C. A. Bowers, and E. Edens (eds) *Improving Teamwork in Organizations*: 9–30. London: Lawrence Erlbaum Associates.

Serfaty, D. and Michel, R. 1990. *Toward a Theory of Tactical Decision Making Expertise*. In Proceedings of the Symposium on Command and Control Research: 257–69. Monterey CA.

Sexton, J. B., Thomas, E. J., and Helmreich, R. L. 2000. "Error, Stress and Teamwork in Medicine and Aviation: Cross Sectional Surveys." *British Medical Journal*, 320: 745–9.

Shapiro, E. R. and Carr, A. W. 1991. *Lost in Familiar Places: Creating New Connections between the Individual and Society*. New Haven, CT: Yale University Press.

Simpson, D., Love, J., and Walker, J. 1987. *The Challenge of New Technology*. Boulder, CO: Wheatsheaf Books.

Sir Norman Chester Centre for Football Research. 2001. *Football Stadia after Taylor: Fact Sheet Number 1*. University of Leicester.

Sir Norman Chester Centre for Football Research. 2002. *Football Stadia after Taylor: Fact Sheet Number 2*. University of Leicester.

Snook, S. 2000. *Friendly Fire: The Accidental Shootdown of U.S. Black Hawks over Northern Iraq*. Princeton: Princeton University Books.

Stein, M. 2004. "The Critical Period of Disasters: Insights from Sense-Making and Psychoanalytic Theory." *Human Relations*, 57(10): 1243–61.

2007. "Oedipus Rex at Enron: Leadership, Oedipal Struggles, and Organizational Collapse." *Human Relations*, 60(9): 1387–1410.

Stokke, E, Haugset, K., Nelson, W., and Bjorlo, T. 1991. *Instrumentation and Control Systems in Nuclear Power Plants*. Halden, Norway: Halden Reactor Project.

Stuart-Smith, The Right Honorable Lord Justice. 1998. *Scrutiny of Evidence Relating to the Hillsborough Football Stadium Disaster*. Presented to Parliament by the Secretary of State for the Home Department by Command of Her Majesty.

Stubler, W. F. and O ' Hara, J. M. 1996. *Group-View Displays: Functional Characteristics and Review Criteria* (Technical Report No. E2090-T-4-4-12/94). Upton, NY: Brookhaven National Laboratory.

Sullenberger, C. 2009a. *Highest Duty*. New York: Harper Collins Publishers.

24 February 2009b. Statement before the Subcommittee on Aviation, Committee on Transportation and Infrastructure, United States House of Representatives. Accessed online on 7 June 2009: http://transportation. house.gov/Media/file/Aviation/20090224/Sullenberger.pdf

Taylor, I. 1987. "British Soccer after Bradford." *Sociology of Sport Journal*, 4(1): 171–91.

Taylor, The Right Honorable Lord Justice. 1989. *The Hillsborough Stadium Disaster: Interim Report*. Presented to Parliament by the Secretary of State for the Home Department by Command of Her Majesty.

1990. *The Hillsborough Stadium Disaster: Final Report*. Presented to Parliament by the Secretary of State for the Home Department by Command of Her Majesty.

Taylor, R., Ward, A., and Newburn, T. (eds). 1995. *The Day of the Hillsborough Disaster: A Narrative Account*. Liverpool: Liverpool University Press.

Trist, E. 1993. "Introduction to Volume II." In E. Trist and H. Murray (eds), *The Social Engagement Of Social Science: A Tavistock Anthology, Volume II: The Socio-Technical Perspective*: 36–60. Philadelphia: University of Pennsylvania Press.

Trist, E., and Murray, H. (eds). 1993. *The Social Engagement of Social Science: A Tavistock Anthology, Volume II: The Socio-Technical Perspective*. Philadelphia: University of Pennsylvania Press.

Tucker, A. L., Edmondson, A. C., and Spear, S. 2002. "When Problem Solving Prevents Organizational Learning." *Journal of Organizational Change Management*, 15(2): 122–37.

Tuckman, B. and Jensen, M. 1977. "Stages of Small Group Development Revisited." *Group and Organizational Studies*, 2: 419–27.

Tyson, A. S. 17 January 2010. "Can This Officer win the War?" *The Washington Post*: B1.

Union of Concerned Scientists. 11 February 2008. *No Space for Aviation Safety at NASA*. Accessed online on 20 January 2009: http://www.ucsusa.org/scientific_integrity/abuses_of_science/nasa-pilot-survey.html

United Airlines. 2003. *Flight Operations Manual*.

United States Department of Transportation (US DOT). June 1998. *Profile: Regional Jets and Their Emerging Roles in the U.S. Aviation Market*. Office of the Assistant Secretary for Aviation and International Affairs. Accessed online on 5 January 2010: http://ostpxweb.dot.gov/aviation/domav/regjets.pdf

United States Government Accountability Office (US GAO). March 2002a. *Commercial Aviation: Air Service Trends at Small Communities since October 2000*. Testimony before the Committee on Commerce, Science, and Transportation Subcommittee on Aviation, U.S. Senate (GAO-05-834T). Accessed online on 18 December 2009: http://www.gao.gov/new.items/d05834t.pdf

United States Government Accountability Office (US GAO). July 2002b. *Commercial Aviation: Structural Costs Continue to Challenge Legacy Airlines' Financial Performance*. Report to Congressional Requesters (GAO-02-432). Accessed online on 18 December 2009: http://www.gao.gov/new.items/d02432.pdf

United States Government Accountability Office (US GAO). August 2004. *Commercial Aviation: Legacy Airlines Must Further Reduce Costs to*

Restore Profitability. Report to Congressional Committees (GAO-04–836). Accessed online on 18 December 2009: http://www.gao.gov/new.items/d04836.pdf

United States Government Accountability Office (US GAO). July 2005a. *Commercial Aviation: Structural Costs Continue to Challenge Legacy Airlines' Financial Performance.* Testimony Before the Committee on Commerce, Science, and Transportation, Subcommittee on Aviation, U.S. Senate (GAO-05–834T). Accessed online on 30 January 2010: www.gao.gov/new.items/d05834t.pdf

United States Government Accountability Office (US GAO). September 2005b. *Commercial Aviation: Bankruptcy and Pension Problems Are Symptoms of Underlying Structural Issue.* Report to Congressional Committees (GAO-05–945). Accessed online on 18 December 2009: http://www.gao.gov/new.items/d05945.pdf

United States Government Accountability Office (US GAO). June 2006. *Airline Deregulation: Reregulating the Airline Industry Would Likely Reverse Consumer Benefits and Not Save Airline Pensions Structural Costs Continue to Challenge Legacy Airlines' Financial Performance.* Report to Congressional Committees (GAO-06–630). Accessed online on 19 December 2009: http://www.gao.gov/new.items/d06630.pdf

United States Government Accountability Office (US GAO). July 2008. *AIRLINE INDUSTRY: Potential Mergers and Acquisitions Driven by Financial and Competitive Pressures.* Report to the Subcommittee on Aviation Operations, Safety, and Security, Committee on Commerce, Science, and Transportation, U.S. Senate (GAO-08–845). Accessed online on 13 December 2009: http://www.gao.gov/new.items/d08845.pdf

United States Government Accountability Office (US GAO). April 2009. *Commercial Aviation: Airline Industry Contraction Due to Volatile Fuel Prices and Falling Demand Affects Airports, Passengers, and Federal Government Revenues.* Report to Congressional Requesters (GAO-09–393). Accessed online on 18 December 2009: http://www.gao.gov/new.items/d09393.pdf

United States Navy Court of Inquiry (COI). 2001. Record of proceedings of a Court of Inquiry convened at Trial Service Office Pacific by order of Commander In Chief United States Pacific Fleet to inquire into a collision between USS *Greeneville* (SSN 772) and Japanese M/V *Ehime Maru* that occurred off the coast of Oahu, Hawaii, on 9 February 2001. Naval Station Pearl Harbor, Hawaii. Accessed online on 22 April 2010: http://www.cpf.navy.mil/news_images/special_projects/cpfnews/coidownloadtranscripts.html

Waddle, S. 2002. *The Right Thing*. Nashville, TN: Integrity Publishing.

Wald, M. L. 1 October 2007. "Fatal Airplane Crashes Drop 65%." *New York Times*.

  7 March 2008. "F.A.A. Fines Southwest Air in Inspections." *New York Times*.

Wald M. L. and Maynard, M. 13 April 2008. "Behind Air Chaos, an FAA Pendulum Swing." *New York Times*.

Wallace, J. 20 March 2000. "Unlike Airbus, Boeing Lets Aviator Override Fly-By-Wire Technology." *Seattle Post-Intelligencer*. Accessed online on 3 January 2010: http://www.seattlepi.com/business/boe202.shtml

  30 April 2007. "Boeing Unit Tries to Speed Pilot Training to Fill High demand." *Seattle Post-Intelligencer*. Accessed online on 5 January 2010: http://www.seattlepi.com/business/313681_pilotshortage30.html

Walvin, J. 1986. *Football and the Decline of Britain*. London: Macmillan.

Weick, K. E. 1993. "The Collapse of Sensemaking in Organizations: The Mann Gulch Disaster." *Administrative Science Quarterly*, 38: 628–52.

  1995. *Sensemaking in Organizations*. Thousand Oaks: Sage.

Weick, K. E. and Sutcliffe, K. M. 2001. *Managing the Unexpected*. San Francisco: Jossey-Bass.

Weiner, E. L. 1989. *Human Factors of Advanced Technology ("Glass Cockpit") Transport Aircraft*. (NASA Contractor Report 177528). Moffett Field CA: NASA-Ames Research Center.

Weiner, E. L., and Curry, R. E. 1980. "Flight-Deck Automation: Promises and Problems." *Ergonomics*, 23: 995–1011.

Weiner, E. L ., Kanki, B. G ., and Helmreich, R. L. (eds). 1993. *Cockpit Resource Management*. San Diego: Academic Press.

Weitzel, T. R. and Lehrer, H. R. 1992. "A Turning Point in Aviation Training: The AQP Mandates Crew Resource Management and Line Operational Simulations." *The Journal of Aviation/Aerospace Education & Research*, 3(1): 14–20.

White, B. 28 January 2009. "What Red Ink? Wall Street Paid Hefty Bonuses." *New York Times*. Accessed online on 5 June 2009: http://www.nytimes.com/2009/01/29/business/29bonus.html?scp=5&sq=bonuses&st=Search

Wilson, K. A., Salas, E., Priest, H. A., and Andrews, D. April 2007. "Errors in the Heat of Battle: Taking a Closer Look at Shared Cognition Breakdowns through Teamwork." *Human Factors*, 49(2).

Wilson, M. and Baker, A. 16 January 2009. "In Icy Water, Quick Rescue Kept Death Toll at Zero." *New York Times*: A1 & A25.

Wilson, M. and Buettner, R. 17 January 2009. "After Frightening Splash, Chills, Heroics and Even Comedy." *New York Times*: A1 & A18.

Wright, P. T. July 2001, "Commentary: *Greeneville's* Collision Is There a Better Explanation." *US Naval Institute Proceedings*, 127: 28–9.

Youngs, G. 2007. *Global Political Economy in the Information Age*. London: Routledge.

Yu, R. 23 June 2008. "United Flight Canceled When Pilot Says He's Too upset to Fly." *USA Today*: 3B.

Zsambok, C. and Klein, G. 1996. *Naturalistic Decision Making*. Hillsdale, NJ: Lawrence Erlbaum.

INDEX

Index